IT RUNS IN THE FAMILY

ALSO BY
RICHARD MANNING

IT RUNS IN THE FAMILY

RICHARD MANNING

St. Martin's Press ≈ New York

www.stmartins.com

Design by Anna Gorovoy

Library of Congress Cataloging-in-Publication Data

Manning, Richard, 1951-
    It runs in the family : a memoir / Richard Manning. — First U.S. Edition.
        pages cm
    ISBN 978-0-312-62030-1 (hardcover)
    ISBN 978-1-250-03136-5 (e-book)
  1. Manning, Richard, 1951– 2. Manning, Richard, 1951—Family.
3. Manning family.   4. Farm life—Michigan   5. Fundamentalism—
United States.   6. Conservatism—Religious aspects—Christianity.
7. Journalists—United States—Biography.   I. Title.
    CT275.M45655A3 2013
    977.4092—dc23
    [B]
                                                              2013009261

St, Martin's Press books may be purchased for educational, business, or promotional use. For information on bulk purchases, please contact Macmillan Corporate and Premium Sales Department at 1-800-221-7945 extension 5442 or write specialmarkets@macmillan.com.

First Edition: July 2013

10 9 8 7 6 5 4 3 2 1

For Josh, Trish, Alden, and Eddy,
for making certain it goes on

CONTENTS

IT RUNS IN THE FAMILY

1

IN THE
BEGINNING

I started this investigation in deep winter of January 2009, when I was in retreat, beaten and broke. My business had failed, as did many in our nation that year. I drank too much. My house was on the market, a forced sale, since sold. Journalism, the good work I had done my whole life, was necrotic. The last of these weighed most on me, my life's work rendered worthless. Nonetheless, journalism was all I had then, so I used it to dig my way out of a hole. This is the process recorded in this book.

Asking questions and reporting answers is how I have always worked, so there is nothing at all unusual in my spending three years so engaged. What was unusual, though, was that the questions, of necessity, probed private matters, because of my own state of disrepair in the beginning and the simple fact that my father had died a few weeks before. He was an extraordinary man, and mostly not in any good sense of the word. Part of my burden that winter was a sense of shame for who he was. The truth is, I had spent most of my life to that point trying to get away from him, trying to ignore him and the rest of my family and trying just as desperately to deny any influence he might have had on the course of my own life. Yet oddly it occurred to me that the time had come to account, not just for my own sake, but more relevantly because of the public's stake in my private questions. I had until then lived most of a life never publicly acknowledging my parents, and now, paradoxically, public events demand I do so, as I will in what follows.

Anyone who had seen my dad in his last days—and I had, finding him literally in a jungle, a homeless, babbling bum lost a hemisphere away from home—would have thought him mad, and he was. He suffered a peculiar and specific madness. He and my mother—she had died a few years before—had lived their lives as fundamentalist right-wing Christians of the exact same stripe that plays an appallingly significant role in American public life. Indeed, in that January of 2009, the very month that fundamentalist-in-chief George W. Bush left office, it was easy enough to see how my father's madness had become a general plague on the nation. It is this parallel that dictated my assignment for the next three years, that I would need to abandon my studied ignorance of my father's life and admit to our common story, our common genes, even admit to the possibility of our common madness.

Now three years on, it is my job to report, but you already

know I cannot bring news of great improvement in the nation's well-being. The troubles imposed by Bush did not end with his presidency; John Birchers, Koch brothers, Tea Party, Fox News, know-nothing fundamentalism, Newt Gingrich—my father's fellow travelers, every one—remain. We remain at war. We are governed by plutocrats, many of us impoverished, and a nation shaken to our financial foundations. The country is not much better off three years on, but I am, and I am as a result of asking questions, of learning and facing the consequences of my story and my kinship with a madman.

Then, though, I could only retreat to watch it snow and wonder what was to be done about me and about the rest of us. So I rented a small cabin for a week on the edge of the Rocky Mountain Front a few hours drive east of where I live in Montana. The cabin backed up against mountains of the vast Bob Marshall Wilderness at the western edge of the howling Great Plains. It snowed, and snowed hard nearly every day of the week I was there. Just up the trail, there was a wintering herd of mule deer, and from time to time I went out to walk among them, grand ghostly creatures circling me in halting steps I took for grace, but know to be their obedience to the demands of winter, a sort of ambulatory hibernation. Step easy and conserve every bit of energy if you are to survive. If there were a third party there to record that scene, it would look like a truce of deep winter's peace between man and animal. Honoring and understanding the terms of that truce have much to do with why I am better off today.

In the cabin, there was a bottle of good Irish whiskey with barely the neck knocked out. I had six bottles of decent red wine, a venison roast, some garlic and parsnips. I have a good wife, beautiful and decent enough to spend this week in the cabin with me out of iPhone range, cell range, a rare electronic silence. Willing even to tolerate my own silence as I retreated to wilderness to think of these things. I had a Filson wool jacket, red-and-black buffalo plaid, competent boots and thick wool socks. I had a stack of books piled before the rimed mullioned panes of the cabin.

There was a wood stove, a Jotul, a clever little Norwegian model and the best I ever used. There were parallel piles of thinly split yellow pine, limber pine, quaking aspen, and a bit of fir to each side of the cabin door. For me and for the long line of northern latitude people I come from, a woodpile is well-being. So my days passed mostly in endless fascination of feeding the fire. Hundreds of generations of my northern European bloodline, facing long, cold winters, bred this little stove, and I am proud of our work, proud of our people, immediate and otherwise, and I connect to them through my father. This, then, is my first realization and admission of kinship to him and the privilege it brings.

The stove has secondary combustion, which means if I get it running just right, it will burn its own smoke in a whooshing roar and with a blue flame one associates with natural gas, not wood, and I do indeed get it running just right. I can build a fire. I can jump-start a pickup truck. Grease boots. Wax skis. Split wood. Dress a deer. Break rock. Right a raft. Incise a clean dovetail in rock maple and fit the joint. Can and did build a house every nail, solder joint, and wire nut. My dad has something to do with this. He and everyone in his line could make things work, a simple fact every bit as relevant as his religion. This facility with real work is the counterbalance to religious fanaticism in the story that will develop here, in my story and in the American story. Owning up to this is part of what made be better.

My dad's death put a trigger in my hand, with a command to sit at this computer's keyboard and fire. The death of both of my parents frees me to tell our collective story, that last adjective a painful admission, but I make it. It is a family story, collective. I am from them. They are finally both dead, and now there must be an account, not because they were unusual, but because in the American context they were not.

2
HOME GROUND

I was born in Flint, Michigan, in 1951. Like many children of that town and time, my earliest memories were of traveling "up north." This was during the height of the postwar boom, which produced an enormous migration of southerners—both black and white—to the north, leaving the poverty of rural southern states for good-paying jobs in automobile plants in southeast Michigan. We called the nearby city of Ypsilanti, also an auto town, "Ypsitucky." There was, however, a smaller but significant exodus from the north. My father and his three brothers, and both of my maternal uncles and my maternal grandfather before them, left their home farms near Alpena, Michigan, two hundred miles north, and all settled in Flint, the town at the center of Michael Moore's film

Roger & Me. (Moore was born near Flint three years after I was.) These former northerners returned home as often as possible, that is, went up north.

My dad didn't work in the auto plants, but had gotten a job first as a Flint city cop, then as a claims adjustor with General Motors' insurance division. This meant he got a new Chevrolet as a company car every year, part of the reason he called his employer "Generous Motors." When I was four or five, we frequently went north propelled by small-block V8s and progressively more prominent tailfins. The trip took a bit more than four hours, allowing for a stop at Pinconning to buy pickled baloney and Colby cheese, smoked suckers in season. If time was right, we—three kids then, my little brother and sister and I, spaced a year apart—could convince my dad to stop at the statue of Paul Bunyan and Babe the Blue Ox, a roadside attraction on U.S. 23 between Harrisville and Ossineke. Bunyan's blue boots were taller than I was, and we were reliably informed that we shared some sort of unspecified kinship with the Bunyan lineage. The legendary logger had probably even worked for a great-grandfather or great-uncle as they oversaw the clear-cutting of northern Michigan's giant white pine in the latter half of the nineteenth century, leveling forests for farms.

My paternal grandparents' house was sided in brown Insulbrick, two stories and full basement. A line of lightning rods trimmed with colored milk glass balls guarded the roof's ridges from heaven's wrath. There was a nickel-plated wood cookstove in the kitchen, a shingle-sided outhouse behind, a piano in the parlor, and oval-framed sepia portraits of my grandfather and his brothers as young men. The house stood across the highway from where it had been built. About the time my father was born in 1929, my grandfather had winched it across the road with a horse-driven windlass to clear the right-of-way for a highway. It was a fine old house and still stands on Manning Hill, at 919 feet above sea level, the highest point in Alpena County and officially bearing my family's name for almost a century and a half.

My great-grandfather settled the land, about two hundred acres, in the 1870s. His marriage record in Alpena County says he was English, by which it meant a subject of the queen. He had not been born in England, but in Huron, County Ontario, and I cannot trace his lineage beyond that simple fact. This makes sense. That region of Ontario saw a rapid influx of English, Scots, and Irish about then, people who had come from the British Isles seeking farm land. It was a frontier, and record keeping was poor. Technically, they were not immigrants to Canada, because Ontario was still a colony. I can find no record of his birth. He first appears in the 1870 U.S. census in a rooming house in Saginaw, then a lumber mill town in need of good men, so that was when he was lured just across Lake Huron from Ontario to Michigan. Typically immigrants to white pine country logged for a few years while stashing money and waiting for a good shot at a workable plot of cleared land. My grandfather found his home ground atop a hill one hundred miles north of Saginaw.

He married Eliza Ann Boyd, a childhood sweetheart also from Huron County, Ontario, in 1876 in Alpena, and they were on the farm on Manning Hill by 1878. Some of this detail I confirmed with a copy of his obituary that appeared in the *Alpena News* in 1916, the same paper where I would learn newspapering in 1976 by first writing obits. My grandfather Benjamin Wade Manning bought the family farm when my great-grandfather died in 1916. He was then twenty-three years old, the youngest son of the family's nine children. His older brothers had already settled on nearby farms, some of them adjacent. This heritage left about thirty families of Mannings settled mostly within sight of the hill where I grew up. It was locally rumored that my family members suffered a weird sort of Lamarckian evolution: all of us had one leg shorter than the other from living on that hill. It wasn't much of a hill, but Alpena County is mostly swamp, so it passed for prominence by comparison.

My grandmother Esther Collins Richardson grew up on the farm adjacent to my grandfather's. She descended from timber barons who came from Maine and settled in Alpena. In fact, if you were to draw a line from where Ebenezer Richardson, her grandfather, settled in Pittsfield, Maine, through where the Mannings and Eliza Boyd's family originally settled in Durham, Ontario, and then to Manning Hill, you would find the line oddly straight. In fact, it is an important line, the 45th parallel: Manning Hill stands at latitude 45.062789. My whole paternal lineage seems to have an odd affinity for living exactly halfway between the equator and North Pole. I have deviated significantly by living most of my adult life just north of the 46th.

In their time, though, there was a clear explanation for this fact, not the Mannings' and Richardsons' fidelity to latitude, but their shared tendency in trees. Lumbering then from Maine west as far as Minnesota was specifically targeted to white pine, and working the species required a specific set of skills and knowledge. The new mills in Michigan in the 1870s weren't after any man, but men who knew white pine, so recruiters looked east straight down the 45th parallel.

My paternal grandparents were both still alive for those early visits up north, and I remember them well. Ben Manning was taciturn and tough, and everyone deferred to him. He had lost an eye in a farming accident when he was just a kid, so wore glasses with one lens frosted over, the side of the frame shuttered, because his eye socket could no longer hold a glass eye, so long had he lived with the loss. My research turned up a copy of his draft registration card for World War I, and it notes the handicap. When I knew him, I was always terrified he would take those glasses off, and there would be nothing to prevent me from staring straight into a hole in his skull. My grandmother smiled a lot and mostly superintended a bustling kitchen. She too wore glasses, hers rimless, her short-cut gray hair in a netted bun, and housedresses. She had once fed threshing crews, and a family visit was no big thing.

Even better than genuflecting before Babe the Blue Ox and Paul was being put in bed for the night in that Insulbrick house, always at 8 P.M., a rule I would observe until I was in high school. The bed was in an upstairs bedroom, and its floor held a heating register grate, but not the sort hooked to ductwork. Instead, there was an enormous wood-burning furnace in the basement, "down cellar" they called it, with a plenum vented into a four-foot-by-four-foot grate in the living room floor. We called it a "register" and every kid who had encountered it forever had slightly burned feet from standing on it barefoot. The register in my bedroom's floor was simply a ceiling vent in the living room, positioned to catch the wood heat rising. Yet it would also catch the rising conversation of grandparents during those visits, uncles and aunts sitting around the grate and "visiting" on into the night. They laughed often and loudly. They spoke in country words like "dasn't." Their stories were local and immediate, often featuring running battles with "rotten sons-o'-bitches."

The oldest printed English stories are Viking and Celtic. *Beowulf,* first written in Old English in the eleventh century, records a version of events that occurred much earlier in what are now Sweden and Denmark. King Arthur was a Celtic warlord, likely Welsh. Then there is the marvelous body of literature, the Icelandic Sagas, recording events between the eighth and tenth centuries, not just in Iceland, but in Scandinavia, the British Isles, and even in what is now New England. All of this, I think, is deeply relevant to my story, or any English story.

First, the sagas tell us something about Viking expansion 1,200 years ago. The surviving mythology speaks of a bloodthirsty bunch of seafaring whack jobs bent on plunder, and so they were, but the truth is more complex. The Vikings were then in ascendance. They had developed a robust and wealthy culture able to expand. They ruled much of the British Isles for several hundred years, founded Dublin in Ireland, and spread influence throughout the lowland countries of Europe. All of this time they were mixing it up with the Celtic culture already in place, but also with Angles and Saxons, Frissians and Dutch. These are the northern Europeans: Celtic, Germanic, and pagan. This Norse, north culture was the antipodal force to the Mediterranean groups to the south, the Christians.

Because seafaring dominated the north, it makes more sense to see the flow of politics and culture by sea alignments than by landmass. The British Isles have three separate histories, defined by the North Sea, the Irish Sea, and the English Channel. Further, Mercator projections distort actual distance between the key landmasses of this region in our mind's eye, so biased are those projections toward the south. Look down at a globe with the North Sea at the center of your vision, as it was so centered for the Vikings, and you will have some sense of how this history flowed.

This matters because we lose much of history in our gloss of Western civilization biased to the Mediterranean and Christian. This matters to me because this is the lineage I claim for myself and because my life recapitulated the central tension, of Christianity imposed on pagan working people. My compass always points north of the 45th parallel. This matters because these earliest stories of this culture, the sagas, are anachronistic. They were written three and four centuries after they occurred, transcribed from oral tradition by Irish monks. Monks being who they are put something of a religious overlay on the stories, but they nonetheless preserve hints of our pagan past, and religious anachronisms aside, we at least know these stories must have mattered greatly to the people who inherited them. The translation I have of the Icelandic Sagas runs to seven hundred pages, and for three centuries all of these were preserved only in the memories of a very few people. This was, mind you, an oral tradition, not a folk tradition. Those entrusted with the tales were not free to embellish, or add and subtract to suit conditions, audience, and message. The saga of Leif Eirikson records the Vikings' discovery of the New World and remained through three centuries of oral tradition accurate enough to aid modern archaeologists in locating his settlement.

These oral histories had to be accurate because they mattered; they were paternity and, in a few cases, maternity. Each had to contain a lengthy and accurate accounting of who begat whom because they were meant as creation myths of particular places in Iceland. Each family and each community would hand the story generation to generation as a sort of oral abstract of deed, the story that bound them to a particular place and granted their right to occupy it. Paternity served as deed to land.

This fundamental utility of these stories is what makes them seem all the stranger and, at the same time, all the more normal to our ears today. Stranger, because they are mostly not—as the main of literature and history is—accounts of priests, popes, and kings, but of ordinary people doing ordinary things. (To the degree you consider cutting your neighbor's head off with your halberd as ordinary.) Written history is usually an account of elites, and these are not. The novelist Jane Smiley says, "The sagas and tales are full of work. Action takes place in a context of sheep-herding, horse-breeding, weaving, cooking, washing, building, clearing land and expanding holdings, trading by ship with mainland Europe and the British Isles." This is an almost subversive, anti-elitist element that thrived in written literature from the beginning. Mostly, early written English was a tool of religion and of kings to propagate and glorify both. History then, and to a large degree now, was an account of the mighty largely written at the expense of the conquered. The modern view of the Celts as illiterate, bloodthirsty barbarians, for instance, is a simple parroting of propaganda written by Roman historians, especially Julius Caesar.

Yet English has been able to maintain the subversive strain that preserves the story of common people. These are my people. We cut wood and drink *usquebaugh* on long, dark, cold winter nights. We live in the north and call our enemies "sons-o'-bitches."

At the same time, the sagas are epic. They tell of heroism, foolishness, pride, envy, stupidity, failure, honor, and duty. They freight all of this in the patronymic, a lineage of fathers laying warnings and responsibilities on the next generation.

At the time of the sagas, surnames were almost strictly patronymic. That is, if your name was Leif, then your son Eirik became "Eirik Leifson," but his son Olaf became "Olaf Eirikson." The tradition recorded but one generation of heritage, and the sagas took care of the rest. The other Germanic traditions—German, English, and Dutch—allowed some variation on this theme. Surnames could derive from occupations—Smith and Baker in English, but Fleischmann (a butcher) in German—and from place names. Richard of York became Richard York. Nonetheless, English retains the patronymic. My cousins, for instance, were Atkinsons and Morrisons and my grandmother was a Richardson.

My own name is less obviously a patronymic, the suffix "ing" now mostly in disuse, but it shows up occasionally in vestiges like "earthling," a person of earth, in this sense, a place-based name, but earlier a patronymic. A variation of the surname Manning appears in the Domesday Book, the first recording of surnames in the British Isles. There is some disagreement as to what it might have originally signified. It could be an affinity to place, maybe the Isle of Man, but that doesn't have much resonance. I began favoring the interpretation that it meant simply "son of man." In fact, the Semitic root of this phrase is the etymology of "human." This gives me some claim to a universal human story, not just mine.

The better genealogical Web sites will encourage your paid enrollment by telling you for free my surname derives from something quite noble, the Anglo-Saxon adjective for "manly," "manlique." Surnames often derived from descriptions of some ancestor's physical prowess, so this seems likely enough. The Saxons would have used it exactly as it survives in Yiddish (also a Germanic language): "Come on, be a mensch." All of this is completely appropriate to the way I was raised to this name, grew into it as a masculine responsibility. There was work in my story.

Yet I am now settling on a particular story as true, that my name is encoded, as modern British does when a person of privilege speaks of "My man Higgins." A servant, a laborer. The whole business of genealogy, especially among the WASPs among us (I will establish my WASP credentials soon enough) is designed at placing us among kings. I have the opposite intention, a reverse snobbery. The genetic record agrees with me, that the real action was among the common people, the ordinary dirt farmers. The conquerors, the Normans, Romans, and the rest and the royalty they imposed were an aberration. Royalty in feudal Europe was nothing but intensely incestuous and effete, silly had it not been the cause of so much human slaughter. There is a counterstory, and I am claiming it for myself.

The counterstory is, in fact, political. The invaders of the British Isles invariably imposed a top-down hierarchy of rule consistent with Roman imperialism and consistent with the religious imperialism of the Catholic Church. The pagans, however, had a wholly different idea, a system of local government based on shires, small political subdivisions we call counties today. Power in the shires rested with the sheriff; the latter term derives from the former. As long as a thousand years ago, British sheriffs would, on suspecting a crime, recruit a jury of twelve men empowered to arrest, try, and punish a miscreant. Historians suggest the concept of local political power independent of the monarchy was a strong feature in both Viking and Anglo-Saxon people of northern Europe, a counterbalance to monarchy, that provided continuity and kept British society functioning, even in time of upheaval. The Normans, for instance, did indeed impose a French aristocracy, but it relied on the sheriffs to attend to the day-to-day workings of government. The system was too successful and too institutionalized to replace. This is very much the force that would later lead to the Magna Carta, which did nothing so much as limit the power of monarchs. British common law is at its core antiauthoritarian, and I take this to be a part of my story as well.

I can't say for sure who the Mannings were before Ontario; I lose track of my paternal lineage. What did turn out to be a great deal of help in tracing my lineage was my paternal grandmother's genealogy. A relative had done a family history a few years ago, but it stopped with her ancestors in Maine, specifically one Ebenezer Richardson, who was a timber baron in Maine and died in 1864. This was all I knew just a few months ago. It turned out to be relatively easy to go on from there, because these Richardsons are plugged into a prominent lineage. In 1620, John Winthrop led the second wave of Puritan colonists to found the Massachusetts Bay Colony around what is now Boston. The list of settlers included three Richardson brothers, part of a group charged by Winthrop with founding Woburn, Massachusetts. Two of the Richardson brothers were Ezekial and Samuel. Samuel's grandson, Stephen, married Ezekial's granddaughter Bridget, and these are my grandmother's direct ancestors. Yet the lineage, if we accept the standard genealogies, is traceable through a couple thousand years, and extends back to a point in the fifteenth century when Ralph Richardson's father was known as "Bedo Ap Richard," the Welsh form of the patronymic. Then it extends to the Welsh kings, including Llywelyn the Great. His circle of chieftans was the basis of the King Arthur legend. And here, the title of "king" is misleading. These guys were the local warlords who fiercely fought Christian conquerors for generations.

Like my grandfather, the Welsh kings were herders and farmers and raised cattle in rough hilly country and stubbornly and violently resisted imposed authority. The surnames, the lineages, the language, the fidelity to north and to farming intertwine to form a deep history. The Mannings and Richardsons cut trees and had been farmers since farming began. I think my father was the first Manning who was not a farmer since the Manning surname came into use at least eight centuries ago. And even he tried to be one. I believe this was the biggest part of the problem. He not only failed on the land, but on a particular plot of land on the back side of something known widely as Manning Hill. I think this is why he exiled himself to die in the tropics, not along the 45th parallel.

As I write this, an antique Winchester lever-action carbine rifle rests against the wall of my study. It is a precursor (its serial number places its manufacture at 1890) of the legendary model 94, so named because it debuted in 1894. It is a relatively rare caliber, a .38-55. It came to me in 2001 when my mother died, and my father was cleaning out the house. It was the only thing I wanted among their possessions, that and a photo of my father's family and one of my grandmother's, the Richardsons. I had fired the rifle as a teenager, and knew its stories long before then. My great-grandfather originally owned it, then it went to my grandfather—odd, because he was the youngest son in his generation. Maybe because he bought the land, the rifle went with the deal. Primogeniture kicked in during the next generation. My father got it when my grandfather died. Now it's mine. The Internet is, among other things, sometimes terribly useful, and I try to imagine the original owner understanding how I provisioned his rifle. A few weeks after I got it, I was able to locate for sale online a box of custom cartridges in the now outdated caliber. Then a friend of mine who hand-loads his own cartridges consulted, and we were able to refine the load to something that fired satisfactorily, which wasn't easy. Get the load wrong, and the bullets tend to pitch end-over-end instead of whizzing nose-first to the target.

My paternal grandfather was not a hunter; people kept rifles then for protection or, literally, when the sheriff needed some help with a criminal at large. My grandfather wrote off hunting as a waste of time, as he did all sport. He was of that school of farming that considered nature and wild animals as something to be eradicated. He had no concept of recreation. He was a notorious hater of trees, and believed all trees should be pruned at ground level. I am told this was something of a hangover from his youth, when my great-grandfather planted Manning Hill to orchard. It was my grandfather's job to cultivate those apple trees. The brush and trees made a mess of the horses' harnesses, and he had to spend hours cleaning harness after a normal day's work was done. So when he took over the land, he cut down all the trees.

The exception to his rule was the back forty, a woodlot he maintained to heat his house. It was allowed to grow up in aspen (known then and now in northern Michigan as "popple"), birch and maple, a portion of which would be felled and bucked every fall to fuel the furnace in the basement.

Woodlot or no, though, it was still his land and still subject to his rule. A neighbor had a herd of sheep that repeatedly broke down the line fence and trespassed on the back forty. So my grandfather shouldered his rifle, my rifle now, and shot the sheep.

My dad told me this story, so I don't know if it is true.

The buzzing of firewood from the back forty was one of the annual work bees that survived into my childhood. Earlier, before widespread mechanization, bees in general were more common, when neighbors pooled labor and went farm to farm to tackle monumental tasks, the biggest being threshing grain. This was before the invention of mechanized combines, machines that are pulled behind tractors and thresh

grain in the field. Threshing machines were enormous station-
ary mills powered by chuffing steam tractors, and a threshing
crew comprised a dozen or so men.

By 1961, after postings in Knoxville, Tennessee, and Colum-
bus, Ohio, my dad had left his job with General Motors, and
we moved back to Manning Hill. We lived for a short time in a
temporary house in the nearby village of Long Rapids, the
former home of a blind medical doctor who had delivered
babies, including my father. We stayed there only long enough
for my dad and his brothers to build our new house on sixty
acres that had been my grandfather's, my dad's patrimony, on
the back side of Manning Hill, the south side, called the back
side because the highway, M-32, ran on the north side. The
story was my grandfather kept the back side only so he had a
place he could work on Sunday out of sight of neighbors traveling to church on the highway. (My grandfather did indeed
regard church much as he regarded recreation. The term "Puritan work ethic" would be a hopeless contradiction to him:
"Which is it? Are you going to church or are you going to get
your work done?") Still, I doubt the explanation for owning
the back side; I find it hard to believe he cared what the neighbors thought, and likely would have enjoyed goading them by
violating the rule about working on the Sabbath in full public
view.

During that first year in Long Rapids, there was to be a
buzzing bee on a Saturday at my grandfather's, and my brother
and I could think of little else. I was ten, my brother nine,
judged old enough to be of some use. We had heard stories of
buzzing bees, so named because of a frightening device called
a buzz saw. It was a giant circular saw with a blade about

three feet in diameter. Power for this rapacious monster derived from a John Deere B tractor nosed up to the saw. A big steel pulley driven by the tractor's engine turned a stout canvas drive belt maybe six inches wide and twenty feet long. The belt would hop and thwap along the grass as it spun fast enough to power the saw through the popple and birch. In previous weeks, my grandfather had cut and built a garage-sized pile of tree-length wood, the wood to be "buzzed," meaning bucked to stove length. To do so, two of my uncles would muscle up a tree trunk, frog-march it to the buzz saw bed, then feed it along a table a stove-length at a time. Another uncle or maybe my dad would "pull saw," meaning pull that savage, spinning blade straight at himself to make the cut. Another uncle or an older cousin would "throw blocks," that is, catch the wood as it fell from the saw and pitch it into a chute to the basement.

My brother's and my chief fascination with all of this was the magical business of pulling saw. There was a family story about some relative or another who had been engaged in this very craft and had pulled the saw into his stomach, disemboweling him on the spot. We were excited by this prospect and considered it well worth the sacrifice of an uncle or cousin to be present at such a monumental event. So we were ready to go at first light, but apparently had committed some unnamed and terrible crime. As punishment, my dad went off to the buzzing bee without us. No matter. We had bikes and my grandfather's place was only six miles away down well-traveled highways. So we went buzzing, against our father's wishes.

We knew we would catch hell, so went straight for the basement at my grandfather's house, both to be out of sight of my father and to be of some use. The firewood blocks came tumbling down the chute, and we and a couple of other cousins grabbed and piled them, row on row, to fill the basement. The smallest among us, I and my brother, climbed to the very top of the pile like blue-eyed, tow-headed apes, so we could chink in the last few blocks up into the ceiling joists. All of this was wrapped in the indelible smell of fresh-cut Michigan hardwood, ready to warm my family through a winter. And we did catch hell from my dad, but not from my grandfather. He thought our insolence was funny and appropriate.

My father, my father's family, were Depression-era dirt farmers. Each one, man and woman, justified their space taken on the planet by the work they did. I understood this viscerally, even as a very young child, wandering as a happy little pagan among them. Theirs was a work ethic so deeply ingrained it was not an ethic any more than breathing was. Accordingly, we were never schooled or instructed in the ethic; we were simply turned loose among men and told to keep up. What little instruction there was came in parables, and there were but two or three, which is why I can remember them now. The story of my grandfather shooting the sheep is one of them. The story of my great-uncle Frank's suicide—I'll tell that soon enough—is another, but that one was not about work. It was meant as our sole and formal religious instruction. Living there and then was simple enough as to require no religious creed beyond work. The religion in my life would come later, a virus that infected when my father met my mother, the virus that enfeebled and sickened my paternal legacy. Yet these dirt farmer Mannings were not simple people, or the seminal parable would not have persisted among them.

During the Depression, my grandfather raised potatoes, for exactly the same reason potatoes today are a favored crop worldwide for farmers weathering troubled times. They are the surest way to convert rock soil and sunshine to a dependable pile of carbohydrates, and if everything goes to hell in the markets, they'll still feed the kids.

Nobody called potatoes "spuds" when I was a kid, but the etymology of this slang term requires no explanation for anyone who has done the job of planting them. Properly speaking a spud is a tool, a tool more oppressive than a shovel or pick. Is a heavy wedge of steel welded at the end of a solid steel bar the length of a man. One swings it on a vertical axis to open a hole in hard ground, muscling the wedge's point to break rock and open hardpan clay. Because its work is done on a downstroke, its considerable heft is to the worker's advantage. Traditionally, potatoes are grown in new ground, rock ground, hard ground, and so calling them "spuds" captures the hard-fought, hand-to-mouth pitch of the battle.

One fall day at harvest deep in the Dirty Thirties, my grandfather loaded his pickup truck overtop full of rows and columns of stacks of square-slatted crates brimming with red potatoes and drove them to a rail siding nearby where there was a buyer. The buyer offered the going market-crashed rate, which was not enough to cover his costs. My grandfather said nothing, but backed his truck away, pulled across the road and backed into the ditch in full sight of the buyer, dumped every crate into the ditch, then, in a perfect rage, drove his pickup back and forth across the pile to smash every last spud to mush and rot. Sons-o'-bitches. He was not reacting to the assessment of his potatoes as worthless; the price on offer really said his work was worthless.

It would not surprise me at all to find out this never happened, that this story is apocryphal and there are versions of it throughout the Upper Midwest told to my generation. All the better.

3
COME OR BLEED

My father, Harold Manning, was six foot one, handsome, personable, broad-shouldered, and liked to talk to people standing with his arms crossed across his chest. He walked with a marked toe-out, something I noticed even when I was very young, because I liked to follow him, walking in his tracks. I did not know then his habit was a fault, but I noticed, because it was not the way I walked, so I spent years trying to train myself to walk as my dad did. I assumed he walked that way because he was a man and I was a child, a problem I would need to correct, not through time, but by force of will, by work.

I failed in my first attempt at work. I was five, and we were still living in Flint then, probably 1956, but we had traveled up north for a work bee, picking rocks. Manning Hill was laid by glaciers, an esker. Eskers build from a glacier's internal streams of melt when watercourses pile sand and gravel against an ice wall. Once in retreat, the glacier spits out a hump of a hill made of water-rounded rocks and sand. Time, life, and decay apply a thin layer of topsoil, but tillage works the rocks to the surface. On my grandfather's farm, the spare time between planting, haying, cultivating, and threshing was spent picking rocks. A crew walked behind a tractor, which towed a sledge called a "stone boat." We picked up rocks and dropped them on the sledge, then dumped the load at fencerows. Every farm had its stone piles; some of the more elaborate houses, like the one my grandmother grew up in, still standing, were built of stone of this same water-round stone split in half by men and sledgehammers to form one flat facet on each half, laid up in the wall face out.

It was hot this day I barely remember, and my uncles took frequent breaks to drink iced tea. There was no water, just tea, and they told me to drink some, but I refused, got sick of dehydration, and couldn't bring myself to tell them why. Only a few days before I had watched an episode of *Howdy Doody* in which Clarabell the Clown had drunk something that looked like tea, and, as a result, the clown had shrunken small enough to dance on the head of a drum. No doubt, the show offered this as a cautionary tale, in that tea and coffee were at the time widely believed to stunt a kid's growth, at least that's what my mother told me. I preferred dehydration to a life as a drum-dancing dwarf, so refused then to drink the tea, and I still don't drink it.

My failure that day didn't matter much, because boys were still judged pretty useless at five. A boy's time to put away childish things didn't come until he was ten or eleven, old enough and, with some luck, big enough to drive tractor (the indefinite article was always dropped in this phrase).

When we moved back to live on Manning Hill a few years later, my dad had by then somehow acquired a hulking beast of a tractor, a tricycle front-end Farmall H, bright red once, but rust red when it came into our hands, a behemoth of the 1940s. It was top-heavy, ungainly, and not all that powerful, a Model T Ford in comparison to the tractors only a couple of years in the future. By the time I was ten, I could set the choke and throttle, start it, slide it into gear, pop the clutch, and drive. I did so standing on the thick plate steel driving platform that stood maybe four feet off the ground. I was not tall enough to reach the pedals if I sat the hard, steel tractor seat, but there was no real shame in this. Many grown men drove tractor standing up, because those seats were unsprung and delivered a considerable ass beating when working rough ground. I remember only that on my first solo trip, the Farmall was at my grandfather's place, and my dad told me to drive it through the south gate and down the backside of the hill, then through the pasture to where we were building our house on our land, sixty acres, land once a part of my grandfather's farm. So I did as I was told.

In those days and in that place, people who needed a house picked a plot on some favorite corner of family land, ordered concrete and a load of lumber, then brothers and uncles came and built it. I learned to mix mortar and tend mason, the mason being my Uncle Dale. It was my brother's and my job to drive every one of the hundreds of ten-penny rosin-coated nails into the one-by-ten hemlock sheathing that was the subfloor. I insulated and shingled and swung a shovel full days.

My dad was working more or less full-time on the house. He didn't have a regular job, and I didn't know exactly why. I knew we had moved back to Manning Hill because my dad had left his job at General Motors in Ohio to become an insurance adjustor for Farm Bureau Insurance across northern Michigan. The company was a big deal then, not just because it insured the homes and pickup trucks of the many farmers, but it also attached to a social and political organization by the same name. Everybody belonged to a Farm Bureau group and met regularly at members' homes for cake, molded Jell-O, and coffee. But not very long into that job, my dad suddenly didn't have it anymore, and it was the first time I remember hearing phrases that would recur throughout my parents' lives: "crooked lawyers" and "out to get your father" and so forth.

Even as a naive kid, I still knew then there was not much money. The back shed of our temporary house in Long Rapids held a row of, at one point, nine hanging dead deer, frozen stiff in midwinter, our illegal meat supply. Michigan's deer hunting season was in November, an annual, near-religious ritual, when sportsmen were each entitled to shoot one deer, a male, a buck. We were not sportsmen; we were "violators," the local term for people who illegally killed deer. The practice was widely regarded as an egregious breach of the social code, if not deviant and immoral. It was believed to be the modus vivendi of "cedar savages," people who lived in tar paper shacks in cedar swamps, cut cedar fence posts, and propagated vigorously, what we would today call "trailer trash."

And today they cook meth, not venison. We were not cedar savages, but my old man was an enthusiastic violator. He used a .22 caliber rifle because it made so little noise. He would drive around back roads at dusk and shoot whitetail does in the neck, pop them in the trunk of his Pontiac, then back into the garage after dark so the neighbors wouldn't see. Once, as my brother and I looked on, he opened the trunk and a doe that had only been stunned by the shot jumped out and ran. He chased it around the garage and killed it with a hoe. We were, by then, six children.

We would go to work on the new house those cold winter mornings bearing a pot of venison stew. The house was closed in, and we were insulating and hanging sheetrock. We had set up an old potbellied stove in what was to become the living room, and would fire it up every morning with scrap wood, then set the stew on top to simmer while we worked. We marked our progress in tucking the studs in pink fiberglass insulating batts by the house's increasing ability to hold the smell of the stew.

Presently the house was done and we moved in, and there was a series of jobs for my dad, some I was a part of, and some not. I would nonetheless have more work to do in both cases.

Most of his jobs tended to be away, a lifelong pattern. He bought a weird little snub-nosed Corvair pickup truck and trowels, bull floats, and forms and drove every Monday four hours south to Flint to do concrete work, staying the week in a cheap rented house trailer and returning home on weekends. In winter, we worked in the woods, an eighty-acre piece of ground my paternal grandfather had sold to my maternal grandfather. My dad cut cedar posts, and after school my brother and I loaded them on a steel-runnered dray we pulled behind an antique Oliver bulldozer. Once we'd loaded the dray, my brother and I would argue over whose turn it was to drive the little dozer over the iced haul road to the landing. Once a week or so, a truck would come to haul the posts away to the mill to make fencing. Last thing each day, we'd pile up a load of cedar boughs and throw them in the pickup, take them to our house, and pile them in the basement. After supper, we weighed and bundled the boughs. A big flatbed truck would come to the house every week or so, and we'd pile on the boughs, to be sold to florists for flower arrangements at funerals.

The money came as cash. My dad wanted untraceable income to allow him to collect unemployment insurance, what he called "rocking chair" pay, although I never saw him sit in a rocking chair. He did not believe defrauding the government constituted fraud, and never would. The government was always the enemy and deserved what it got. He bragged about a lifetime of lies to the Internal Revenue Service.

Soon, he got more involved in concrete in summers and eventually tried to buy a little concrete supply business in Rogers City, thirty-five miles north of Manning Hill. By then, he had a pretty nice International pickup, which we painted blue to match the concrete trucks, and when there was no school in summer, my brother and I—I was then twelve or thirteen—rode with him to the plant to put in a full day's work. We delivered concrete blocks, unloading them by hand off the bed of an old '51 Chevy flatbed, and sometimes I drove it. We learned to run the front-end loader and the forklift and strip forms from precast septic tanks.

My particular task, because I was still small, was to clean the residue of hardened concrete that accretes inside of mixer trucks. The giant mixer drums had a small hatch, maybe eighteen inches in diameter, on the side. We'd unbolt the hatch so I could crawl through it into the drum that was spiraled with fins for mixing the concrete. Sometimes the concrete had built up a half foot thick on the fins, making them less effective, so I used a little handheld jackhammer and chisel to bang away for hours on end. No one thought about earplugs then. My hearing is so damaged I needed hearing aids in my early fifties, and I suspect I got my start on the problem then.

My dad was always trying to think up some shortcut to a job, and had an idea about cleaning mixer drums. He told me to fill the drum with empty paper cement bags, then we poured about five gallons of diesel fuel on the pile of paper and touched it off. The idea was the heat from the burning bags and fuel would expand the metal fins and the concrete would crack and fall off. Nothing much happened for a few minutes, so I climbed up on the drum and poked my head into the hatch to have a look. About then, the flames inside had heated the fuel to a flash point, and it did indeed flash, sending a burst of fire through the hatch. It blew me off the side of the truck, and I fell about six feet to the ground, thinking the whole way down that I surely was a ball of flame. I had seen such things on TV and, in fact, had heard a fireman tell my class that people who are balls of flame should not panic and run, but should roll on the ground. So I rolled, and after a few revolutions realized my dad was laughing at me and that I was not a ball of flame. I was merely bright red with first-degree burns and had no hair and eyebrows. The skin peeled off and grew back in a few days, hair and eyebrows in a few weeks. The fire did nothing to the concrete, so I had to crawl back in with my little jackhammer.

We seemed to be doing a pretty good business that first year. Maybe my dad had found a niche, but then something happened between him and the man from whom he was buying the business, some contract or another he neglected to sign. And I heard more talk at the dinner table about "out to get your father" and "crooked lawyers" and then we didn't have the business. So my dad went back to construction jobs in Flint, was gone again most weeks, this time in winter.

When he built the house, he had equipped it with an old green Bryant hot water boiler, secondhand, that was forever breaking down. That and we ran out of fuel oil often, so I learned to take the boiler's fuel lines apart, bleed out air, and relight it. Sometimes it didn't work at all, and I'd fend off the Michigan winter by building a fire in the fireplace, always a problem, because my dad never cut enough wood. Winter was the hardest. Northern Michigan's winter cold is deep and complete at night; no child is the equal of it.

In November of 1961—I was ten—my school's principal came to my classroom, whispered something to my teacher, Mrs. Himes, then pulled me from class. Long looks all around suggested something bad had happened, and everyone knew what it was but me. My grandfather had died. Like every man I knew of that generation, he died of a heart attack, all of a sudden.

There had been some heart trouble before, and he was not

supposed to work, so he no longer farmed, but didn't leave the farm either, choosing to live on in that brown Insulbrick house where he'd been born. Installing one's storm windows to defend against a northern Michigan winter was not really work, more of a chore, and the doctor hadn't said anything about chores, just work. He had been hauling a window up a ladder to a north-side, second-story window when the coronary hit him, and he fell off the ladder and died. He was sixty-eight.

They laid him out at Bannan Funeral Home in town—the Protestant funeral home, the place for all Manning funerals. My parents took me to see my grandfather in his casket, so I would know what dead was. After, I hung out with my cousins in the parking lot and marveled at the elk. The Elks Club was next door, and the lodge kept a life-sized bull elk statue in the parking lot. I had never seen a real elk; they were gone from Michigan then, since returned, but the statue was impressive enough. The high school was nearby, and boys from there had taken it upon themselves to glue fuzz to the elk's realistic-looking scrotum, a service maintained on through my high school years.

A few weeks earlier, my father had taken me to visit my grandfather after supper one night, the occasion being my first report card at my new school, straight As, a highly uncommon occurrence in family lore and the township in general. My grandfather looked at the card, did not say a word (he seldom did), but dug into the pocket of his bib overalls, pulled out a beat-up coin purse, extracted a folded-up dollar bill, unfolded it, and gave it to me. And he smiled, and I was no longer afraid to look at his missing eye.

My grandmother lived on in that house for another six

years until liver cancer killed her. She would not go to the hospital and died in bed at my aunt's house a mile from where she lived all her adult life, a mile and a half from where she had been a child. In her last years, we three oldest kids in my family were frequent visitors. She was always happy to see us and spoiled us as a grandmother should with sugarcoated cookies. Occasionally we would bring our pet goats, and she was never happy to see them; they ate her hollyhocks. Sometimes we would ride our horses, and she would lecture us about them. She reasoned it would be a lot more sensible to sell them and buy motorcycles in that we would no longer have to put up hay, and when you're not using a motorcycle, it just sits there and doesn't use gas, but a horse always needs hay.

She herself would make no such concessions to modernity. It took a considerable harangue from both my aunts to convince her to get a telephone. Everyone had telephones by then, but she had lived her entire life without one and didn't see a reason to change. When she finally did get one in the late 1960s, a party line shared with one of my aunts, she still wouldn't use it to make calls. She had agreed to get it in case she got sick, and she wasn't sick, so what was the point. If people wanted to visit they could damn well stop by and visit.

Nor would she even consider the radical idea of getting a television set. Radio was fine. In fact, she enjoyed radio and was an avid fan of the Detroit Tigers, listening to the game every night they played. This only deepened her resistance to the television set, because one time one of my aunts explained that the television also had the Tigers and she ought to see a game, so she did. She was shocked to see that the Tigers had numerous players who were Negroes, including her longtime personal favorite, Willie Horton. I don't know that she thought it a bad idea to let Negroes play professional baseball, but it did unsettle her worldview, and she stayed away from the television after that.

When we were much younger and stayed at her house on visits from Flint or Ohio, we took baths in the clawfoot tub in the only bathroom in the house, and she would always come into the bathroom, sit on the edge of the tub, and wash my brother's and my backs. And she would tell my mother that it must make her happy to have boys with meat on their bones. We weren't fat. Just normal kids, but her boys had been rail thin. They ate well enough, but farm work took it right back off. Whenever I am tempted to think of this as a small thing, I remember that my grandmother had ten children in that house during the Great Depression, and only six lived to be adults.

One's right of passage in that world that raised me came not from work but from getting paid for it. By that standard, I came of age when I was fourteen. One of my aunts, my father's older sister, Ellen, was married to a hardworking and respected German dairy farmer, John Behling, and the summer I graduated from eighth grade, he had Aunt Ellen call my folks and see if I might like to drive tractor for a couple of weeks at pay to help him haying. He milked maybe thirty Holsteins twice a day, but I would be spared that, much as I liked doing it. Milking was done before and after a full day's work, and he didn't want me up at five and in bed at nine like he was, so I was called down to breakfast after he was done milking.

He chopped his hay, as opposed to baling it, meaning he drove a tractor pulling a machine that ingested windrows of hay, diced it up, and blew it through a chute into a huge, high-sided, four-wheeled wagon behind. My job was to hook a tractor to the filled wagons, run them to the barn, dump the hay into a conveyor and blower that shot it up into the mow, then bring back the empty wagons. On days it was too wet to hay, I picked rock or shoveled shit out of the calf pens.

The work went on for a couple of weeks, then I got paid and it was time for me to start high school, a major event in that I would no longer attend the little school in my community, but would be bused the fourteen miles into town, Alpena, to attend the county high school, in the same building where my father and mother had gone.

But it was still a week or so before school started, and money was burning in my pocket, as I recall, the whole $30 that was my two-weeks wages. My mother took me to town in her hulking Pontiac station wagon, then I was on my own at Sidewalk Sale Daze, and I went to the J.C. Penney store, bought black peg-legged jeans, white socks, and a shirt like men wore to church on Sundays. I went to Alvin Ash's music store and picked through the records, knowing exactly what I was after, the entire Roger Miller oeuvre, on a single and newly issued album *Golden Hits.* His hit "King of the Road" was getting major airplay on the sort of stations we listened to. Rock 'n' roll was well into its heyday, but for some reason it could not penetrate the airspace of northern Michigan, so I listened to Roger Miller. I had spent my head time on my uncle's farm making up new lyrics to his song, but an entire album opened a whole new world of wordplay, and I memorized every word, can still do "Dang Me," and "Do Wacka Do." These are my literary roots, but I at least knew I would enter high school in solid command of a cool body of work.

I held a similar opinion about my black peg-legs, but learned a few days later this wardrobe that had consumed my hard-earned cash was the equivalent of a hick uniform. It didn't matter; at least my mother hadn't picked it out, or at least I thought it didn't matter, but it did. There was a sharp divide at that school between town kids and farm kids. This much I knew, but I had assumed the farm boys were judged to occupy the top half of the pecking order, because we were in command of tractors. I couldn't imagine a social milieu where this was irrelevant. Nor did I have to imagine, because it was spelled out to me in plain English soon enough. During those same few days, I learned about bullies (I was small for my age): hazing, hard punches to the gut, and about having my girlfriend from the year before dump me for one of the bullies. In fact, I think it all happened during the same day.

A few months later, television did something to me like it had done to my grandmother. There was a broadcast of Arthur Miller's *Death of a Salesman* with Lee J. Cobb reprising the role he had made famous on stage. The story inhabited a world so far removed from Manning Hill, yet it illuminated a corner of my odd little existence that would never be dark again, both in a general, but also in a very specific sense. I had no trouble, even at fifteen, recognizing that my dad was Willy Loman. It's not that the details matched up, or they did the same things. But on TV, I somehow knew something wasn't true when Willy said it was true, and then I knew all along it had been the same with my dad. In watching Biff discover

Willy's infidelities when he met him on the road, away from home, a bit more snapped into place, that from shouted arguments between my parents I had overheard, I knew more than I thought I knew. I suddenly knew why my father liked to work away from home and leave me alone to tend to that goddamned furnace.

I was sitting there watching a made-up story on TV one minute and I was a different person the next. What sort of power is in story? It frightened me, for a good reason. I was just a kid, and yet I could see clearly my dad was Willy Loman. And now it had been on television, so I knew everybody else would see it too.

Now I have brought my life to high school, a time of coming of age, and yet I have told but half of the story of what was happening in those years. I have spoken mostly of my paternal lineage and of work, which, in my mind and, I think in the minds the people of that lineage, were the same thing. I tell of work and Mannings first, because this is the easy part to tell. I understood them, and they are my foundation. I imagine many readers regard the details of my upbringing as troubled. From where we sit today, from our time, from the standards by which we raise kids today, some of this is indeed troubling. Yet I do not regard it so, not the work. The fact is, I believed mine was a life of great privilege. I was raised among brute animals, tools, and simple machines. I was raised by people who were heroic.

When I was a child, "work" meant something more than minimum wage at a 7-Eleven, bundling subprime mortgages, or punching keys. Both Marxist academics and editorial writers for the *Wall Street Journal* fail to grasp this deeper significance of work and the people who did it. During the course of about a century, for better or worse, the people who founded our generation imposed the industrial revolution on a wilderness with not much more than muscle and will. I understand fully the objections of revisionist history to the frontier myth, even raise some of the same objections: capital, disease, greed, theft, racism, and violence all had much to do with bringing a wild and merciless landscape to heel in the nineteenth and early twentieth centuries in North America. Yet beneath the academic bickering over these matters lies an undeniable reality, and the bickerers miss it when they call it "labor" instead of "work." "Labor" is from old French, a term imposed by Norman aristocrats. "Work" is Anglo-Saxon from old German and Norse. Labor is work seen from above.

A close reading of the elemental detail in the record of day-to-day life in lumber camps, mine pits, rail grades, and threshing crews does nothing so much as rehabilitate the adjective "heroic." These people who did this work were a different species, now extinct, for the very reason most species vanish: their habitat is gone.

In my life I knew a man, my Grandfather Manning, who was born in the nineteenth century and learned his work at the very height of this time of bloody-knuckled conquest. He learned from a man, a farmer and logger, born in wilderness early in the first half of the nineteenth century. There is nothing I would trade for this legacy.

As a child and young man, I was privileged to be present at a series of events, a type of event really, that boils this legacy to an essence. Through the years, the situation varied, but it always had essential elements: a) something stuck that needed to be unstuck and b) a force for unsticking like a big, hard hammer—irresistible force or immovable object, but the gods to be tested by this ancient conundrum were just simple machines: lever, wedge, and screw, and muscles, internal combustion, steam, and vocabulary.

Maybe it was a dray load of logs slid sideways on ice to wedge in the pinch between trees, maybe a tractor axle assdeep in mud and no help for miles save a hand-crank coffin hoist and some burlap bags for traction. Or maybe a live shaft broke on a combine cutter head, a rust-bound bolt, and gathering clouds promising downdraft winds ready to smash flat a year's crop to lodged, worthless straw in minutes. Whatever. The nut has to come off, and the dray has to give. So maybe a frayed wire cable gets hooked to a full-throttled bulldozer, the front end chained to a tree to keep it from going airborne in the lurch. Then tracks dig and spin and engine roars and cable thins threatening to part. Or maybe the worn box-end wrench on the frozen nut of the combine fails, so the two of you, you and a brother, slide a six-foot-length of pipe on the end for leverage, then both sets of boots braced against anything that might not slide and heave for all you are worth.

Among the people I knew, there was a common battle cry reserved for such moments, an incantation set to the rhythm of the rings of progressively larger hammers. Breathless and face flushed full red, we commanded: "Come, motherfucker. Come or bleed."

And mostly it came, whatever it was, and there'd be a story

to tell over dinner. Or it wouldn't and there'd be busted knuckles, a lost field of wheat, or an arm snatched off a kid in half a second because he didn't have enough sense to stand clear of cable's bight. Or the horse-drawn roller would catch the edge of a ditch. The tongue snapped and flipped 180 crushing the man at reins dead as a hammer, which is what happened to one of my great-grandfathers.

These mostly unrecorded and ordinary events made us who we are, a birthright, collective as a nation, but mine too, personal. I think of both in context of who we are today. Yet in both general and specific cases, the birthright is not and was not inalienable. I did not realize what was happening then, what I was seeing as an adolescent. I understood only that I was living on a firm and unshakable foundation of family, land, and work. So was my father, and this had much to do with my deep childhood attachment to him, this and a fact obvious to everyone around me but not to me, that I was more than most sons, his genetic echo.

I was a child, beginning to recognize he was becoming dishonest, and by this, I mean something more than someone who fails to tell the truth. His dishonesty was less willful; it required self-deception, and I watched him acquire the skill. Good work, on the other hand, requires, above all, veracity. The work people did then daily measured itself against the demanding realities of the physical world, real and present. Mistakes were self-correcting. Either it worked or it didn't, and the sooner you faced that fact, the better it was going to be. There was an accounting at the end of every day. An action was right or not, and if wasn't right, whatever it was you'd worked on would break again, and you'd have to do it all over.

The problem was, my father's marriage drew him into a world, into a habit of mind that required self-deception. For I also had a mother, and that's the half of my story I turn to now.

4

MATERNITY

These past few years I have searched repeatedly and yet come away finding fully drawn memories of my mother's side of my family are simply not there. Or there, but exist more as photographs than as moving scenes: a few snatches of sounds, smells, constrained motion, but mostly shadows. Most of the images are of my grandfather.

This is odd, because my immediate family was close to my maternal grandparents, as families were then close. George and Loie Mayo lived not much more than a mile south and east of Manning Hill on eighty acres of gravel and cedar swamp my paternal grandfather had sold them. I expect they were the reason my mother pressed so hard to move back to Michigan, the family she referred to when she spoke of missing family, as she often did when we lived away from Michigan. After we moved back, she was at their house almost daily, and often so was I, especially when I was younger, before I went off to work with my dad.

My earliest memory of them comes much earlier than Manning Hill. We were then still living in Flint, so I was younger than five. My maternal grandparents were living there as well, as they would off and on, most of their lives. When he worked at all, my grandfather was an autoworker punching a clock at various incarnations of General Motors in Flint and Detroit beginning in the 1920s. I have only this fleeting wisp of a recollection—a forgivable lapse, I was not yet five years old—of visiting them in a little bit of a house, and even more in shadow was an old woman, wrinkled and dark. I was given to understand she was Catholic, so likely of another species. I understood on my own something more significant. I had seen *The Lone Ranger* by then, and I knew an Indian when I saw one, and my great-aunt was one. I don't remember that she was ever spoken of again in my life.

My grandfather Mayo was born in 1905—somewhere in the Upper Peninsula of Michigan was the family story, Manistique was what I remember him saying, although I cannot find a birth record. Likely it was the little settlement of Garden near Manistique. Nothing strange about missing records; the Upper Peninsula was then a near-frontier and he was of a hidden subculture of half-breed Indians. I do find the family, however, in the 1920 census, living then in Grayling at the center of the Lower Peninsula. The author, Jim Harrison, was born in the same town in 1937, and his novels wander back and forth across Straits of Mackinac from northern to lower peninsula, from wild to less wild, from Native to white, following the lives of Chippewa half-breeds. Grandfather was a teenager in 1920, living with his father, Joseph, and mother, Julia Lamotte, his sisters Agnes and Rose and brother Albert. These four children are the only ones on the record, although my grandfather said there had been thirteen children total, seven of whom made it past age ten. No clue as to what happened to the rest. All of these names I do know are only from the census record, not as people. The family had moved to Grayling to work in timber. The census says Joseph worked for DuPont, which had started a large plant there in 1915 to make charcoal out of tag alder, beech, and maple. The process also produced wood alcohol, acetone, and by-products that DuPont used at other plants to make explosives.

The family surname Mayo had been anglicized from "Maillioux," most likely when Joseph and Julia immigrated from Canada in 1872. I have found a church record that appears to place Joseph with his family in Quebec when he was a boy, but I cannot be sure. My grandfather referred to himself, even in old age, as French Canadian, as did Joseph and Julia in the 1920 census. They listed their race as "white," a common practice for Natives then. Frontiers allow new personal stories.

Family lore says both Joseph and Julia were half Chippewa Indian, or as the tribe is known today, Anishinabe. There is no way to sort this out and every reason to doubt the precision. There are no tribal enrollment records for either of them and even those records rest more on claims and self-identification than DNA. Quebec and Ontario and even the Upper Peninsula of Michigan produced a unique Native history, largely because of the practices of the early fur traders in what was then New France, beginning as early as the sixteenth century and peaking in the eighteenth and nineteenth. It was common for fur traders, both English and French, to marry Native women. Eventually this produced a distinctive culture still officially recognized as "Métis" in Canada and to a certain extent in the U.S. Periodic land grabs and shifts in policy—in fact the very land grab that I suspect brought my paternal ancestors to Ontario—pushed Natives back and forth across the border between Canada and the U.S. People tended to become more Caucasian with each crossing, each new spelling, and each new version of their story. Eventually, the main body of Métis migrated north into Manitoba, where they fomented a rebellion under the leadership of Louis Real, who was prosecuted and hanged. A large body of Métis migrated south into the U.S. and Montana territory and founded some the state's first towns on the plains. It was common, however, for Métis in Montana to deny their heritage for fear of political reprisals and many claimed to be "white," the exact word that labeled my Métis great-grandparents in the 1920 census. I think my grandfather was wound up in this great continental diaspora, but settled out in Michigan, as many of this tradition did. They simply called themselves "French Canadian," and it was widely assumed Native was part of that deal.

When I was a boy, my grandfather owned a suit of heavy woolen clothes: mackinaw and pants, buffalo plaid, antique, even then in the 1960s no doubt acquired at considerable sacrifice during the Depression, when good wages were a dollar a day, probably a week's wages to a Traverse Bay Woolen store. He hunted deer with an old octagon-barreled Winchester model 94, a .32 special, a cut above the standard 30-30 most everyone else carried. I came of age following him around that eighty acres he had bought from my other grandfather, a parcel of cedar swamp so sodden it would never stand a plow, and so my other grandfather had no use for it. Grandfather Mayo had bought it, house and land, for $2,000 in 1944, no doubt flush with wartime wages. Probably the only time he was flush.

My Grandmother Loie was born in 1907 and raised a Methodist, I'd always been told, around Flint. But the 1920 census also found her and her parents, Ray and Effie Baldwin, living in Grayling. There she met my grandfather. The story is they met at a dance. Now I have to think of my grandmother as anything other than dour and obese and someone a person might ask to dance. Apparently it happened. They married in 1923, and then my grandfather found work in a Buick plant in Detroit a few years later. When the crash came in 1929, my grandfather was away from Detroit, had gone north with $600 he had saved to buy apples and pears from the orchards around Bay City to haul back to Detroit and sell house to house. That's how you got by. He returned to find the plant shut down, and he was holding his life savings as bushels of fast rotting fruit he could not sell, as worthless as my Grandfather Manning's potatoes.

But George Mayo could always make a few bucks in the woods, so he moved the family from Detroit, two kids then, my Uncle Robert—Bob, always Bob—and my Aunt Lorraine, north to Schoolcraft County in the Upper Peninsula. He trapped beaver, mink, and rabbit for 50 cents a pelt and worked for a dollar a day and some food at a farm. These were the circumstances of my mother's birth in 1931, and here, as far away from any Spanish-speaking person as one can be in the United States, they named her Juanita, a name they liked when they heard it in a song.

In 1934, a rumor came saying the auto plants may be hiring again. My grandfather walked from Manistique to the Straits of Mackinac, close to one hundred miles, then hitchhiked to Flint and got hired on. He stayed until the mid-1950s when, not yet fifty, he was in car wreck that left him disabled with phantom pain in a shoulder that a string of chiropractors never seemed able to fix. Not MDs—they were not to be trusted—chiropractors. I remember him most sitting in a green plastic rocking chair, smoking a pipe, an arm limp, an occasional grimace, and watching TV. He laughed more than he talked, an explosive, infectious laugh. My grandmother did the talking. She also did hair. Through the week, most of the women from the Baptist church would come to her and have their hair done up for Sunday, how she made the money that stretched my grandfather's pension and disability pay. This also made her something of an information hub, and the most prized sort of information in her circle were details of the failings of people not in her church and of surgeries. The former was quickly dealt with in clucking censure, generally by citing specific details of whose car had been spotted parked at which "beer garden," the notorious Duby's in one direction, or the Spratt Tavern in another. Medical matters, however, were explored in far greater detail. It was, in fact, a legitimate claim to status for a woman in her circle to have undergone any sort of procedure. "Female trouble" and gall bladder operations seemed to be particular favorites. Details of an individual case were often rationed out over the course of months, to be savored until another fortunate acquaintance went under the knife.

Aside from the great gulf between the beer garden crowd and church people, there was a second significant social cleavage in her world, the sort of women who came to her beauty shop—a special sink and a hair dryer in her basement—and the sort who got their hair done "in town," meaning Alpena fourteen miles east. My paternal aunts were in the latter category. I never recall hearing my Grandmother Mayo speak well of anyone, nor can I conjure her face in anything but a glower. When I was an adult and marking some significant achievements, I went to visit her and my grandfather. The only thing I remember her saying was, "When are you coming back to church?" I cannot remember ever seeing her smile or hearing her laugh. I am not saying she didn't or that I didn't see her do so many times. I am saying my head won't tolerate the memory.

This was in a time before food stamps, and poor people got by on what were known as "commodities," surplus lard, flour, and powdered milk. I learned to recognize their packaging in my grandparents' house. Years later, fresh from a first year at university, I was visiting them and chose to demonstrate my newfound and profound understanding of the world's workings, gleaned from a poli-sci 101 lecture as to how Franklin Roosevelt had laid the grounds for the modern welfare state. My grandmother and grandfather lit into me simultaneously, I think the only time I had ever heard them agree on anything. I was flatly informed that FDR was only one notch below Jesus Christ in the pantheon, and the real problems of our times were owing to the collusion of Communists and Republicans. (My grandfather believed the Republican Party was nothing but a front for the Communist Party, and he often said as much.)

The great compromise of their marriage had been to become Baptists, what my grandmother must have decided was the midpoint between Catholic and Methodist.

The grainy gray stills that are my first memories of these people began to take shape, color, and motion in the old house, the one my Grandfather Manning had sold them at the end of the Second World War. I came to know it maybe ten years later. It was a shack really, a tin-sided shack with a door at one end, two front rooms, one for eating, one for visiting around a space heater, and maybe a couple of tiny back bedrooms with windowpanes that were more ice than glass in winter. It had no running water, and every morning during our visits I followed my grandfather when he lugged a two-and-a-half-gallon galvanized steel pail a couple of hundred yards over a hill to a free-flowing spring of clean water. We drank from this bucket using a long-handled steel dipper with a hooked handle for hanging it on the edge of the pail. We ate venison my grandmother had canned in Ball jars with zinc-cladded lids.

These early visits must have been my first of what would become years of following my grandfather in the woods, mostly on his eighty acres of cedar swamp, a scattered ridge of hardwoods above an impenetrable tangle of brush in the swamp below. My grandfather was elfin, wiry, dark, and quick. I'd follow him step for step, and still somehow never manage to keep up. He seemed to cut through tangle and brush like it was water and he was a trout, without snapping a twig or moving a limb, silently and without effort. He hardly ever spoke when he was in the woods, but when he did it was to instruct. He spent most of a winter's afternoon showing me how to make little wire nooses, how to spot a bottleneck in a rabbit trail that was an ideal spot for rigging these snares, and how to fence off the trail with bits of twig to steer the rabbit into the noose, how to rig it to an overarching branch as a little gallows frame for the loop so the rabbit's dying flops would not generate enough purchase to snap the wire. Snaring rabbits was illegal, but this didn't seem to matter in the swamp. The next day, our trap line held three or four winter-white snowshoe hares, and we skinned them and ate them for dinner.

In spring, he taught me the proper search image that allows one to spot morel mushrooms peeking forth from the forest floor. Find the first few, then you quickly realize you've been walking by them by the dozens because your brain had not yet learned to grasp what your eyes were seeing all along. At about the same time, ferns would be opening their palmate fronds just enough to form ancient-looking arthritic fists that he called "fiddleheads" because of their resemblance to the carved peg head of a violin. We fried the ferns and the morels in butter.

He advised me that if I were to shoot a deer and the deer did not die stone dead right there, I shouldn't run off after it immediately, but should sit "quite" (that's how he pronounced "quiet") for a few minutes and have a cigarette so as to give the animal time to die. I was about thirteen at the time and had not yet taken up cigarettes, but I got the point. When I did start smoking, it was Camel straights, same as him.

Somehow, I learned from these walks with my grandfather that wildness was a state of mind that time would teach me to inhabit. Like morel mushrooms, you had to learn to see it, even when it was all around.

He collected and saved all sorts of things, from tin cans to rocks he liked. Nothing was without value. The old barn on his place was worn out and sagging and finally came down in a heap; for years after, he pulled it apart, sorting the hardwood boards into piles, pulling and straightening all the nails to be used again. When it came time for the house to come down, he did the same with that, and we used the nails to build my grandparents a new house just behind the remains of the shack. As was the custom there and then, my grandfather recruited some guys from the neighborhood to lay up a concrete block foundation, then set joists on the plate and sheathed in what later would become the subfloor of the second story. He covered the subfloor in tar paper and tarred the seams to make a flat roof, and my grandparents moved into the foundation until they could afford to press on. A couple of years later, my dad built the rest, a neat little frame house on top of the foundation, two front rooms, one for visiting, one for eating, two small bedrooms, but with central heating, flush toilets, and running water. Then my grandmother set up her beauty shop in the basement.

My grandfather's station was in the living room, that green plastic chair with an ashtray beside. His roots in Catholicism seemed to grant him some special dispensation against the strict Baptist prohibition of tobacco, and he hung on to his Camels. One of his fingers had been caught in a press in a car factory where he worked, and it had been broken in a way that left it bent sideways at about thirty degrees from the second joint. I always thought it an ingenious accommodation of his cigarette, creating a neat little hollow that wrapped it. Jesus and my grandmother eventually convinced him of the wickedness of the Camels, and he gave them up, thereafter smoking a pipe. He reeked of equal parts tobacco and Ben-Gay.

The chair was his throne for television, which he engaged as if seated front and center at live theater. He was addicted to soap operas, a habit developed from shift work at car plants, and would weep openly as the plot thickened, but mostly to comedies, especially Red Skelton. He liked sitcoms and variety shows and would cackle and twinkle constantly. Fibber McGee and Molly jokes from radio days were still regarded as perfectly good jokes, and he recycled them frequently. He was less animated when folks were visiting, occasionally interjecting an understanding nod at the details of someone's surgery. When company came, he was more engaged with the children, demonstrating all sorts of special powers, such as the ability to steal a child's nose and hold it out in front the child's face, as if it were hanging in thin air. His granddaughters in particular were entertained with knee-bouncing games and tickling. He called his grandsons "Bub."

My best estimate is my grandfather worked the auto plants in Flint until at least 1960; my evidence for this is a blue Corvair. The line he worked on Fisher Body had a hand in making Corvairs, and the third one off the line happened to be destined for Applegate Chevrolet, a dealership in Flint, so he got off work and bought it for just under $2,000. The Corvair was Chevrolet's answer to the Volkswagen, the only air-cooled, rear-mounted engine ever mass-produced in the United

States. Ralph Nader would make his name as a champion for consumers by writing a book condemning the odd little Chevy. It was a compact, quick car that fit a compact, quick little man. Both of my grandfathers, in fact, were madly eccentric drivers of the sort whose first experiences in locomotion involved horses. They both drove as if cars were sentient beings and had some responsibility for their actions.

My Grandfather Manning's weapon of choice was a powder blue Studebaker Lark, a car distinguished at the time by the fact that, although it was compact like the Nash Rambler, could accommodate a big V8, and he had one. His style was full-out all the time and was something of a terror up until he died, taking back roads and blacktop alike in the low eighties. Speculation was widespread that this would be how he would die, and a few neighbors with him.

Grandfather Mayo was not so much about ultimate speed, but about what football commentators like to call "quickness" as distinguished from speed. He was the sort of driver who was in third gear before he cleared the end of the driveway and could decelerate from fifty to zero in the last three inches before the stop sign.

I know all this because the Corvair was to become my first car; I bought it from him for $100 in 1965, when I was fourteen and had a learner's permit. The most appreciated and unique feature of the Corvair was, because it was air-cooled, it needed a heater independent of the cooling system, a problem Chevy solved by equipping it with a gasoline-fired heater. And although Chevy may not have intended this, the independently fired heater allowed one to keep the car reasonably warm without idling the engine, greatly appreciated when the car would find itself parked for long periods on back roads on winter Saturday nights, an integral part of any high school experience.

The Corvair's downside was it had no frame, but was built up on a sheet metal body pan. In Michigan then, cars did not wear out; they rusted out. The state was unique and profligate in its use of highly corrosive salt on winter roads, meaning one needed to buy a new car every three or four years. This looked suspiciously like planned obsolescence to some of the more cynical residents of the auto-making state, but we were assured this was coincidence. The governor who would have overseen this coincidence was George Romney, a former auto company executive. My grandfather's Corvair had indeed suffered what was known as a "cancer" of the rocker panels, a problem that in most cars was simply ugly, but in a Corvair was threatening of structural integrity because it affected the body pan. All this came to a head one Friday night after a football game when I and fourteen of my closest friends piled into the Corvair, clown-car style, and the car simply broke in half at the middle.

But I also knew this car as well when it was under my grandfather's guidance. Occasionally, it would be my great honor to ride with my grandfather. My brother too, Mike, a year younger. My brother and I were inseparable. He was just a year and nine days younger, and we made for a pair of bright blond boys who looked alike and my mother dressed us alike until we were old enough to stop her.

My Grandfather Mayo was the only adult male I knew who went fishing. Everyone else—the lifelong farmers who dominated the community—considered fishing a near-sinful waste of time. As in all other tasks, the Corvair was suited perfectly. My grandfather fished for pike with a cane pole maybe ten feet long, no reel, just a length of monofilament and a big red-and-white bobber. He bent this rig over the roof of the Corvair and lashed its ends to bumpers fore and aft. He jammed a couple of cheap bait casting rods in the front-end trunk for my brother and for me, along with a tackle box full of all sorts of arresting paraphernalia. There would be a coffee can full of black earth alive with gobs of night crawlers dug from his worm beds made of salvaged wood in the fallen-down barn. And we'd stop at the bait store to buy a dozen little bait fish, he called them "minnies," then take pains to keep them alive and vital in a specially made minnow bucket.

The Corvair would take us to Fletcher Pond, a nearby impoundment named for the Fletcher family that owned the power company that created the dam and like everything the Fletchers owned, was named for them. (I was later to encounter a scion of the tribe when I was a young reporter and then confirmed that arrogance in these people was bred to the bone.) My other grandfather had made some spending money during the Depression logging off the backwater of Fletcher Pond before it was flooded, and now we fished around the submerged stumps he had made.

My grandfather rigged up the big rod with a minnie for bait and set it as far out as he could cast, waiting for a decent northern pike to strike. Often this could take a whole afternoon, but he would simply squat on a rock, sometimes on a plastic cushion he called a "dry ass," smoke Camels, and stare without once wavering his gaze from the red top of his bobber. My brother and I, meantime, fished for sunfish and crappies with worms along the shore, but the process always began with a fight to settle which one of us would fish the mermaid. The mermaid was a bobber float, not a ball, but a more elaborate plastic representation of a mermaid, green on the bottom half with mermaid fins, naked on the top with glorious 1940s tits. We could not imagine how he came by such a thing, and less could we imagine what would become of my grandfather if my grandmother were to ever have a look inside his tackle box. Likely his old life would end on the spot. But the mermaid was the foundation of my lifelong fascination with fishing.

I did not love my mother. I no longer find this sentence sad or troubling, simply true, difficult to form, it took years, but a relief when it finally appeared. Writing it freed me from the obligation. People expect people to say they loved their mothers, and I don't know why that should be true, either the expectation or the fact itself. It is obviously true that a significant number of our population is made up of failed humans, so it follows some of those will be mothers. My memories of her are consistent from the time of first dawning of memories until the day she died in 2001, from my end never once of any warmth or attachment or affection, always at odds, a force to be avoided or defeated. I have a tenable life today only to the degree I was able to defeat her.

I can only make sense of this now when memories place her in context with my grandparents. She was never really happy away from them, which was, I think, the dynamic that drove my parents back to Michigan after those early years when we lived in Tennessee and Ohio. She was unable to engage other people on anything but a superficial level, and could only exist in the tight little world of my grandparents, especially my grandmother.

My mother was a short woman, five foot one, tending to fat even early, and as she aged, obese. She had a smile of sorts but it never seemed to be able to fully bloom, always an overlay on her more dominant demeanor, a stubborn set of jaw. If you were to meet her on the street today, you'd see the jaw set right away, but what you would most remember would be her speech. She so mangled grammar and pronunciation that you could believe you were hearing not English, but a new language in the making. This was not a standard northern Michigan dialect. It was, in fact, the language of my grandparents. They spoke the same way, and no one else I knew ever did.

For a long time, I was merely ashamed of this, held it as an obvious sign of ignorance that I was escaping. And ashamed of myself for pointing it out, even here. These were poor people, products of the Great Depression, and the bare facts of this life mean they had much more on their minds than correct diction and pleasant speech. Were it simply that, I would not lean so hard on it, but I finally realized the language was the key.

I was raised in that tight little world, because my mother spent more time with her parents than anywhere else. When I came of age, I was often embarrassed when I would innocently mispronounce a word as I had forever heard it. Yet this embarrassment was the mark of my emergence, that even as a very young child, I was developing an ear for the larger world and learning its tongue, not my mother's. Language is how we enter the larger world. We attach to our circle of humanity with its notes and rhythms. My mother's eccentric speech was not so much a mark of her ignorance as it was her inability to tune her ear to the larger world. She simply could not attach, and I cannot blame her for this. It was the emblem of her isolation, and now I realize she must have lived alone all her life. My lifelong anger is aimed at her religion, which became a sort of madness, but something more fundamental was in play.

My Grandfather Mayo's lineage is the one that stumps me, although I know more now than I did growing up. I have the few tidbits like the 1920 census. That same census also enumerated the family of Ray Baldwin in Grayling about the same time. This was toward the end the great timber boom in Michigan, and Grayling was a timber town, so likely both families had come for work. Only one census earlier, the Baldwins had been in nearby Traverse City, my grandmother included. This now taps into the other line of DNA, mitochondrial DNA that tracks from mother to mother's mother and so on.

I remember my mother always maintained her mother's lineage was "Heinz 57," meaning a mixture, but she also maintained we were related to presidents and such along the way. This seemed an unlikely story for tar-paper-shack Baptists and probably needed some fact checking, which I finally did a few months ago.

My maternal grandmother's father, Ray Baldwin, continues a line of family from people with names like Swift, Crane, Hopkins, Wise, Partridge, and Fox, stretching back to the 1600s in Connecticut and Massachusetts, then to England. Ray's wife, Effie Higbee's, lineage runs through names like Rose,

Norris, Williams, Harrison, Boone, and Talman—even to an Abraham Lincoln, not the president, but the president's great-grandfather. The Boone family is part of Daniel Boone's line. Part of her lineage traces back to the 1600s in Virginia, then to England, then back through peerage records to people with names like Ap Comyn, which morphed through a few centuries to the French surnames of the nobility after the Norman conquests. Many of my grandmother's ancestors fought in the Revolutionary War, which is to say my grandmother had a pedigree to qualify her for the Daughters of the American Revolution, literally.

The DNA bears this out. I sent in a cheek swab myself in order to learn this. I share mitochondrial DNA with about half of the European population, drawn from an ancient group of settlers who arrived from Asia to southern Europe about 25,000 years ago. They rooted in almost the same place as did my paternal line—my cheek swab confirmed this part of my lineage as well—up against the ice sheet until glaciation ended, then north into Europe and the British Isles. The long list of surnames in my maternal grandmother's genealogy make the British Isles more likely, just as does my own surname and what I know of my paternal grandmother's genealogy. But deep down, we're all Cro-Magnon in this European line; the DNA confirms this as well.

This, of course, ignores my Native American blood, but as I think of it, it's not all that different. First, a good part of that heritage is, in fact, French, so traces to exactly the same people as the rest, but Native people evolved jammed up against the ice sheet in Asia, then crossed into North America to live as hunter-gatherers about 13,000 years ago, maybe longer. Natives spread south from Alaska through the tropics to the very tip of South America, but somehow my strain stayed north, from what I can tell, very near the 45th parallel. In all of the thousands of names I can locate in my genealogy and in the DNA, I can find evidence of only a couple of generations, some colonists in my maternal grandmother's line, who lived as far south as Virginia, then moved north, to Pennsylvania, then Indiana, then Traverse City, Michigan, on the 45th parallel. I have no explanation for this remarkable fidelity to north that seems encoded in my genes.

Nor can I explain the religion, but know now it did not emerge of a sudden with my grandparents Mayo. There is one long, straight line in my Grandmother Mayo's genealogy that follows her maiden name, Baldwin, an old-line American name, follows it straight back to the Winthrop colony that landed in Boston and included three Richardson brothers, one of which was Ezekial Richardson, my paternal grandmother Richardson's ancestor. Ezekial had a daughter, Phebe, only the tenth child born among the British colonists. She married Henry Baldwin in 1649 and these people are my maternal grandmother Baldwin's ancestors. Both of my grandmothers descend from Ezekial Richardson, a stalwart of the Winthrop colony. Whatever else this story might be, it is deeply American, and so accordingly, it is deeply religious. Always I have held my story as framed by opposite poles of maternal and paternal lineage, of the clash between religion and simple working people who got things done. My deeper story is written by the tension between these two deeply American poles.

A lot of us take some pride in tracing ancestry to the Plymouth Colony, but in the process forget these were the Puritans, religious zealots, every one. The zealotry waxes and wanes through the American story. My maternal grandmother's lineage included Quakers and a string of French Huguenots, who fled persecution in France. My paternal ancestors the Richardsons, Puritans from the beginning, would go on to found first a Baptist church near Manning Hill, then the Reorganized Church of Jesus Christ of the Latter Day Saints, the church my grandmother was buried in. This weird little offshoot of Mormonism was founded when James Jesse Strang split with Brigham Young and removed to Beaver Island in Lake Michigan, where he had himself crowned "King James I of the Kingdom of God on Earth." Today it is called Community of Christ.

Nor was my father's family, the taciturn working men, the Mannings, immune from religious schism. For instance, there is this:

THE ALPENA NEWS, April 26, 1924
Widely Known Young Farmer Succumbs To Self-Inflicted Attack

Frank Manning, aged 32, died last night at his farm home on the Salina road in the west part of Alpena county from a self-inflicted wound in the neck done with a razor while in a despondent mood, believed to have resulted from brooding over his wife's ill health.

The body has been removed to the home of his brother, Ben Manning, who occupies the old Manning homestead on Manning hill, west of Lachine on M-32. The funeral will occur at 1 o'clock Monday afternoon from the home with interment in Evergreen cemetery in Alpena. Rev. R. A. Allen will officiate.

He is survived by a wife and five children, the oldest of which is six years old. He is also survived by three sisters, Mrs. Ralph Thompson, Mrs. Jennie Morrison, Mrs. George Wallace, and four brothers, William, Fred, Harry and Ben Manning. According to meager information received from the scene, Mr. Manning sent a note to his father-in-law, requesting him to come to the house, and when the father-in-law arrived, Mr. Manning, who was at the edge of a woods some forty rods from his house, inflicted the wound. The father-in-law saw him fall and immediately went to his side.

A call was sent to Alpena for medical assistance, and before Dr. D. A. Cameron had departed a second call was received to the effect that death had taken place. Accordingly he continued to the Manning home in his capacity as coroner, accompanied by W. E. Williams, undertaker. Two other physicians went to the scene.

Upon arrival it was found that Mr. Manning was alive, though in a very weakened condition from the loss of blood. Examination showed that the jugular vein had not been severed and hope was expressed that his life could be saved. The loss of blood, however, proved too great a handicap to be overcome, and death ocurred several hours later.

Mr. Manning figured in a serious accident last fall, when an auto overturned on him in a ditch, pinning him beneath the machine, where he was found some time later in a weakened condition.

The newspaper clip, which I first saw as part my research for this book, was not my first encounter with this story. My father told me a version of it when I was a child, but with the added detail that the suicide resulted from a dispute with the Fitzpatricks, his wife's family, hence the summoning of his father-in-law. The Fitzpatricks were Catholics, and the dispute was about which religion the children would be raised in. A couple of my relatives, unprompted, recall this story the same way I did, that Frank's wife's "illness" was mental and she had tried to kill the children by putting them in an oven. My father offered it as a cautionary tale as to why I should never date Catholic girls. If the details of this story are correct, Frank was laid out in my grandfather's parlor, the very parlor I knew well as a child, the place where I heard the chatter of ancestors rising with the wood heat. Now I can't help but wonder about the story of my great-uncle's suicide from my grandfather's perspective. How did he learn of this? A whispered conversation on the front stoop with the authorities? Did he have to hitch horses to a wagon to get Frank's body and bring it the couple of miles to home, or was there a truck by then? Now it's too late to ask.

The Greely Baptist Church does not look like the center of conflict, nor did it on first sight look so to me. It was instead an innocuous and fitting fixture standing near the west foot of Manning Hill, visible from the vantage of my Grandfather Manning's farm. In an early-twentieth-century photo I have of my grandmother's childhood house, the Richardson house, the church sits on the background's horizon line. The church was built on a little plot near my great-grandfather Richard-son's farm, a simple little frame structure that still stands, as does the parsonage next door. I have sorted this structure into my maternal lineage, but in fact it was founded by a great-great-grandfather in my paternal line, A. R. Richardson. No Richardsons remained on the rolls when I attended, but a few Mannings who happened to become religious through mar-riage did attend.

Greely was my first real brush with churches. I have some memory of being dragged off to a Baptist church in Flint when I was younger than five, but in the years we lived in Ohio and Tennessee, I can never remember going to church. Instead, we played Little League baseball and rode bikes and went to air shows at Lockbourne Air Force Base, or visited the Great Smokey Mountains to see bears and picnicked at Norris Dam, like normal people. We lived far from the pressures of my mother's family and accordingly lived normally.

Fundamentalism tends to run in cycles in family lives and in longer cycles in our national history. Young adults slip away, lured by the joys of dancehalls and beer gardens and of being young adults. For my dad, who had never been religious (only my grandmother attended church in his family, and the rest called it "grandmother's church"), this was a natural course of events; my mother, however, had been raised in and con-tinued to state fundamentalism as her credo right up until she died. Yet I do know there was some significant backslid-ing, especially by my father. Once, as an adult in my fifties, I found myself in Knoxville, with time on my hands and a rental car. We had lived there when I was five and six, and I was able to recall a fragment of a street name and a school name, checked a map and drove there, found the house easily. It triggered memories, and they were not particularly peaceful, of my mother telling three crying kids my dad was going away; they were getting a divorce, and she and we would move back with "my folks." That's what she always called her family, her "folks."

Not long after my visit to Knoxville as an adult, after my mother died, my father was for some reason telling me about his discovery of the evils of alcohol, admitted some experimentation and repeated an often stated family belief that some people are predestined to alcoholism and, upon taking even one drink, would almost instantly slide into a life of sin and degradation, and that he knew that he was indeed one of these people. Then he detailed an event at that house in Tennessee, of waking up on a Saturday morning and seeing his brand-new Generous Motors company car parked on the lawn of the little frame house on Dove Lane and not remembering how it got there.

I grew up never seeing so much as a six-pack of beer in the refrigerator. People would give my dad bottles of whiskey for the holidays, and those got stacked in a bedroom closet, unopened, or at least unopened until my father and mother got into one of their screaming fights in the night. Then my mother would pour some of them into the kitchen sink as if she had studied technique with Carrie Nation. A family's cycles of fundamentalism are often driven by alcohol, and I suspect from memory fragments I can recover, it was no different in my family. The spin of this cycle is likely what finally drove us back to Michigan and to settling on the back side of Manning Hill not much more than a mile from Greely Church.

The church was then fundamentalist although all of its members likely were not. Since at least 1919, there has been a clear statement of what that means, composed by the World Christian Fundamentals Association. The tenets include the inerrancy of scripture, the deity of Christ, accepting the virgin birth, believing that Christ died to atone for all sin, the resurrection of Christ, and a belief he will literally return. Citing this list, William Martin, the historian of the religious right in modern America, says:

> The keystone was and is the inerrancy of scripture, meaning not only that the Bible is the sole and infallible rule of faith and practice, but also that it is scientifically and historically reliable. Thus, evolution could not be true, miracles really did happen just as the Bible describes them, and on Judgment Day all who have ever lived will be assigned for eternity to heaven or hell, both of which really do exist. Any attempt to interpret these or other features of Scripture as myths or allegories strikes at the very root of Christian faith and must be resisted with every fiber of one's being.

My mother, her parents, and all of her siblings would have checked each of these boxes. So would my father, at least later in his life.

In recent years, "evangelical" has become the preferred term to "fundamentalist." I suspect this is a euphemism that allows us to reserve the latter term for describing Muslim fundamentalists, but the distinction is unwarranted. Evangelicals and fundamentalists are the same, believe and act the same, and the taint implied by a connection to Muslim fundamentalism is deserved.

Like all kids so blessed as to be imprisoned in fundamentalism, early close contact began with Daily Vacation Bible School. This meant that as soon as summer vacation from school began, I did not give my days over to horses, bicycles, and fishing poles. Instead, for two weeks I went to church all day every day. That is, depriving us of the freedom and fun being enjoyed just then by our peers was supposed to make us into devoted Christians, an odd assumption that gave us some reason to suspect the basic logic of the people in charge of fundamentalism.

Bible school meant you learned a Bible verse every day and manufactured useful household implements with glue and sucker sticks, maybe a trivet with "Jesus Loves Me" spelled out in gold-flaked macaroni. And you sang:

Jesus loves the little children
All the little children of the world
Red and yellow, black and white
They are precious in his sight
Jesus loves the little children of the world

(Most of today's right-wing fundamentalists sang this song in Bible School too, but somehow the doctrine therein has failed to make it into their political planks. Or maybe the belief is Jesus does love the brown people only as long as they do not become immigrants.)

Then after two weeks of this, there would be a program. Parents would come, we'd recite some verses, sing some songs, everybody would go home with sucker stick utensils, and we would finally be left to the customary pursuits of young savages for what was left of summer.

Yet over the course of a few years, the early 1960s—when elsewhere, Bob Dylan was already in Greenwich Village, Negroes were at lunch counters and the front of buses, and a bright young Catholic president was charting an ambitious course—my parents dug more deeply into fundamentalism. They went to church more often. My maternal grandparents were always there, my grandfather sort of hunched forward in the pew, his arms crossed, nodding sagely to the preacher's pronouncements on all matters except cigarettes, my grandmother scowling. My father became a regular and a deacon. My mother taught Sunday School. They were saved.

Yet none of this had the hard edge we would come to know in today's fundamentalist churches: no amplified guitars and shouting in tongues, no politics, no railing and moaning. Elsewhere, fundamentalism mutated through the 1970s and 1980s, but Greely was still a simple country church presided over by the Reverend Norris Beck, a bald, soft-spoken, humble man. Mostly it was a place to gather for service on Sundays and for potluck suppers in the church basement every now and again. My mother, in fact, acquired a set of copperylooking Jell-O molds in a variety of attractive shapes, just to serve her responsibilities in this regard.

Or so it seemed, but as some awareness dawned, it became clear to me, in fact was made clear that somewhere along the line, Bub, you're gonna have to come to the Lord, accept Jesus Christ as your own personal savior, join the church. This last term made no sense to me. Join? Wasn't I already there? Against my will, but I was there. They had something more in mind. A line had been drawn, and I was a young heathen on the wrong side of it. I was separate from them. Nonetheless, unlike my younger brother and sister, I resisted the altar call.

This is a pivotal event in Baptist services. At the end of Reverend Beck's gentle little sermons he'd offer up the lure of life everlasting and invite the unsaved among his flock of thirty or so people, the same thirty or so he'd seen all their lives, to accept the Lord, and then Virginia Green would lay down an intro on the piano and we'd sing, in unison:

> *Just as I am and waiting not*
> *to rid my soul of one dark blot*
> *to thee whose blood can cleanse each spot*
> *Oh lamb of God I come, I come*

Then we'd go home and have chicken dinner and read the Sunday comics (we called them "funnies") in the *Detroit Free Press* that we'd buy at Bob Gleason's General Store in Lachine.

The Baptists I knew didn't call themselves "evangelicals" back then but they did indeed have evangelists, a custom long predating my brush with the church. The archetype, at least in my parents' and grandparents' mind, was Billy Graham. My grandparents had once seen the great man in person, in 1945 at the North Baptist Church in Flint, an event that welded them to the church. I can see how that might be so. Graham began his act in the 1940s and his biographer William Martin has written about those early revivals, which featured "Bible quizzes, patriotic and spiritual testimonies by famous and semi-famous preachers, athletes, entertainers, military heroes, business and civic leaders, former hoodlums and miscreants, and such specialty acts as magicians, ventriloquists, and a horse who would 'kneel at the cross' and tap his foot twelve times when asked the number of Christ's apostles or three times when how many persons constituted the Trinity." I can see how such a horse could make a serious spiritual impact and wish I could have seen this. Greely Baptist and even Alpena, Michigan, however, were far too remote to attract Graham, but as kids we were ordered to sit in front of the television every time a national network televised one of Graham's stadium-filling revivals. Same deal as church: "Just as I am without one plea," but thousands of folks would stream forth to be saved, which must have made the Reverend Beck envious.

We couldn't book Graham, but Greely did do revivals, which was something like having a bar band replaced by a headliner act for a week's run. My attendance was mandatory. Our backwater Graham was a man named Gleason (no relation to the general store Gleason), and I cannot remember his first name, only that he had a large number of children about my age, and they played trumpets and clarinets and such. Gleason trucked in a bit more hellfire and brimstone than the Reverend Beck; probably had to because he had to hustle for a living.

Usually, just before the free-will offering plate came round, he'd tell some story about his family, about being down to the last potato in the house and not knowing where the next meal was coming from, so the family group knelt in a circle and prayed to God for potatoes, and just then a kindly believer would pull up the driveway with a whole sack of potatoes, not to mention a decent roast of beef. But Gleason was not in town to have dinner, but there to save souls, which involved a sort of windup and pitch.

The windup was some pithy bit of hellfire from the Book of Revelation about Jesus returning at any moment, and if we had not offered up our souls to him via Gleason, we, even we children, would burn in everlasting hell. I tried to imagine everlasting, tried even to imagine a lake of fire that would not burn me up in a heartbeat and instead make me everlasting; I could not. But the Lord tarries. And then he'd launch into a story from a recent headline, maybe about kids exactly my own age who had been killed in a car wreck on the way home from church after once more resisting an altar call, thus condemned to the lake of fire. It could happen.

Then we'd be singing:

Just as I am, though tossed about,
with many a conflict, many a doubt . . .

And then, without explanation, it happened. I found myself standing at the front of that little church, shaking and weeping uncontrollably, the most embarrassing possible position for a twelve-year-old boy, but I couldn't stop shaking. I had no idea how I came to be there, but there I was. I think this was indeed about acceptance, that if Jesus could manage such acceptance, perhaps my mother and her family could accept me just as I was.

———

There was a rite of passage not limited to Baptists, but available to every male child of the 1960s in rural northern Michigan. My dad did not hunt, at least not with regular sportsmen during the season, which began then as it does to this day on November 15. My two uncles from Flint, my mother's brothers, would show up maybe the day before with their faded red jackets and scoped military Mausers they had customized themselves. There'd be talk about calibers, bolt actions, and telescopic sights that penetrated the murk of dusk. Both uncles were crack shots. My grandfather would suit up head to toe in his red buffalo plaid and oil up his octagon-barreled Winchester. And I'd be given some old hand-me-down shotgun and the job of driver, meaning me, my brother, and my cousin David would fan out in a line and stumble through swamps trying to push deer toward my uncles and grandfather waiting on the opposite side. Drivers seldom saw deer.

But by the time I was fourteen, I could hunt on my own. I was old enough to buy a hunting license, but my dad told me I didn't need one to hunt my own land, so wouldn't buy me one. This was, of course, false. I had a cheap, single-shot 20-gauge shotgun, a round of buckshot in the breech and two more in my pocket. The shotgun, an ancient XLCR made by Iver Johnson, sits in the corner of my office as I write this. Armed with it I wandered the oak-copsed ridges on the south side of Manning Hill and topped a ridge to see a small young buck stepping up the opposite slope, headed straight away from me. I had seen my uncle make such a shot, hitting a doe square in the anus and breaking her spine. I know many hunters today, and not a one would consider this a legitimate shot, but then I had few examples, so saw this as my chance to come of age. I fired a round of buckshot, hitting just off center. Buckshot at close range does not make so much an entry wound as it does an excavation, and I saw one open on one of the buck's hind legs, the right. At the center of the hole I could see a shattered top of femur.

The buck fled on three legs, the wounded leg swinging as if on a hinge over its back, to my horror, running faster than I could run, and I ignored my grandfather's advice about sitting and having a cigarette and instead gave chase. Every now and then I heard the animal collapse in a crackle of leaves a few hundred yards ahead, and then I came up over a ridge and it would spot me and would jump and run and I would fire a useless shot, and this happened over and over until I had no more shells. Then I tracked it with a few spots of blood all across our land, then onto Alman Eagling's place, where I was forbidden to go, then out across Manning Hill road where anyone could have driven by to see this shameful event unfold, then onto the Klein place, maybe three quarters of a mile of breathless, panicked scramble, fearing I would lose the trail and hoping the deer would die somewhere where no one could see what I had done. Then finally I found it near-dead and collapsed, looking up at me, and I had no more shells for my shotgun, so I broke loose a chunk of fallen poplar tree and bludgeoned it to death. I have been trying to atone and make my peace with deer ever since.

This event would become, literally, a recurring nightmare, one of two that plagued me well into adulthood.

5

EDUCATION

A blue-and-red bus picked me up at my house on Bristol Road in Flint, and took me to kindergarten class where the routine was always the same. Each child deployed a sheet of fibrous, wide-ruled paper and a fat pencil and wrote the alphabet, caps and lowercase, followed by the numerals, one through ten. As each accomplished this and turned in his assignment, he was freed to play with toys. I follow an analogous routine today as a writer, so perhaps it's true what they say about the importance of patterns in early life. In kindergarten, though, I was mostly left alone to play with toys for long periods each morning, while the other kids struggled at their desks. I wondered what they had against toys. Teacher had walked us through the ABCs and the numbers, so why didn't those other kids simply do the drill and get on with it?

Reading was taught with a big illustrated flip chart, our introduction to Dick, Jane, and Sally and their dog, Spot. Being able to read seemed a sort of magic that allowed me to crack codes all around, deeper mysteries like the contents of street signs and advertising posters in store windows. All of this was obsessively entertaining, and from then on there was no place I would rather be than school. That's where my friends were. That's where I learned to play softball, and that's where I could read as much as I wanted. I've forgotten most of the specifics of these early school years, but among the snatches I can recall there is not a single unpleasant memory. I think I was probably a good little kid, something of a teacher's pet, certainly precocious.

There was a florescence of awareness in about sixth grade, when I was eleven or so and my family had returned to northern Michigan and Manning Hill. I was then riding the school bus every day to Green Township school, driven by my dad's double cousin Oden. (Their fathers were brothers, their mothers, Richardson sisters. Oden lived on the farm next to ours, a place that had been his father's before. It was adjacent to my grandfather's, both places once part of my great-grandfather's farm. The Richardson farm, on which both Odens and my father's mothers were raised, had been adjacent to my great-grandfather's.) The school's construction had been superintended by my Grandfather Manning only a couple of years before, so it was brand-new. He was on the school board, which then meant climbing onto a scaffold and overseeing masons himself to ensure the job was done right. I saw him do this. It was how conservative Republican farmers discharged responsibility to community.

Sally Knorr was my teacher that year, and she taught a method of learning language now viewed every bit as arcane as the Palmer penmanship class that was also required curriculum. We diagrammed sentences, parsed them, as it is known now. It was a stunning revelation for me, that mysteries and intricacies of stories could be disassembled as cleanly as a small-block Chevy engine, the power revealed and available to all. And so I went through my days fully engaged in shooting horizontal lines to underscore subject, verb, and direct objects, vertical lines to separate them, angled lines to split off phrases and subordinate clauses. It was obvious to me where everything belonged and deeply satisfying to assign each part of a thought to a place.

My teacher the next year was Ardella Herron, my bus driver Oden's sister, therefore also my dad's double cousin. The student population was small, so required doubling up grades, which was fine with me. I could finish my work and listen to what the older seventh graders were doing, which seemed a good bit more interesting than my assignments. We began learning what was called then "the new math," a curriculum that became controversial simply because it seemed more pretentious than good old-fashioned 'rithmetic. It was abstract and taught algebraic concepts, and I liked it. Like diagramming sentences, it began to crack more puzzles and unravel more mysteries. Math was like Tinkertoys, and plugging the pieces together was entertaining.

Our reading program was called SRA, for Science Research Associates, which was based in Palo Alto, California, and a few years later employed a young writer, Raymond Carver. The program was a "reading box" that held a student's individualized program. It broke up the old reading group system and allowed each of us to proceed as we would, and I proceeded. This suited me fine. I was reading what was available outside of school, which in my house was a shelfful of Bible stories, luridly illustrated, and the *World Book Encyclopedia,* complete with annual updates, and naturally, the Bobbsey Twins, the Hardy Boys, and Nancy Drew. My omnivory, however, caused some discomfort at my school.

My parents belonged to a Farm Bureau group, as most adults did. These were a sort of rural equivalent of bi-gendered book clubs, an excuse for a circle of friends to meet at someone's house once a month to eat Jell-O molds and cupcakes and drink coffee brewed in an enormous urn. Somehow or other, one such meeting at my parents' house produced a stack of magazines and pamphlets largely concerned with telling the story of a Baptist missionary who was also an intelligence officer and was killed by Communists in China, a fellow named John Birch. I read the magazines like I read everything else, took them to school to share this information, as my father said I should, and the principal, Bill Bates, told me it was best if I would take it home. The John Birch Society, still with us, began only in 1958, so this would have made my dad an early adopter.

In November of seventh grade, Bill Bates made an announcement on the PA that the president had been shot.

I found myself especially liking school in these years because of the cows. The cows had come to terrorize my life at home, and at least at school I was away from them.

My dad always fancied himself a farmer, so we had chickens and a couple of horses on our sixty acres, but then his farming never went so far as raising crops to feed the animals and us. Every spring, he busted up an enormous patch of weeds and rocks, maybe an acre and a half, and we dutifully planted it to garden. Within a month, the weeds had usually reclaimed it. A few years on, he decided to build a barn in the side of the hill and hired someone to lay up a foundation, maybe twenty by thirty feet, of concrete blocks. He topped this with what were to be the floor joists of the second story, sheathed and tar-papered the whole business to serve as a roof until he got around to completing the second story, typically a hayloft. But he judged progress sufficient to accommodate milk cows and bought at auction a half dozen stove-in specimens that drew no competing bids, an eclectic mix that included an Ayrshire, a Brown Swiss, a Guernsey, and a couple of Holsteins. All serious dairymen in our area milked only Holsteins, but my dad believed all gains were made by working the margins. He bought a busted-down air compressor to power a couple of antique DeLaval milking machines and an old cream separator, which was a simple centrifuge for pulling cream from skim milk. We sold the cream and fed the skim milk to hogs. He haywired some tubing to a couple of posts, plumbed in some petcocks, and our compressed air system was ready to drive the two milking machines, one for my brother and one for me. Then he left us, taking off to wherever it was he was working construction.

Cows must be milked twice a day every day, and there was no one else to do this but my brother and me, then eleven and twelve. So we did, up every morning at five to find the cows in their pasture in the dark, drive them to what passed for stanchions in my father's barn, milk, feed hay, catch the bus to school still smelling like cow shit, off the bus at four, repeat.

Dairy barns are usually impeccable places despite the storied ability of cows to produce great quantities of shit. Under normal circumstances, this miracle of sanitation is accomplished by concrete wrought into neatly lined stalls and a gutter system strategically placed and sloped. Our barn's concrete floors and gutters, like its hayloft, were still in the planning stages. This proved to be more than an inconvenience when my dad was backfilling the barn's foundation walls with a little bulldozer, and it slid downslope, collided with the barn, and caved in one wall, knocking the lid askew. He thought this a bad bit of luck and planned to get around to fixing it. Meantime, the roof leaked, first in fall rains, then the drip from winter's snows. Thus, we boys did the milking twice daily in a quagmire of cow shit and mud until winter finally froze the whole business solid.

My dad's plans also included a line fence on our land's north edge. There already was a fence of sorts, one built by his father probably before he was born, and we did spend some time patching and propping as we could, but it was no real match for our cows' increasing athletic skills, especially in periods when my dad forgot to buy hay. They preferred to ramble in the early morning hours, and this is when the party-line wall-mount phone in our kitchen would jangle us awake, a call from a neighbor whose garden was under attack by our cows. My brother and I would be rousted, dressed, and dispatched into the night. And we were to some degree relieved these matters occurred in the dark, because even at our age we knew a certain shame attached to faulty fences. After some years of this, the cows quit giving milk and went to the slaughterhouse. I was glad to see them die.

I left Green School after the eighth grade to go to high school in Alpena, the city, but the bus I rode, still driven by Cousin Oden, circled the entire township, then went to town, so it was an hour-and-half ride every morning and the same every night. The ride made me an available captive for a couple of bullies, and apparently I deserved beatings because I was little and smart. This former problem ran in the family. My dad was so small when he entered high school classmates hung the ironic nickname "Hippo" on him, but he ended up six foot one. I still didn't mind going to school, and a couple years later got my growth.

Testing had sent me to Robert Kelly's advanced placement English class for freshmen, and I got a D on my first writing assignment, the first D I had ever seen. But I listened to what he said about simple declarative sentences and the power of short words and wound up with an A for the class. I took Latin, all the hard sciences, played the saxophone in marching band and in jazz band. We read Orwell, Sinclair Lewis's *Elmer Gantry* and *Babbitt,* Dickens, *Lord of the Flies.* We staged Thornton Wilder's *Our Town,* and I played the lead, the stage manager/narrator. I reveled in math, especially math, my favorite, at least until I discovered sex. Then, there was nothing to my mind more satisfying and elegant than a simple geometric proof, that beginning from a few known facts and unwavering laws of logic one could advance, step by irrefutable step to the conclusion, QED. This, probably more than any other single influence, decided that I would spend my life writing essays, not fiction. By my senior year, I had learned enough calculus to place out of freshman calculus my first year at the university. I had learned enough Latin and enough of Sally Knorr's diagrams and enough of Bob Kelly's disciplined sentences to be formidable in debate with adults. And I had learned enough of everything to understand war with my parents—and through my life, a long string of analogs of my parents—was imminent.

The first concrete benefit of my accepting Jesus Christ as my Lord and Savior was it got me laid. I only later learned this was a well-known phenomenon among fundamentalists, but had I learned this sooner, I would not have been so resistant to religious fervor. I'll not go too deeply into analyzing this phenomenon, but I know the empirical case well enough to hypothesize. Fundamentalist girls tend to be a bit on the easy side. This is especially true in the case of daughters of ministers, otherwise known as a "pk" for "preacher's kid." These children especially have reason to rebel and tend to do so liberally when hormones urge them on.

Some of the credit for this, however, attaches to the limited activities available to children indentured to this religion. One quickly outgrows the allures of Daily Vacation Bible School, activities not completely satisfying for girls with developed breasts. In the normal world, this would be the period when dating commences with movies and dances, but we were not in the normal world. In those days, Baptist kids were forbidden both dancing and movies. The substitute was a social network organized under the rubric of Youth for Christ. Thus, our elders assumed we would be dissuaded from the devil's temptations available at sock hops and picture shows by providing us with more opportunities to sit in circles and study the Bible. These weekly events would be offset by periodic opportunities to carpool to towns a couple of hundred miles away, stay at parishioners' houses at some new church under strict rules of gender segregation, and have more full days of opportunities for Bible study and reflection. These events were called retreats, and my parents made me go to every one on offer.

The weight of all this yielded the widely understood phenomenon, even among the Catholics and Lutherans, that Baptist girls couldn't dance or go to movies, so they filled the void with sex. Whatever the reason, I was grateful for the result. The passion raised by praising Jesus is powerful and transferable. The authorities' prohibitions are not enforceable. Sooner or later there would be a church social at someone else's distant house, then long car rides where an hour can slip by unaccounted, a walk in the woods, first rub of a bare breast, a squirm to shuck jeans in a backseat, and then an epiphany: if religion prohibits this, then religion is wrong.

Fundamentalist Christianity is not about negotiating the ethical intricacies of life; it's not even about being a better person. It is at bottom about belief—literal professed belief—in the details of a two-thousand-year-old story. Jonah did get eaten and spit back up by a whale. There was a flood and two of every kind of every animal on earth fit into one boat. Evidence be damned, the earth is six thousand years old. Christ did walk on water and there is a place in the sky when we die.

When I was among the faithful, these matters were generally discussed and revealed to us in an order of increasing absurdity, a sort of conditioning that prepares initiates to eventually swallow the larger whoppers. It is relatively easy to accept that Jesus loves me and therefore will not let me die, but exploring the ramifications of this idea raises logical problems. This is likely why the convert doesn't hear much about the Book of Revelation until he is well into and fully conditioned to the world as rendered in funhouse mirrors.

The Book of Revelation is a bizarre bit of literature that stands as evidence that hallucinogens are not unique to our time. For fundamentalists, however, the Book of Revelation is not literature, but a literal description of the last days before Jesus returns to claim the faithful. It is an account of the Apocalypse, when the wicked among us will be cast into a lake of fire, when Jesus will rule for a millennium that will usher in eternity in heaven for the faithful. All of this is set in what is now the Middle East, logical, because the authors lived there and did not yet know any other place existed.

I was pretty taken with Revelation and tried to imagine what the final days would look like. My Sunday School teachers had primed the vision, and I'm sure I embellished a bit. For instance, I could never leave it at four horsemen; in my mind's eye there was a whole phalanx of fiery stallions riding down out of a blazing orange sky, a scene I could easily imagine from the edge of Manning Hill when clouds and dust painted a particularly dramatic sunset. It was an easy matter to merge this scene with similar visions most kids had then, as we tried to make some sense out of what our parents had told us about the Cuban Missile Crisis, duck-and-cover drills, and why there was a bomb shelter sign on our school. Our God had always promised to rain down hellfire and brimstone on a wicked world and now there were tools for doing so. Apocalypse was a real possibility.

But by then, I knew more geography than the guys who had written Revelation. Because this event was to affect the entire world, Cubans, Chinese, Australians, the whole deal, it seemed highly unlikely I would see the horsemen on the Michigan horizon line near Manning Hill, or that four guys on horses could get the job done. And blazing sunset was just sunlight refracted through water vapor and dust, a real enough phenomenon that did indeed portend darkness, then sunrise the next morning and another day.

My faith dissolved under logic, literally, as I sat on Manning Hill late one day watching the sunset. The same thing had happened only a few years before as I did the math on Santa Claus—total number of chimney-bearing households in North America and Europe and average distance between, factored against reindeer velocity, average time per visit, that sort of thing. That couldn't be right. If you can do the math, you can avoid a lot of really bad ideas. This was not a crisis of faith, but a simple dissolution of faith. I was not a bit torn or troubled. Nor was I for a second tempted to seek out some more moderate interpretation than fundamentalism, something that would keep God in my life through the expedient of a less than literal interpretation of scripture. I did indeed know that moderate churches existed; we had been warned against them explicitly. I also knew the moderates read the King James version of the Holy Bible; I knew what it said, and it simply wasn't true, wasn't even very interesting to read. Even at fifteen I had a firm conviction there is nothing to be gained in believing something that is not true. Now, if I meet someone who professes faith in Christianity, I sometimes ask them about their position on Santa Claus and the Easter Bunny. From that day on, I was an atheist.

My emancipation from my mother's fundamentalism was founded as much on pig shit as it was education. When I was fourteen or so, my mother got a call from Don Manning, a distant cousin. He'd heard I was a good worker and would I be able to come by his shop the coming Saturday? Don owned the slaughterhouse Manning's Meats, which he had bought only a few years before from George Manning, another cousin distant from both Don and me. George was at retirement age and neither of his sons, Harmon and Victor, wanted the business, but they both still cut meat and slaughtered hogs, sheep, and cattle. Nothing so refined as this, however, awaited me that Saturday. Don kept hogs and the pens needed mucking out, so I did this deed, for days on end, load on load heaped on a wheelbarrow with a pitchfork, then wheeled up a plank and into the manure spreader.

I was dogged enough in this that Don called a few weeks later and I was put to work in the slaughterhouse, for the first few days at such chores as cleaning the bandsaw with a steam hose, pulling up the wood walking slats over the concrete floor and scraping them clean, unloading fresh smoked slabs of bacon and hams from the smokehouse. Then a few weeks later Don taught me the quick roll and tuck of the butcher's wrap, so I was then skilled enough to stand whole days at a counter and wrap packages of meat in waxed paper, ready for the freezers of my cousins and neighbors. I worked every Saturday and after school.

This was not the standard pound-of-this-and-a-few-slices-of-that deli business, although we did some of that. The bacon, hams, and sausage were good enough that we drew some trade from outside the community, especially in the summer when people from the auto plant cities were up north camping at our lakes. The primary business, however, was to serve as an essential hub and infrastructure of a traditional farming community. Almost everyone kept a few cows and fattened a few on surplus grain; most kept a few hogs and in fall sent them to us for slaughter, to hang in long rows in our coolers for a week or so. Then Harmon and Don would cut them to steaks and roast and grind burger, and I'd wrap. This was more than a process. Loading the beef your farm had raised into the freezer was an annual ritual and validation. Most of the Mannings and Richardsons and Morrisons around Manning Hill raised Herefords for beef, like most beef cattle, a British breed named in the nineteenth century for the town of Hereford at the edge of Wales. The Welsh had been seminomadic pastoralists raising beef cattle even before they were Welsh, maybe eight thousand years, and the Mannings, Morrisons, and Richardsons were direct descendants of these people who had stored cuts of beef against long winters for millennia. I had a literal hand in this tradition about the time it ended. What I learned to do then was very much like the process today resurrected in the better boutique meat markets of urban foodies.

My Grandfather Manning's farm was fallow then, and he was dead, although he had mostly quit farming a few years before he died. None of his sons was interested in carrying on, for a good reason. The sort of farming that had supported that place through a century was falling to the industrial monocrop agriculture that would claim a way of life in a matter of a decade or so. Industrial-scale agriculture requires flat, long fields of thousands of acres with no fencerows, and such places were few and far between in the glacial terrain of northern Michigan. Industrial agriculture requires pesticides and chemical fertilizers and produces food my family would be ashamed to eat. The land around Manning Hill was marginal at best and the winters long, so farming simply went away, migrating to the flat, fertile, south-of-the-state places like Iowa, Indiana, and Minnesota.

My Grandmother Manning refused to eat irrigated strawberries, always a major crop on the farms around the village of Spratt about five miles south of Manning Hill. Strawberries—she called them simply "berries"—were a big deal to her, and as long as she could, she picked her own every June into July, working under a floppy sun hat, picking into a wooden flat that held eight quarts, heaped. Then she fired up her summer canning kitchen and rendered them to jam, which she would oversweeten. She treasured sugar, a vestige of rationing during World War II. She left as many berries as possible fresh for table and served them for breakfast during sunny summer months, sugared.

Thus it had been for generations, but irrigation was a new

wrinkle in this, a measure some of the more forward-thinking farmers had adopted to ensure commercial viability. My grandmother thought this a dangerous sort of heresy, an intrusion of technology as suspect as the telephone. She believed irrigated berries did not taste right and would not eat them.

Likewise with eggs, and this was not just my grandmother's prejudice, but a community standard. Not everyone kept chickens, but everyone knew who did and how they fed them, and everyone was careful where they bought eggs, certainly not from the A&P in town. One bought them from a neighbor, and not just any neighbor.

The Purina feed company was at the time beginning to market package deals for egg farmers, a contract to supply feed and financing for long, aluminum chicken coops with caged chickens fed on an assembly line, chickens that did not go outside. Almost all eggs are produced this way today. A farmer named Bye was among the first to enter this devil's bargain with Purina. No one who valued eggs could imagine any good would come of this, and they bought their eggs elsewhere.

There were no feedlots; cattle were pastured and hogs rooted sod in the sun. Winter feed was hay from your own mow and silage chopped from your own fields in fall. Hammer mills on your own barn floor driven by ancient John Deeres smashed up oats and corn for finishing cattle and laying just the right amount of fat on a hog's side bound for Don Manning's smokehouse.

All of this proceeded more or less independently on dozens of farms but it had a couple of hubs, the most important being the Friday livestock auction, every week at the auction barn in Emerson, about five miles east of Manning Hill. Even after he had no cattle, my grandfather went every Friday to sit on the bleacher seats, to visit with this man and that and to inspect his neighbors' cattle, nod and give advice. He was unnecessary to transactions, but necessary nonetheless, and people showed respect. There was a hamburger stand about the size of a horse trailer next to the auction barn, and a couple of times I sat at the counter with him, and we had burgers.

The slaughterhouse was the same kind of place, a hub, and as I grew enough to heft a half of hog, I was allowed my own knife, shown how to hone it vicious sharp with a couple of quick flicks across the steel, taught to run a bandsaw, how to slide a knife just behind the bottom rib in a side of beef to split it to quarters, how to slice salami so thin each piece had only one side, how to angle the cut around the vertebrae to not ruin any T-bone, where the rib eye split from the chuck and how to take off the round with one clean slice so that the top of the femur's ball joint would produce a disk exactly the size of a fifty-cent piece. At fifteen, I was being trusted with the care of my neighbors' meat.

This was, of course, blatantly illegal. Child labor laws existed and explicitly prohibited kids my age from cutting meat. With cause. One day I was wrapping, and my cousin Victor—a lifelong meat cutter and never called "Victor" but "Buck"—sliced off an inch worth of his index finger on the bandsaw. He shut off the saw, picked up the end of his finger, and flicked it into the bone barrel.

Like the auction house, people showed up at the slaughterhouse more or less regularly, sometimes with no business, sometimes just to have a cup of coffee, sample the latest batch of Thuringer, and predict the weather. I mostly took no notice of this and simply cut meat, got the job done, and made two bucks an hour. This was the point. I had become a working man, a man of means. The money paid for clothes of my own choosing. The money paid for burgers and dances and movies, dates. But mostly the money gave me status in my parents' eyes, enough status that on Sunday mornings I could slip away into my own day, not forced to go to church. The theology of my heritage was more complicated than most in that it granted two pathways to salvation, Jesus or work. I took work, especially because the vehicle that navigated that road was a powder blue '57 Chevy, a product of my wages.

The Chevy had cost me exactly as much as most high school kids' cars cost in those days, $100. Aside from transportation, it delivered me some status, because it was regarded as something of an antique, retro and cool. Understand, the car at the time was less than ten years old, but a ten-year-old car was a rare thing, especially in Michigan's planned obsolescence of rust. Aside from the rust, the critical internal systems of all cars—starters, alternators, brakes, water pumps—were expected to fail and need replacement at thirty thousand miles. An engine that lasted 100,000 miles was a rare beast and usually venerated in discussion at the auction barn. Cars last easily twice as long and go twice as far today, even American-built cars, but planned obsolescence then meant I could afford a '57 Chevy.

It got me to school every day and out on Saturday nights, but its most outstanding role emerged on Sundays. Somehow, I had made a social life for myself, a circle of friends, which is pretty much the point of high school. It was the group easily identifiable at most high schools even today, not the popular kids, nor the bad kids, known then as "hoods" or "greasers." Not the jocks and prom queens and cheerleaders. Mine was the edgier crowd, dressed a little weird, voluntarily read novels and spoke of them, was interested in theater and music, listened to Dave Brubeck records, achieved but did not overachieve. A core of this crowd coalesced and labeled itself the "Sunday Afternoon Sinkhole Society." The name derived from the layer of limestone that underlay our glacial terrain.

Sinkholes occur in limestone when a source of groundwater triggers a simple chemical decay of the carbonates that hold limestone formations together. This creates a void not far below the surface, and eventually the lid of the void collapses, creating a steeply sloped pit, sometimes several hundred feet deep. This had occurred in a number of places just north of Manning Hill near an area of massive limestone and shale quarries that fed Alpena's cement plant. On Sunday afternoons, my friends and I piled in my Chevy. I threw a long rope I had cadged from my father's tools in the trunk, and we explored sinkholes. Or sometimes not. We also knew a deserted beach on Lake Huron north of town and walked it for hours, talking kid nonsense and growing older by the hour.

Our number varied upward sometimes to eight or so, but at the core, besides me, were two. One was a guy who would become and still is my closest friend. The other was, of course, a girl, and I like thinking of her as a girl again. Petite, slight, pretty, blue eyes, and deep intelligence, cautious as a doe. She started out high school as the center of gravity of the popular kids, the town kids, the kids we understood to have status, but her dawning rebellion gradually drew her into the Sinkhole circle, rebellion that did not stop her from graduating at the top of our class with a perfect 4.0. One night, shorn of Sinkhole colleagues, just her and me, she showed me some secrets, parked in the '57 in her driveway, and we were inseparable after that. She was my wife for seventeen years and the mother of my only son, now grandmother to my grandchildren.

The Icelandic Sagas are odd stories, probably because of their antiquity. They are ornate and detailed in their genealogy, which is why they were necessary. They existed not in writing but in telling for three hundred years, passed to succeeding storytellers charged with strictly memorizing who belonged to whom, a pedigree meant to keep track of inherited rights, especially property rights. Yet a pedigree is not much of a story; it is a diagram of an incomplete sentence. The pairs of parallel horizontal lines that signify coupling come together at neat angles, intersect and flow to the next line, to progeny, without a hint of the chaos that often explodes at this most crucial of all human intersections. Most stories are about the people closest to us, most of them unreachably close. This is not an account of the people closest to me. This is a saga. A saga ignores some intimate relationships, maybe because the teller understands there are some he will never understand, or the teller understands this is not his story alone, and he has no right to tell it.

In any event, the Icelandic Sagas employed a blunt and eccentric device by simply announcing "Now Snuri is out of the saga," often by using the simple expedient of cleaving Snuri's head with a halberd. So it goes. Now this woman, my first wife, is out of the saga.

———

Ray Feher was my school's basketball coach, but looked nothing like a player. He was built more like a linebacker and looked as if he had at least one parent who was a gorilla. Unlike most coaches who taught subjects like history, civics, or health, Feher taught math, real math, which meant I couldn't avoid him. I took learning seriously enough so I could see no point in athletics or all the nonsense that went with them. Pep assemblies, school spirit, and even cheerleaders seemed to me silly, even as a kid, a sentiment that slowly built to a lifelong loathing of sports. Spare time was for earning money and school time was for learning, not as a result of my determination or drive, but simply as a matter of interest. And from the beginning I set myself up for every hard class in the building, advanced English all four years, a gantlet of hard sciences—biology, advanced biology, chemistry, physics—but especially I liked and excelled at math.

Feher, as I recall, taught trigonometry and one day walked into class to announce that there would be an immediate test on a chapter he had not yet covered and the score would weigh heavily in our grade. It was his idea of a joke. Then he proceeded to ask a few of my classmates what they thought of this idea. They mumbled. Then he started straight at me with his heavy ape eyes and asked me the same, and I said, "I think it's the damnedest thing I ever heard of."

He scowled. The class went silent, and he jerked back a clenched fist with a thumb pointing me into the hall. I was his height, so it was an eye-to-eye discussion of a single volley:

"Mr. Manning, I take it this means you are no longer a Christian," he said.

"No. I am not."

That was it. He signaled me back into class, and we resumed. I have no idea what my faith or lack thereof had to do with trigonometry or how the use of the mildest of expletives revealed that lack. I had no idea he would know I had ever been anywhere near Greely Baptist Church. He didn't know my family, and I didn't know his. Apparently these matters were bruited about among teachers. Nonetheless, I knew it was none of his business and if he pressed this, I had the upper hand. He had no right asking anything like that. This was a public school and we both knew it. I earned an A in his class.

About this time, I took a trip south to Lansing with a couple of other kids from school. For reasons unexplained to us, we had been selected to attend leadership training sponsored by the state 4-H Club. As a farm kid, I had always belonged to 4-H. My dad taught the woodworking class. I got a marksmanship certification and was in a horse club. But leadership was a new thing. In this class, a bunch of kids I didn't know sat in a circle centered by two adults, but the adults didn't say a word. Silence. Until one of us kids figured it out by taking the leadership and speaking. That was about it. I told my dad about this, because I was sort of proud that someone considered me leadership caliber. He exploded and began screaming at me at levels I thought would turn to violence. He announced that I had been "brainwashed," and the 4-H session in Lansing was obviously nothing but a thinly disguised "Communist training camp." About the same time, he took to showing a Birch Society photo purporting to show Martin Luther King entering a Communist training camp in China.

Also about this time, some infraction of mine at home had infuriated my mother, so much so she lost it. She grabbed a steel-handled kitchen broom and began swinging, knocking at me, working her way up my legs and arms. She was all of five foot one; I was five ten, cut meat, picked rock, and slung bales of hay. I caught the broom handle, took it away from her. We stood and stared for a moment, then I handed the broom back to her. She started flailing again, and we did a couple more cycles before she gave up and walked away.

More feared in my school than Ray Feher was Mike Yedinak, equally simian with slits for eyes, but he was the football coach, the authority figure for the privileged gland cases on his team and accordingly not students in the classes I took. Still, the lines of our social stratification were not so sharply drawn, and over the years eroded in simple kid business, meaning I made a few friends on the football team. This was a normal enough situation, but at the time, playing out against an increasingly troubled society. November 1963 had smashed national innocence, but was then a single isolated event, not seen when it happened for what it was, the foreshadowing of what would become real upheaval, Vietnam, civil rights, and race riots. As kids in the mid-1960s in a dinky, isolated, and naive town in northern Michigan, we had no context for reading these larger events. But some of the adults did, and had begun sniffing around kids for telltale signs of proto-rebellion. I had, in fact, been early identified as a Communist in the making by a subset of the high school staff. I was completely oblivious to this then, but a teacher I stayed friendly with for years after explained it to me. Yedinak took juvenile red-baiting the furthest of any of the school's teachers and one day convened his football team to announce he was forbidding them from any association with me. A friend on the team reported this to me the next morning. For some reason unknown—and much hinges on knowing it—I did not hesitate. I did not stop to think or to consider the matter. It was pure impulse, my core impulse. I simply walked to Yedinak's class (nominally, he taught civics, and it would take some years for me to fully appreciate the irony of this), called him out in the hall, and challenged his right to say any such thing to anyone who happened to be my friend. I shouted it right straight to his angry, bulging, no-necked face.

I was becoming who I would become. The reaction was not willed, but instinctive, as if hardwired.

I have a springer spaniel, an old guy now. Through the fifteen years he has been with me, he has taught me much about living properly, perhaps the most important piece of wisdom when he was a pup. I had begun the work of his obedience training when he was eight weeks old, and it went well enough: Sit, stay, heel, and a come back call. Clearly he was a knothead, a willful animal, but I knew that when I picked him as a pup. I had wanted a good hunting dog, and a willful animal will not be stopped by the brush and briars of the field. Stubbornness has its upside. But then training foundered when he and I got to the business of "down," a command that is supposed to make a dog collapse fully prone, as compliant and limp as a rug. He simply refused to comply, so I sought out the help of a trainer. She watched me work my dog, then interrupted, incredulous. "What are you doing with this dog? He is superdominant and will be nothing but trouble. Most people would have taken him to the pound by now."

This is not really a matter of breeding or breed, not a fault in either nature or nurture; litter mates of such animals are usually completely docile and compliant. Just in some dogs, the genes align and they are instinctively this way, and he was. In dog society (more likely in wolf society, because all dogs descend from wolves) having these hardheads around served some purpose, or the trait would not have survived. Then she explained my problem with the "down" command. Staying, heeling, and sitting are all neutral pieces of business in dog society, carry no social stigma. "Down," however, requires the dog to adopt what every dog knows to be a submissive pose. It is a public act of submission to authority the equivalent of bowing on knees to kiss a ring.

Then the trainer showed me a special spiked training collar, a medieval device that pinches flesh. It does not injure, but quickly inflicts enough pain to deplete an animal's reservoir of fight, obstinacy, and pride. So I used it, and even then, my dog would not do "down," at least not for a week or so, but I was determined my dog would be properly trained. We repeated the process day on day and finally he did. But not with a submissive drop of his eyes I expected. Instead, he went prone and stared straight into my eyes from deep in the depths of his, communicating nothing so much as betrayal. I could see what I had done, and I was sorry for it.

As I write this, he sleeps at my feet, now well into his dying days. Between that day and this, I have never asked him to do "down" again, not once.

Besides the Birch Society's *American Opinion* magazine, my parents subscribed to the *Reader's Digest,* but they never seemed to read it. I did, because I liked the jokes and would memorize them and try them on my friends. Some of the stories were okay, but I was especially intrigued by the periodic announcement of sweepstakes, in which one could win fairly interesting things like new cars and vacations. So I'd find a pencil and dutifully fill out entry forms in my over-round cursive handwriting, a big loop in the "D" of "Dick." I was never known as Richard. One day a registered letter came for me, a relatively rare occurrence in our household. As far as we had previously known, only the IRS sent registered letters.

I had won a stereo, an RCA console stereo, an iconic bit of late 1950s kit that had more to do with furniture than music. It was a maple box the size of a hall table with speakers built into each end hidden by tweed speaker cloth. The top slid open to reveal a turntable and a radio built inside. We unpacked it and put it in an open hallway, a sort of balcony above our living room. My parents had some albums of Tennessee Ernie Ford singing hymns.

The stereo was not yet in my household the instrument of subversion such equipment would become in the late 1960s, but I liked it well enough. I already had my collection of Roger Miller's entire works and found that "Dang Me" and "Do Wacka Do" sounded particularly wry on this new machine. I went to Alvin Ash's music store and added some Al Hirt and Herb Alpert and the Tijuana Brass. One day I found Peter, Paul and Mary's *In the Wind,* and bought it because they looked like interesting people, especially Mary. I of course did not know then I was buying into Albert Grossman's cynical attempt to capitalize on the folk music scare in Greenwich Village by creating a group from whole cloth. I didn't know that what prompted Grossman to do so was the success of another client of his, Bob Dylan. I didn't even note the fact that a song I liked on the album, besides "Stewball," was something this Dylan guy had written, but then there was a lot coded in that album I played constantly on my sweepstakes stereo I did not understand, particularly exactly what it was that was blowing in the wind.

I'd had some inkling even earlier that music was prying open a crack in our world. One of my family's Sunday night rituals was to drive in our big station wagon, by then six kids of what would become seven, from the south side of Manning Hill where we lived a few miles north to the very toe of the hill, where my Aunt Leafa McEwen lived, adjacent to my grandfather's farm on its north edge. She was my father's older sister; her husband, Keith, farmed some and drove road grader in summer and snowplow in winter for the county. They did not, so far as I know, have a console stereo, but did have an impressive console color TV and Sunday nights were for Ed Sullivan. This is how I got to see the Beatles, but the consensus of those assembled is these guys didn't amount to much and in fact looked like girls. I suspected there had to be something more to it than that, given the reaction they drew from actual girls and so took it upon myself to go to Alvin Ash's music store, where I also took accordion lessons, and order up sheet music for "I Want to Hold Your Hand." I tried to learn to play it on my accordion, but never could make it sound anything like what I heard on Ed Sullivan. Meanwhile, rock 'n' roll still refused to penetrate the rarefied airwaves above the 45th parallel, so my exposure remained limited. After school, the radio stations played polkas. This would be corrected as the 1960s simmered on to full boil.

My gradual radicalization would eventually be stimulated by Alice Lyche, although she probably never intended to do so. Alice Lyche was a quintessential old maid English teacher, one of two in our high school. The other had the wonderfully Dickensian name of Blanche Hockett, but it was Lyche who taught Dickens. Both women had taught my parents. My father had told me a story about Lyche, that when he was in school, every day she would walk into class and daub out a gob of hand cream from a jar she kept on her desk and one day he had put ink in the hand cream and the class roared. When I went to her class my sophomore year, sure enough, there was the hand cream used as advertised, and I soon heard the same story from just about every kid in my class. I don't think we had yet learned the word "apocryphal."

Alice's innocent act of subversion was to insist we become writers, and the only way to do so was to become readers. She did not see much of value for us to read in the popular press, particularly not the *Reader's Digest,* as I may or may not have suggested. She was, however, if not a fan, at least tolerant of something called an "essay" that would appear each week in *Time* magazine, and if we were to be serious about our writing, we should read this. The library's copy had a subscription form. I appropriated it, filled it with over-round caps, bought a stamp from the drugstore, and sent it off.

In July of 1967, my cousin David Mayo was staying with us when he was up north from Flint, where he lived. He was a year younger than me, but nonetheless much cooler in that he lived near a city, could play guitar, had already started his own rock 'n' roll band, and could do a passable version of "Gloria." My parents had a pop-up camper trailer, which was always parked behind the house and in summer popped up for company. My brother, Mike, David, and I spent most of one afternoon holed up in the camper reading the issue of *Time* just off the press. The cover story explored the matter of hippies, and was full of all sorts of astounding news from a world we could not imagine: marijuana, LSD, and readily available sex. There were photos and some of the girls were naked. Quoting *Time*:

> San Francisco's Haight-Ashbury district—a throbbing three-eighths of a far-from-square-mile—is the vibrant epicenter of the hippie movement. Fog sweeps past the gingerbread houses of "The Hashbury," shrouding the shapes of the hirsute, shoeless hippies huddled in doorways, smoking pot, "rapping" (achieving rapport with random talk) or banging beer cans in time to ubiquitous jukebox rhythms.

Perhaps Alice Lyche was right in advising we read the essay and nothing else in *Time*.

Two weeks later Detroit exploded in race riots. President Lyndon Johnson sent troops and Governor George Romney sent in the National Guard, one of which was David's father, my Uncle Bob. He had fought in the Pacific during Word War II and stayed in the Guard for more than twenty years, but never talked much about it. Mostly he talked about hunting and fishing. The week of riot leveled more than 2,000 buildings, jailed 7,200 people, injured 467, and left 43 black people dead. My Uncle Bob would later maintain this last number was a government lie, and that his Guard unit alone killed more than a hundred, which seemed to be a matter of pride to him.

That fall, my English teacher was Bob Buchner, a short, muscular man with a bald head and round face, a practicing stoic, but occasionally he could muster a wry smile. Our school was bermed and his classroom was on the first floor, meaning the belly-high bottoms of the windows were at ground level on the outside. Buchner periodically made his entrance to class by stepping in through a window. Also periodically, and with a frequency that must have been expensive, he would calmly and without pause in his lecture pick up a pair of scissors from his desk and snip his necktie in half.

My closest friend then as he would be for most of my life was David Werth from the Sinkhole Society, a tall, gangly kid with a head of bright red hair, profoundly and weirdly intelligent. That year, his habit was to carry at all times a carved stick, an inch or so around and about six inches long. It was always in his hand and he never said why. His other habit was to go to Buchner's blackboard just before the teacher made his entrance through the window and letter in clean, sans serif block type "T. M. Quinn is coming." None of us was even remotely hip enough to figure out that "T. M." stood for "The Mighty" and we would periodically ask Werth who the hell is this guy. Buchner one day heard this question and answered, without even breaking into his wry smile, "Just some Eskimo." It is deeply embarrassing to realize that in 1967 the old guy who taught me English knew Dylan better than I did.

I am sure we learned something about English from Buchner, but I am also sure he understood he needed to fulfill a more significant role in facing the twenty or so bright adolescents in his advanced placement English class in 1967, coming to grips then with riots happening in our state, a war raging, a war some of us would soon join, an antiwar movement raging, and some of us would join that. *Hair* opened that fall. And all of this came up in class, and Buchner let us struggle with it, in our own way and time. Then came that awful spring of assassinations and even adolescents could not help but consider a world beyond their own, first Martin Luther King, then Bobby Kennedy. All the history and literature we had learned had told us of a very different story, of civilization resting on law and progress, but we were jolted from complacency by pervasive violence and a society in upheaval. It was a different time. Being seventeen in 1968, at the crescendo of all of this, meant adopting the public as personal. Coming of age just then dictated a life of public engagement for many of us. It did for me.

Neuroscience has only recently learned of a process called synaptic pruning. The brain's prefrontal cortex, the rational part, the place where we learn English and self-control and trigonometry, is mostly absent in infants, but grows in place for our first twenty or so years. Neurons connect through synapses, wiring the circuitry of thought, ability, and memory. The greater the number of synapses, the more a brain can hold. Oddly, though, the process of increasing these connections is not lifelong. In fact, we achieve our greatest number of connections in late adolescence, and then the brain adjusts, suddenly, almost violently, with synaptic pruning, severing the connections that are trivial and random, cutting those that matter least. This is how we become who we will become. Mercifully, the brain shields us from memory of this process, but the process amounts to a sort of sudden onset of mental illness and accounts at least as much as hormones for the erratic behavior of teenagers. It's okay to be a kid with a brain firing off in all directions, randomly and wildly, but too many synapses prevent the formation of tight precise networks of thought we need to live lives that matter. Childish things must be put away, and evolution has equipped our brains to effect the process.

6

LIBERATION

I took the most important drive of my life in late August of 1969, a short trip of eighty-six miles mostly south on U.S. 23 from Freeland, Michigan, to Ann Arbor. There were but three of us in the compact car, a dark blue Ford Fairlane worth $200, my father's car. He was driving, my mother as front-seat passenger, and I in the back, each of us silent. None of us had any precedent to allow us to fathom the distance that day. My parents and their parents and their siblings knew nothing about universities, not to mention universities with thirty thousand undergrads, braless women with unshaven armpits, a regular running hashish festival, raving socialists in Army surplus jackets, and a national reputation for aggressive intelligence.

In the trunk of the Fairlane were all the clothes I owned packed in two slate gray, hard-sided J.C. Penney suitcases my parents had bought me at high school graduation. There was a cheap portable stereo I had bought with my first summer work paycheck. A Smith Corona portable typewriter, nothing more. I had spent that summer with my father, who was working as a tramp lineman, guys who traveled to short-term jobs building power transmission lines. He worked for a contractor at the Dow Chemical plant in Midland, Michigan, a controversial place because of Dow's manufacture of napalm for the Vietnam War, but not yet the controversial place it would become for spewing an unimaginable list of chemical pollutants into the Titibawasee River that flowed near my parents' house.

As soon as I graduated high school, my dad got me a job as a laborer with another Dow contractor, Collinson Construction Company, as a simple pick-and-shovel man. Dow's sprawling chemical plant was dotted with what were called "tank farms," a patch of steel tanks of varying sizes that stored the mix of chemistry running through the place, the raw materials of everything from aspirin to Styrofoam insulation to napalm. I was deployed to a tank farm that happened to be heated to a bit more than a hundred degrees. Its base was covered in about a foot of hard, Saginaw Valley clay, a liner that engineers had decided needed to be removed and replaced with limestone gravel. There was not enough room between the bottoms of the horizontal cylinders that were the tanks and the clay below for machinery to operate, a problem solved with eighteen-year-old kids, number two round-point shovels, and wheelbarrows. I made four dollars and thirteen cents every single hour.

About a week into this, my shovel bit off a lump of clay, and suddenly a stream of clear, foul-smelling liquid started pouring across my boots. The safety inspector, a company man always watching us work, poked a big red button on a black box and an ambulance came, hauled me off to an infirmary, where they took all my clothes and my boots and made me stand in a shower for an hour. I got a new pair of boots out of the deal.

My dad had a cheap apartment that always smelled of leaking natural gas upstairs in a house near Freeland at Auburn, but we didn't spend much time in it. Every night, we would eat at a diner, and he would read the classified advertising in the Midland paper. He told me often that the only way to know anything about what was really happening in a town was by reading the classifieds. Sometimes we would drive around and look at a used car or a tractor that had been advertised. He didn't really need any of those things, but believed seeing the actual goods enhanced the information.

Weekends we returned to Manning Hill, and finally I convened my siblings and mother and reported what I knew then of my dad's loneliness. I convinced them to do what my dad had wanted to do for some time, that they all would leave Manning Hill and their schools and move to Freeland, and they did, to a falling-down farmhouse he had found in the classified advertising.

But it was not shoveling alone that sent me to Ann Arbor; it was the fortunate fact I lived in better times than now.

Michigan was then a progressive state dominated by the political power of the United Auto Workers. The union has since ossified and its members became less progressive once they forgot the solid wages they made resulted from hard years of sit-down strikes, billy clubs, and German shepherds in the 1930s and 1940s. But in the 1960s, autoworkers lived well and meant for their children to do well. Part of that was paying for an education system. I had been solidly educated at Alpena High School because people then believed in paying for public schools. I won a regents alumni scholarship at the University of Michigan, a full academic scholarship. My annual budget, tuition, room, books, and board had been set at $2,000 by the financial aid office, of which scholarship covered all but $400. I was later to learn the office had neglected the budget for beer, but even with this oversight, I could make the nut by shoveling and have enough to buy a $100 stereo on the side.

I later learned that when I was much younger, just after that incident when my grandfather gave me a dollar for making all As on my report card, he had decided I was special among all the grandchildren. He told dad he had put aside $5,000 worth of stock he owned to pay for my education. The stock was in the local farmer's co-op, which sold gasoline, diesel fuel, and heating oil to all my neighbors. The co-op was managed by the elder—what they called the lay preacher—in my grandmother's church, the Reorganized Church of Jesus Christ of the Latter Day Saints. The elder, of course, knew about the stock, but it is not at all clear if he knew of my grandfather's intentions for it. In any event, just after my grandfather died, the church launched a drive to raise money for a new church building. The *Alpena News* photo of the groundbreaking shows my grandmother wielding the first shovel, so large had been her donation to the effort. Not clear if she knew my grandfather's intentions, either, but I didn't need his money; I had his work ethic and the support of a just social system that believed the American dream is a hollow promise if not backed by money for poor kids' education.

What that scholarship really was, though, was the price of freedom, and the people glowering in the front seat of the Fairlane and the smug guy in the back certainly realized this that day in 1969, our lack of precedent notwithstanding. So we made our way in deepening silence to the Main Street exit of U.S. 23 at Ann Arbor, followed the university signs that jigged up Huron Street to State, then across campus to the South Quad dorm. I can only guess at their layers of emotions and cannot reconstruct all of mine, but we all must have been feeling something besides resentment and anger. I was the eldest of seven kids, the first to leave, entering a world profoundly alien and frightening to them and to me, for that matter. Even in anger, there were still bonds of affection to be broken. Some shame maybe, a beat-up little Ford parked in a line of bigger, shinier, newer Cadillacs and Buicks with trunks much fuller. On my parents' side, pride maybe, I hope some grudging pride in what I had become.

But maybe not. The best evidence I have—both in their scowls that day and what they would do later—said mostly I was seeing the anger of defeat, that I had won. Not long after the family moved to Freeland, my parents pulled all the younger kids out of public schools. My younger siblings were to be punished for my emancipation by being sent to fundamentalist academies that were then and are now the American equivalent of madrassas. The right wing's destruction of American public education, the long-term trend of the last forty years, rode on a wave of stories just like mine. Education and fundamentalism cannot coexist. No one is more aware of this than the fundamentalists, who have now made religious academies and homeschooling into common and institutionalized forms of child abuse.

The 1960s and early 1970s hardened my parents' religion, and they were not alone. Nationwide many of the fundamentalist Protestant denominations were headed in exactly the same direction. Religion became far more conservative and political, and this almost immediately produced a renewed assault on the nation's long-standing wall between church and state, to the point that today it is common to hear from movement conservatives that the Founding Fathers never intended such a wall. Clearly they did. Thomas Jefferson and James Madison were explicit in reasoning that such a separation was necessary in a pluralistic society, but more to the point, the Baptists in early America were the leading supporters of the wall. The denomination believed any state-established religion would work against them by giving inordinate power to the dominant Church of England.

The Baptists continued to support separation right up until the 1970s, when especially the Southern Baptist Convention took a sharp turn to the right. They formally reversed their position on separation. Likewise, they withdrew their support from the 1962 and 1963 Supreme Court decisions banning public prayer in schools and for the first time opposed teaching of evolution in schools. Public schools became the battering ram for the religious right, and my personal history says exactly why.

There is some long-standing precedent of hostility toward schools by fundamentalists. For instance, the prototype for modern-day televangelists was Billy Sunday, who did his preaching just before World War I. Sunday once said that if someone gave him a million dollars, he would give all but one dollar to the church and the rest to education. Nonetheless, that sentiment didn't harden to full-blown battle until just about exactly the time I was making my way to Ann Arbor in 1969. That year, a real culture war erupted in Kanawha County, West Virginia, over textbook selections in public school. It would eventually lead to what amounted to a general strike by coal miners, shootings, physical assaults of school officials, and firebombings of schools when the school board refused to do the fundamentalists' bidding. The event sparked national prominence for an obscure Southern Baptist preacher from Lynchburg, Virginia, Jerry Falwell, who stated bluntly in one of his books that his goal was to destroy public schools. All of this founded an explosion of Christian "academies" in the early 1970s, reportedly a new school at the rate of one per day. Falwell once claimed a new school every seven hours, when the movement was at its peak.

Indeed, my own elementary school, the one my grandfather, the conservative Republican, helped build, suffered declining enrollments, so the school district sold it. It became a Christian academy. In 2011, I finally summoned the will to visit it and found it was no longer a school, but had been converted to a full-blown, Bible-thumping Baptist church.

The core of this movement, however, is not so much about opposition to teaching evolution and sex education, and really never has been. During the Kanawha County battle, the fundamentalists were explicit in opposition to teaching critical reading skills. That is, they demanded that kids be given only books that fundamentalists regarded as absolutely true and that students be taught to regard all books available to them that way. Fundamentalists understand that if you teach a kid to think for himself, he will leave the church, and they are absolutely correct about this. This is the fundamental impetus behind creation of homeschools and Christian academies, and there is no more subversive element in our society. Democracy cannot exist among people who cannot think for themselves. Forty years of this subversion explain much of where we find ourselves today. This is the infrastructure of know-nothing politics, and fundamentalists have been deliberately assembling it for a long time.

As far as I knew in 1969, people went to college to prepare for one of three professions: doctor, lawyer, or schoolteacher. I chose doctor for the science. This made matters pretty easy, because the University of Michigan's course catalogue spelled out a crisp curriculum of four year's worth of work called "pre-med." I signed on. The heart of this beast was an inorganic chemistry class that I elected to take in its advanced placement version. I had tested out of freshman calculus, and took a math class so abstract as to defy any anchors whatsoever to this planet and promised, at its outer reaches, to reveal the faces of several gods. I tossed in a German and a literature class, all of this without talking to a single soul for any sort of advice. What more did I need to know about planning a college career? My general experience with my parents had taught me adults were unreliable, and I had long since learned to keep my own counsel. I had read the catalogue. I bought a big pile of books and a new, supercharged slide rule in a black leather case, then carefully disassembled it and slicked up its running surfaces with graphite. Let the calculations begin.

South Quad was an eight-story brick warehouse for 1,250 students, mostly freshmen. The building was bisected then to be segregated by gender, but it proved to be a porous barrier. Somehow, though, the university's placement people had made some further attempt at segregation, so that I was assigned to a floor and wing occupied mostly by football players and double Es. The latter, I quickly learned, was the label for an odd subset of humanity majoring in electrical engineering. My own assigned roommate was a double E and a fundamentalist to boot. These guys were objects of considerable ridicule. They did indeed wear pocket protectors, their slide rules were bigger than mine, and they were usually seen late at night trailing long streams of fanfold paper behind them like exotic kites. Double E was the designation for what would become computer science, and each of the nerds I ridiculed then is probably today retired to a multimillion-dollar mansion on Maui.

Sandwiching such people in dorm rooms between the members of Michigan's football team was a perverse bit of humor. The football players were only in the dorm because of some sort of archaic rule. Willing alumni would have cheerfully fronted for an apartment for each, as they did for cars, and even seemed to arrange for some companionship for them. Michigan was then in ascendance. Bo Schembechler had assembled a pantheon of demigods to challenge the hated Ohio State, and I was too much a rube to appreciate how great was my fortune to be placed among them. In particular, I was assigned a room directly across the hall from two standouts, Billy Taylor and Thom Darden, both halfbacks. Darden went on to play for the Cleveland Browns. Taylor broke Michigan's record for career rushing yardage, was named All-American, developed a drug habit, spent two and a half years in the penitentiary on an armed robbery charge, and wound up homeless on the streets of Detroit, but then found religion, earned a doctorate, and overcome addiction. Then, though, his and Darden's room was always filled with stunning blondes after home games. Some mornings Taylor would pound on my door a half hour before his calculus class, and I would fill in a few answers for him on an assignment as he said goodbye to a departing blonde.

This was a miscalculation on Taylor's part, because had I known anything about math, I could have calculated my very long odds at succeeding in that chemistry class I had signed on for. Michigan was then regarded as a place for bright kids, and not just from Michigan, maybe the top 5 or 10 percent of high school graduates. Of those, only a small percentage of chemistry zealots signed on for inorganic chemistry. And of those, only a very small percentage insisted on the advanced placement status I had chosen. None of this had occurred to me, nor had the most important consideration: this class would be graded on something I had never heard of, a curve, meaning that it is of some relevance how well one knows his stuff, but even more relevant is how brightly shine the other 299 bulbs illuminating the lecture hall three mornings a week. I got a D on my midterm. The test had been deeply shocking, even as I took it. It was full of material the lecturer had not covered in class, and we had not investigated in lab. In fact, it demanded that I not simply spit back what I knew, but that I synthesize what I knew to invent new levels of chemistry right there on the spot. Apparently there were people in the room who could do this thing.

The shock of all of this set me on an uncharted course. For the first time in my schooling, it became clear I would have to work at learning, and work I did, riveted to every lecture, obsessively compiling notes. Every night I would learn it and learn it again, working my slide rule until it smoked and then spat out long strings of scientific notation. I scored well enough on the final to raise my overall grade to a C, and I was crushed. I had seen Cs before, but only when I found some idiot high school teacher/coach's assignment so banal as to be not worthy of my attention. Never when I wanted so much to succeed. It was clear that at eighteen years in, my life was a failure, and I abandoned at the end of the first year my pre-med plans, again without talking to a soul about this for academic counseling. Facts were facts. Years later I became friends with a guy who was halfway through U of M's elite medical school on his way to becoming a urologist. I told him the story.

"You got a C in that class? That's a hell of a grade for that class. Most of us in med school got Ds," he said.

In 1969, the most interesting things happening in Ann Arbor were not happening in the classrooms. The town was a well-known center in the antiwar movement, but we were also still feeling heavy rumblings in the fight for civil rights, the Detroit riots having occurred only fifty miles away and two years earlier. My first day in the streets was spent in the latter cause, a student strike in what was called the Black Action Movement. The goal was a series of steps in recruitment and remedial courses designed to increase black enrollment at the university. We won, and pretty quickly. The dominant cause, however, was the war, and there were regular marches, sit-ins, and actions against it. On my eighteenth birthday I had, as required by law for all males of my cohort, appeared before my local draft board and registered. My enrollment in the university granted me a student deferment, 2S status, which would end if I left school, say, took a year off to bum around Europe, or graduated. This was an imposition on my life I resented fiercely, but now think it was probably a good thing. It made the war more urgent and immediate in each of our lives, not like Iraq and Afghanistan today, remote events we are able to ignore. The burden was shared. Most families had someone in Vietnam and so most would follow Walter Cronkite each night with closer attention. It was commonly believed that rich kids could get deferments, and they did, the draft boards being local, but nonetheless, Vietnam was not so much a war fed by the bodies of poor Americans, as are Iraq and Afghanistan today.

All young men had draft cards in their back pockets, and this propelled a lot of us into the streets. Besides, where else would a young man full of rage against authority be other than in the streets, confronting the cops and the billy clubs, the German shepherds and tear gas? More than marching was involved, and I began showing up at some meetings here and there. I was not simply a peacenik; the flower child paci-fists were a big element in the movement elsewhere, but not so present in Ann Arbor. I was reading Marx and taking poli-tics seriously. I began the steps to declare myself a conscien-tious objector, a deferment reserved for pacifists, but got not far in the process and decided I was not, in fact, a CO. I was a radical and began throwing in my lot with the folks who ear-nestly spoke of revolution.

Students for a Democratic Society, the New Left group that had formed in the early 1960s, was in the process of breaking up in 1969 and becoming the notorious Weather Under-ground, a name derived from a Dylan lyric. Those various factions and splinters were, of course, in and around Ann Arbor. SDS's national manifesto was the Port Huron State-ment, drafted in a Michigan town just north of Detroit. SDS's last major gathering in 1969 had occurred in Flint, the town where I had been born and where my relatives had been auto-workers. This locus seemed to infuse SDS with a lot more la-bor politics than the rest of the antiwar movement, and labor was a key element of the foment in Ann Arbor. SDS's disarray notwithstanding, one could still find plenty of people who called themselves SDS and one could attend regular meet-ings with these people, and I did, and of a sampler of various evolving socialist groups. None of it seemed nearly as enter-taining as the streets. I read the tracts and listened to the speeches and teach-ins, diatribes that would go on for hours, hoping for some turn of wit or humor and finally just found it all boring and irrelevant. Then came a sense of having been here before. That young man with the short haircut and the Army surplus jacket leading tonight's cell meeting in a long encomium to Marx began to sound to me for all the world like a hellfire-and-brimstone Baptist preacher. And I walked out. Revolution was fine, as long as I didn't have to go to meetings. I was a radical for about half of my freshman year, but Daily Vacation Bible School had inoculated me against this sort of thing in a way the preachers had not intended.

My new declared major was political science, adopted because of one class I happened to like and because it seemed to be a good idea to be political just then. Unlike all my other pivotal decisions, I did talk to someone about that one for advice, a teaching assistant in the political science class I happened to like. He told me not to do it, that Michigan's program was dominated by the narrow band of thought that crops up from time to time in the social sciences, by social scientists who think they really are scientists. Mostly these are guys with slide-rule envy who believe the complexity of the human experience, the grit and gravel of politics, can be divined by surveys and questionnaires and reduced to neat formulae, regression analysis, and statistics. My teaching fellow had already quite correctly read me as someone who would not get along with these people. I didn't have the intellectual tools to say why, in fact, no one did, because complexity and chaos theory would be a few more years in the making. I was just viscerally and instinctively opposed to the reductionism that drove this line of thinking.

Nor did I object on the same grounds as others who were simply mathaphobes. Just the opposite. I was perfectly comfortable chasing formulae and had some sense of what real science looked like. That sense, more than anything else, told me social sciences are not real science, a position I maintain to this day. I was far more interested in studying political history and philosophy, the sweep of big ideas, and my teaching fellow finally admitted that if I picked and chose properly and wandered liberally outside the department, I probably could assemble that sort of education at Michigan.

Indeed, there were some outstanding experiences. In 1972, when Richard Nixon made his groundbreaking trip to China, I happened to be in China scholar Allen Whiting's class on the history of Mao's revolution. During the trip, Whiting showed up as a commentator on national network news broadcasts. I had solid courses on Latin American politics and on bureaucracies. By chance, I wandered into and then enrolled in a philosophy class on logic that was taught by a gifted lecturer, Lawrence Sklar, and I can remember absorbing his classes with the reverence I was supposed to have felt in church. The rules of logic seemed to me the central glue of civility, the core habit of mind our society needed then, even more now.

Perhaps, though, the most telling bit of education came in a course I hated, an introduction to sociology taught by a statistics guy with all the academic arrogance he could muster. I could muster some back and on my blue book for the midterm filled in the course name as "Social Engineering 101." His sole comment on one of my papers was "You write like a journalist," and he did not mean it kindly. Nonetheless, I warmed to the words, even if I didn't yet understand them as premonition.

Mostly, though, I remember little of this. The truth is, I would have not received much education at all had I not encountered the McKee brothers. Both were engineering students, Rich and Scott, and they were living in South Quad in a room where they had assembled an epic stereo system, most of which they had built themselves with scrounging and soldering irons. The cubicle-sized room had been converted to a shop where they cobbled together motorcycles, usually Triumphs, from literal basket cases. I encountered them late in my freshman year, and they invited me in on an apartment deal they planned for the following year. Split four ways, my share of rent would be $65 a month. The new quarters were big enough to allow disassembly of more motorcycles, and I soon had a Triumph of my own, a 500 with dual carburetors, spread out on the floor, its battery cooking in the oven to harden the epoxy that repaired a crack.

The relationship was pivotal, however, for more reasons than motorcycles. The McKee brothers had part-time jobs at an institution called Campus Corners, a combination liquor store, beer store, pharmacy at the triangular corner of State and Packard. The McKees set me up with the owner, Jim Mitchell, and he found out I could drive truck, so hired me.

Campus Corners's most vital role was to supply beer and wine in quantity to Ann Arbor, most prominently on football Saturdays, standing, as it did, between Michigan's main campus and its outsized football stadium that then seated 101,000 people, some of them not altogether sober. There was a game day ritual called something like the "sea of green." At halftime, an aerial view of the stadium would show a decided green cast to the crowd, created by everyone hoisting largely empty Boone's Farm wine bottles, a popular brand that could be had for 99 cents a bottle at Campus Corners. In the couple hours before a game, we would stock, sell, and bag one hundred cases of Boone's Farm. This was clearly high tide, but there was a steady rhythm of cresting waves every other day of the week, mostly in beer. That's where the truck came in. Management was especially keen on the bullet point in my résumé that noted my upbringing on a farm. It meant I could heft a half barrel of beer, 150 pounds of dense deadweight that needed to make it into the truck and out of the truck and up the narrow flights of stairs to the third-floor apartment where the kegger was in progress. Or a dozen of these kegs every Friday to the law school, so heft I did for three lovely years of my life.

About twenty of us worked at Campus Corners, and we had an attitude. We were gritty and smart. We smoked Camel straights. Our drug of choice was alcohol. We wore jeans, flannel shirts, and work boots. Everybody had a nickname and was known no other way. We played poker until dawn. When a blues band played Mr. Flood's Party downtown, we'd buy a long line of pitchers of cheap beer and close the joint, then finish off the night at the Fleetwood Diner just across the street, those of us who had not found some new young thing at Flood's who happened to fit nicely on the back of a motorcycle. One could and did get laid in the alley behind.

What drew me into this life, though, was a core group of men mostly cooler and a bit older than I was, David Lutton, Richard Gold, Peter Bowen, Michael Smith. The core and their girlfriends evolved into a tight circle of friends, potluck dinners, football games, and concerts, and I was part of it. They were my role models, and for the first time I seemed to be learning how to live. It was a rough and rowdy way to live, which made it all the better. This was the beginning of an education. Oddly, though, what would make it truly educational and the beginning of a lifelong thread of inquiry was music.

Our crowd, to quote the great Mississippi Fred McDowell, "do not do no rock and roll." More likely, the turntables would spin the Nitty Gritty Dirt Band's *Will the Circle Be Unbroken,* or something by Spider John Koerner, Dave "Snaker" Ray, and Tony Glover, a trio of white Minneapolis acoustic bluesmen who influenced Dylan on his way out of Hibbing by way of Dinkytown. Often at our gatherings, guitars were present. Both Peter Bowen and Michael Smith were solid performers. Peter, an art major then, a long, lanky cynic of frightening intelligence, was from Montana and sang and spoke of the West in ways that made it mythical to me. Now I live here, and Peter had much to do with it. He became a novelist, and I lost track of him only a few years ago. I will always wonder whether it was his alcoholism or IQ that did the most damage.

Michael was still in Ann Arbor last time I checked, still in music. He played a Martin guitar and could summon tunes from Jimmie Rodgers and Hank Williams.

I only learned to play guitar a decade later, long after I had moved from Ann Arbor and felt the loss of homemade music so acutely I labored long to fill it, flailing away at a series of increasingly antique and increasingly expensive Martin guitars. These guys cost me a lot of time and money, and I thank them for it.

But the more vital contribution of the Sunday afternoon picking sessions, the bluegrass nights at the Pretzel Bell and the trips to Detroit to hear Merle Haggard and Doc Watson, were the foundation of a solid education. Folk music became a valid path of inquiry I would follow forever. Dylan is mostly responsible for this, not just for me, but for all of us.

My engagement with folk music came after the Great Folk Music Scare, so named by Dave Van Ronk and the term we used even then. It refers to an explosion of popularity of the genre brought on by bands such as the Weavers, Pete Seeger, and later purely commercial opportunists like Berle Ives; Peter, Paul, and Mary; and true horrors like the television program *Hootenanny*. It was music as imagined by professors and Communists, and required a sort of loyalty oath to authenticity. It was unctuous and pretentious aping by urban intellectuals of threads of songs such as the Childe Ballads and the famous collections of John and Alan Lomax. It was hermetically sealed in leftist politics like a museum specimen.

What Dylan—and some key iconoclasts like Harry Smith, Van Ronk, Koerner, Ray and Glover, and David Bromberg—did was to restart evolution. They followed the threads to a much broader tradition, grabbed not so much the authentic as what they happened to like, what fit, what informed and what rocked and stirred the mix—even with electric guitars—and then let it roll on.

The beginning of American roots music came in Appalachia when a couple of tectonic plates collided. Appalachia was unique in the South, because its rugged terrain wouldn't support plantations. It would support a number of contrarians, Scots and Irish people who had fled successive attempts to tax whiskey on the British Isles and in lowland America. They brought with them fiddles and a repertoire of ancient tunes played out on modal scales in a strict form. Appalachia's ruggedness also supported a large number of free blacks who had escaped slavery one way or another, and they brought an African instrument, the banjo, and the pentatonic scale. It was the overlay of the pentatonic that produced the weird notes, the flatted thirds, fifths, and sevenths, that bluesmen, bluegrassers, jazzmen, and rock 'n' rollers exploit, over and over, to this day.

The fluid scale, but also the inherent democracy of the music, virtually forced creativity, endlessly inventive, both in lyric and music. This music, still practiced in almost pure form among traditionalists today, but also in permutations such as bluegrass and jazz, provided a sort of droning grid that allowed recombinations of stories, lyrics, and licks to suit the occasion. It created a framework for a true evolution driven by selection pressure, just as biological evolution is activated by what endures. What was good was what survived, what you remembered, what came up again Saturday night after Saturday night as something you could dance to.

What at first vivified, then eventually killed this process was the phonograph. Not long after Thomas Edison invented the phonograph, they became ubiquitous in American households, even, almost especially, in poor, rural households. This and commercial radio gave a long-deprived people access to more music than they thought possible, so people spent surprisingly large percentages of their income on the machines and records. Interviews with prominent bluesmen from the time, legends who played with Robert Johnson, tell of the enormous influence of this newfound eclecticism. They were no longer bound by regional styles. They sucked up everything they heard. Johnson himself played a wide variety of music from polkas to church hymns. A craze for Hawaiian music around 1900 spread the sliding notes of slack key guitar through the South and soon enough black bluesmen were playing their guitars with everything from steak bones to whiskey bottle necks to mimic the sound.

At the same time, though, recording froze music in place and commercialized it. Thus when recording companies were able to establish lucrative categories like "race music"—and it was lucrative—producers stopped people like Johnson from recording anything other than blues. More importantly, though, performers were able to copyright material, to exert authority and control over it. No longer were people free to pick and choose snatches of musical DNA and watch it recombine and evolve through the generations. Music got stuck in place, subject to the demands of commercialism.

All of this explains why people like to call Dylan a plagiarist. In terms of modern commercial music he is, and the advent of Google has given people all sorts of opportunity to fire cheap shots. He cribbed this lyric from a French poet, this one from Japanese gangster books, this one from a nineteenth-century hymn. Surely he did, and this is not so much irrelevant as it is a non sequitur in folk music. The irony here is that what most of the world means today with the term "folk music" is simply wrong. What the term means today is a singer-songwriter playing an acoustic guitar, and this is irony, because Dylan himself was the prototype of the modern singer-songwriter. In modern terms, the term "cover" is a sort of insult, a mere cover band not offering "original" material. In real folk music, there is no original material. The arrogance of claiming to write a song shows a lack of respect for who we are and where we came from. It ignores the history freighted in traditional music. To know folk music means something far more than mastering a canon; the point is to inhabit it like an evolving ecosystem.

It took no less than a legitimate historian to sort all of this out in Dylan's case. Sean Wilentz, author of such conventional surveys as *The Rise of American Democracy: Jefferson to Lincoln* and biographies of Ronald Reagan and Andrew Jackson, has been a lifelong follower of Dylan and wrote *Bob Dylan in America* in 2010. Much of the book is a decoding of the weft and weave of Dylan's allusions and sources through the years, an analysis that shows his work draws on this deep history. Writes Wilentz:

> Open to artistic inspiration where he found it, Dylan was not so much a sponge (although he has always absorbed prodigious amounts) as an alchemist, taking common materials and creating new art. Nothing that came within his field of vision escaped: French films, 1850s minstrel songs, the works of Shakespeare, Dolly Parton, Saint John of Patmos, Muddy Waters—anything of beauty, no matter how terrible, became something to seize upon and make his own.

Probably the most interesting part of this was no one was immune from his love and theft, not even Dylan himself. He continues to perform endlessly, but taking his old material, standing it on its head and delivering it back as something new.

Just as important to my attachment to Dylan is the central point of departure from his mentors, the folkies of the 1940s and 1950s, and it wasn't electric guitars. People like Pete

Seeger, Woody Guthrie, and even Joan Baez were lefties quoting politically correct music. They were urban, educated people with a constrained and distorted picture of rural and working people. In their view, music was meant to protect a heroic working class and blacks against the perfidies and oppression by bosses and government. Dylan summoned a much broader cast of characters. He peopled his songs with poets, outlaws, gamblers, minstrels, kings, lovers, vagabonds, orphans, and thieves. Coupled with context, this made them legitimate histories, even superior histories to accounts of kings, presidents, and wars, accounts of the elite. This opens a door that extends well beyond Dylan, an ability to unravel the deeper sources to tell us something about who we are.

Therefore we can know that "Cocaine Blues" is not just some flip drug song we heard a lot in the 1960s, but winds back in versions to at least the early nineteenth century. The song was popular in folk traditions in the South because cocaine was popular, freely provided to sharecroppers to keep them working. Many had returned to the fields after World War I already enamored of cocaine. Or that the ubiquitous bouncy fiddle tune "Soldier's Joy" was popular in the late nineteenth century and takes its name from a euphemism for morphine, the ironic "joy" of amputee Civil War veterans.

You can one day learn that when Robert Johnson sings the phrase "her 'nation sack" that this is a truncated term for "donation sack," a sort of pendulous purse that prostitutes draped from their waists, front and center, so that it hung across the central commodity in the exchange, the idea being that nothing went into one before something went into the other. Then you know something about the relationship he is lamenting when he reverses the normal direction: "I've taken my last nickel out of her 'nation sack."

You can gain some small appreciation of the creativity of the folk process when you hear Mississippi John Hurt lay down a tight little short story in two lines:

> *I did all I can do, I can't get along with you*
> *Gonna take you to your mama come payday*

Hurt did not write this, and probably no one knows who did. Better to say it somehow got written.

Or develop entire novels knowing Brady and Duncan were real, Tom Dooley was really Tom Dulla and did hang. Or that the dead girl Delia who appears in various versions of her folk autobiography throughout the Caribbean and United States— songs recorded dozens of times, including by Dylan and Johnny Cash—was fourteen when her lover, called Curtis in the songs, shot her in the Yamacraw neighborhood of Savannah, Georgia, in 1900 in what was probably a whorehouse fight. And Curtis was probably really named "Cooney," but no one in a long time has wanted to apply that term to a young black man (he was only fifteen at the time of the murder).

Or hear the account of the black boxer Jack Johnson being refused passage on a ocean liner because "this ship don't haul no coal." Then hear the reversal in Johnson's retort: "Fare thee, *Titanic*, fare thee well."

Or that the roundly and deservedly ridiculed Kumbaya is widely regarded today as overly precious simply because the Great Folk Scare got it wrong. It is not an African song, but a hymn sung by slaves who spoke Gullah, a dialect of the islands off the coast of the Carolinas. The collectors simply misunderstood their own field recordings. The people were singing "Come by here, oh Lord come by here," not an assertion of unity, but rather a plaintive cry from enslaved people wondering why God was always elsewhere.

Or one can hear Dylan's version of "World Gone Wrong," an old tune, a cover:

> Can't be good no more
> Once like I did before
> Can't be good no more
> Honey in a world gone wrong

And know we are not alone in the despair of our times. Somehow I found all these things to amount to a richer and more accurate story than that on offer in Sociology 101. Somehow it occurred to me that you can make a valid story by listening to what ordinary people say, especially the part that endures. This had much to do with choosing to spend my life carrying a skinny notebook and writing down what ordinary people had to say.

The odd thing is, I can't remember what I drove that night in late May of 1972, or the route from Ann Arbor back to Freeland. No one else would consider this lapse odd, not to recall the specifics of a single trip forty years previous, but my brain has one standout quirk: it organizes memory according to roads. Often and with no warning, a vivid visual of a single stretch of road will pop into my head, and I will know I am supposed to remember something about that day and will follow the mental image of the road with a sort of GPS of deep memory to take my path of logic where it needs to go. If I have been someplace, ever, I can usually go back, as when I was visiting Knoxville, Tennessee, when I was in my fifties and drove to the house I had lived in at five.

My best guess is the vehicle was a maroon-and-white Volkswagen bus; I was in a Volkswagen phase then and had not yet learned the considerable limitations of the bus. And almost certainly I would have driven that night straight north from Ann Arbor on U.S. 23, then cut west on 10 and south to Freeland, the shortest route, but I can't say for sure.

My brother Mike and my dad, who had passed that same general direction a few hours previous, did not go this same way, this I know for sure. And I know what they were driving: lime green Mustang fastback, nearly new, my brother's car, bought with power line grunt's wages. Grunt was also then a term of art for foot soldiers in Vietnam, but that's not what he was. Power linemen used the same term for ground men, the guy who stands beneath a pole and uses a pulley and a long loop of three-quarter-inch hemp rope to lift tools and fittings to the lineman working above. My brother had just got the job that month, and was working on a crew run by my dad, so they left work together. I know there would have been forest green hard hats bearing Laundra Electric decals flung in the backseat along with the empty lunch buckets. My dad would have been wearing blue twill work pants and shirt, because that's what he wore. My brother, blue jeans and a T-shirt. His pants would have been muddy, because then power lines were switching from overhead to underground, and grunts pushed a shovel.

Other than this reconstruction, I know almost nothing of my brother's life then; I had lost track. We had become different people, I, the sort who went off to universities and flew red flags; he the sort who went to the neighborhood community college to learn to be a pilot and got a job that would make payments on a brand-new lime green Mustang.

Their route home that day avoided the four-lane that runs from Saginaw to Freeland, a short commute of maybe ten miles. Instead, they cut north on the section-line grid of narrow two-lanes, then straight west on the same grid. This would have put them into dry bean country where table-flat black-earth fields of prime Saginaw Valley fields drain to deep, steep ditches on each side of the road, crowding out the shoulder. They leave not much room to maneuver when an oncoming truck takes his half out of the middle, so my brother's front wheel caught the ditch and the Mustang rolled. His window was down, and his arm rested out the window. My family believed seatbelts, then mandatory in new cars, were a devious government plot to trap decent folks in burning vehicles, and they refused to wear them. The roll of the Mustang caught my brother's arm and jerked him through the window cleanly enough to let the car roll across his head. My dad stayed in his seat for the full roll, the car came to rest upright, and the first thing he could see was his son was missing, and he went looking for him. He was not far, driven head down into the black soil, sucking for air, and my dad got him upright and cleared his airway. Passersby stopped and stood, but no one would help my dad, though he asked, other than to call an ambulance. My dad scraped dollops of gray brain tissue from his blue twill shirt.

All this I heard from my dad on arriving at Freeland. I think it was my sister who had called me in Ann Arbor to say that something bad had happened, and no, Mike was not dead, but in intensive care after several hours of neurosurgery and no one was sure how this would work out. I first saw my brother the next day at the Saginaw hospital. His ICU cubicle was more dominated by electronics and machines than any promise of life, and he was largely unrecognizable. Comatose, lying on his back, he was a mechanical man, the only movement a precise call and response, his chest rising as the respirator's bellows fell. His head was bandaged where the surgeons had stitched on half his skull, his face swollen to twice its size, and I knew he was good as dead.

For some days my parents talked mostly at first about the prospect of a long course of physical therapy, and searched for signs of a retreat of the swelling that was crushing his brain, as we sat in a waiting room outside, every half hour or so, filing into the room and seeing everything was the same. After ten days of this routine I began looking for excuses to be elsewhere and was for a day; when I returned I could not help but notice a panel truck pulling away from the hospital freighting what I recognized immediately as my brother's respirator, needed somewhere else now that all had admitted his death.

This was long before cases like Terri Schiavo's had dictated marching orders for the religious right, so people like my parents were free to act as humans in matters that ought to be private. My brother had died the day the Mustang rolled, and they made the decision to acknowledge that ten days later by removing the artificial support of his breath. They did well.

Then we sat three days later in the funeral home at Freeland, the six remaining kids, the two parents, and both branches of the extended family behind. A Bible thumper presided and mostly we sat stone-faced. The preacher offered nothing that made sense of the reality, nothing, even for my parents, who claimed they saw the world the way the preacher did. I had some sense a preacher had a job to do in a case like this, to at least ease my parents into what would be two separate lifetimes of grief, but he simply announced that we had nothing to worry about. My brother was not pinned under a lime green Mustang, but already whooping it up in heaven. Then he began the windup I remembered from all those Sundays years ago, that there were young people hearing his words that afternoon and those young people should know that this could happen to them, maybe even that very afternoon, and he gave an altar call so those young people might step forward and be saved, so my brother's death would not be in vain. He offered nothing for our grief but did hope to use the specter of my brother's present and closed coffin to increase his evangelical batting average.

Rage can temporarily offset grief, and I was at that moment glad for clarifying anger, as I looked down the row of grim siblings to see one of my younger brothers, just a boy then, bent over double and heaving in sobs.

Then an hour or so later, after the trip to the simple little country cemetery a couple miles south of my parents' house, a place I would see only two more times in my life, a scene played out in clear geometry that argued a proof for everything that would matter from then on in my parents' life. The yard filled with relatives, the Mannings and the Mayos and just as quickly segregated into two distinct lumps, sorted by blood, my mother with hers and my father with his. Then my father did begin grieving, and his siblings began dealing. He began weeping and openly blaming himself for the accident and his sisters began talking him out of this. My mother was nowhere near, nor was he near to her. They never looked so helpless to me, and I made a decision. I would put this thing out of my mind for a time. Had to. There would be work to do, and no one else to do it. My parents were helpless in this.

Now comes the second dream into my life, the bookend of the wounded deer I would chase through the years. It began a few months later and plagued me regularly into my fifties. It's a simple dream, really, and requires almost nothing of my imagination. I dream that I am sleeping, always in exactly the place where I am sleeping. If it is a pleasant summer afternoon with an open window sending breezes to the couch where I am napping, then in my dream, it is a pleasant summer afternoon with a window sending breezes exactly to the couch where I am napping. But then I become aware of some sort of threat, a menace just outside the window, maybe a rustle and the edge of a face in the window, but I am paralyzed, cannot move, even tilt my head to properly identify the threat and protect myself and those I am charged to protect. I try to cry out some sort of warning to my wife but the paralysis is complete and no sound, not even a groan, will come. I even have some sense I am dreaming and need more than anything else to wake up to end the terror. Over the years I learned to struggle with making the sound and eventually it will come. My wife has learned to hear it and wakes me up. Then, often as not, I go back to sleep and the dream begins immediately again.

It seemed to me what needed to be done in that summer was to work with my dad, so I got a union card from the International Brotherhood of Electrical Workers and signed on as a grunt, my brother's vacant job on my dad's crew. I dug holes and pulled underground power lines through conduit pipe. We also still built some overhead lines, so I borrowed a pair of hooks, the set of braces that hold the spikes at the arch of a lineman's boots, and learned how to lever them against a buckstrap, a long leather waistband that wraps around a pole to provide a lineman's purchase and perch. Then I humped my way up some poles. All strictly against union and safety rules, but you got to learn to climb somehow. Mostly though, I think my job that summer was to steer my dad's conversation and activity to something like a normal daily routine. Work is good for that. Then in the fall, I went back to my life in Ann Arbor for my senior year.

A semester passed without my noticing it. I had taken extra courses through the years, so was looking at a final semester of about a three-quarter load, which was fine with me. Then the draft ended, and I had no idea why I was in school, nor an idea where I was headed. I had managed a 3.0 grade point average, which I considered to be a failure. I was about to get a degree in political science, which as far as I knew was worthless, especially with unspectacular grades. Again, I spoke to no one about this; it was my own naive assessment. I had no idea that a 3.0 and political science degree lined one up nicely to enter Michigan's prestigious law school, or any graduate school anyplace in the country. I had no real concept of a graduate degree or what one did with it, other than to teach at a university. Climbing power poles or digging ditches seemed a lot more appealing than the academy. I was stuck in a sense of worthlessness, of seeing no future and unable to face the simple business of going to class each day, doing the reading, and writing those last three papers.

I think it was the first time in my life I had hit this wall, but at the time, thought it no cause for concern, just normal. I did not see anything unusual. All through my childhood, my dad would periodically enter bleak moods when he wouldn't say much of anything for weeks, and no one dared speak to him. This set of feelings, really lack of feelings, would revisit all through my years. Not long after that first episode, I developed a name for it, the "black hand," a crushing feeling that would descend on me like the palm of a giant, invisible hand and press down as a near-physical burden. Nearly fifteen years of these cycles intervened before I would learn that others named this black hand "depression."

Halfway through my last semester of my senior year, I could not summon the will to go on. I simply walked out of class and did not return. I didn't graduate.

7
RABBITS
EATING WELL
IN GREENBUSH

Sometime in the early 1960s, but for sure the day was a Tuesday, my family was gathered with neighbors at the Greely Baptist Church for an evening event. Not prayer meeting, that was always on Wednesday, but some sort of a potluck. I slipped out, because I knew what was going on across the highway at Green Township Hall. People were counting votes. I had heard of such a thing in government class, but had never seen it for real, and it sounded more important than church. Besides, I had a stake in the issue, a bond issue, a vote to decide whether the county school district would borrow enough money to build a brand-new high school, which would be my school. I borrowed a paper and pencil from someone, and as the clerk read off the final tally, I wrote it down, then walked back across the highway to the church, interrupted whatever meeting was in progress, and filed my story. I was twelve, and this was the first time I had committed an act of journalism.

By the time I left the university, I had been a tractor driver, a shit shoveler, and a meat cutter. I had carried hod, rattled jackhammers, and poured concrete. I had lugged beer barrels and hiked power poles. I had been a deckhand on the *J.L Reiss,* a Great Lakes freighter longer than a football field, a lumbering hulk of a steamship that had fitted out in 1909, by far my favorite job. These distinctive long, flat-bottomed boats, giant canoes really, tool around the Great Lakes in one- or two-day hops, lugging limestone or iron ore or coal. Many were self-unloaders, meaning a long conveyor belt runs the length of the ship at its very bottom, then a bucket conveyor relays the load above deck and dumps into a boom conveyor that pushes the load over the side. One of a deckhand's jobs is to swing around on a chain at the bottom of the wet, angled steel sides of the hold, just above the screaming conveyor belt, to knock loose any cargo that sticks in the corners of the hold.

Up on deck, there is a short boom with a seat like that of a playground swing at the end of its rope. The deckhand mounts that seat when the boat pulls into port, launches out over the side, and is straightaway lowered to the dock, thirty or so feet below. It's his job to pull two-inch-thick lengths of cable from ship to dock to tie up. All good work if you can get it.

In Ann Arbor, I had friends who had bought a gas station and made some money doing brake jobs and tune-ups on Volkswagen Bugs. I hung around, learned the moves, and got by that way for a while, then worked as a Chevrolet mechanic after I quit school. I had been married a couple of years, then my wife was pregnant, and then a homing urge kicked in, and we moved back to Alpena. I was a Volkswagen mechanic there, then took a job as a machinist in a local factory, where I ran a giant drill press for a year or so, learning to land smooth, precisely bored holes within a few thousandths of an inch of spec. Then there was a lockout when the aristocrats who owned the plant tried to bust the union. So I called my dad and got back on a power line crew near Saginaw, making it home on weekends, just as he had done most his life. Thus I had set myself up to repeat his existence, aligned on a normal course for my family. Then my father-in-law intervened.

My wife's father owned a dry cleaning plant in Alpena, but he was an old-school, small-town burgher who perceived his role as more of a seat of civic responsibility than a business—Rotary, a term as a county commissioner, a booster. He made it a point to know the names of every customer, and he made a good living, raising five exemplary daughters, a decent human every one. One of his friends managed the local radio station and told my father-in-law that he needed to hire a news director. Did he know of anyone?

I had heard the news on the radio a couple of times, and it seemed like something I could do, so I went to visit the station manger, Ralph Diethelm, a tall, bald man with a perpetual smile and genuine good nature, good enough to take a chance on a kid who knew nothing about what he was doing. I spent a week getting some tutoring from the outgoing news director, then went on the air.

Actually, news director greatly overstates the case, in that it implies there would be others to direct. I was a news department of one at station WATZ, both AM and FM. When I was growing up, my grandfather's barn, sitting as it did directly beside the main highway atop Manning Hill, was a place of some prominence, and through all of my memory there was a billboard nailed to the front corner of the barn, a cutout of an RCA ribbon microphone—it looked like something Calvin Coolidge might have used—emblazoned with the call letters WATZ. My first day on the air, I spoke into what looked to be that very mike. The whole station's operation fit in a strikingly square concrete block building the size of a garage. There were five World War II vintage steel desks jammed in a front office that would have been tight space for a kitchen. The expanse was working quarters for Diethelm, two ad sales guys, a guy who scheduled commercials, and me. I had a cheap reel-to-reel tape recorder on my desk and a roll of Scotch tape and a razor blade for editing tape, then done with a literal cut and splice with the Scotch tape. There was a portable typewriter where I learned to write copy, and next to my desk a rattling Teletype machine supplied by United Press International, the link to the larger world. Four times a day I ran to the control room to sit and address the RCA ribbon mike and broadcast to the masses what UPI, my Underwood, and the razor blade had given. Meantime, disk jockeys in the control room behind a glass panel directly in front of me would lend their support by ignoring my cues, leaving for a smoke, or by standing on a chair directly on the opposite side of the glass and dropping their pants.

The town's undertakers brought me obituaries, and I read those. I'd call the weather bureau four times a day and talk to Bill Gilmet, who also happened to be the town's mayor. On days he was not angry with me for something I had said about the city council meeting, he'd give me the forecast, and on days he was he wouldn't. I called the local elevator and got the grain prices. On Saturdays I read the results of Friday night bowling, generally a long list of names like Louis Wisniewski, Casimir Arczyszewski, Frank Pysczynski, and Rudy Wieczorkowski. But working in close quarters in a small town, which I came to call "hand-to-hand journalism," I soon realized that this is the only public mention Casimir Arczyszewski will get, so best not to mangle his name when you are announcing to the larger world that he did indeed convert the seven-ten split.

The writing largely consisted of pounding out thirty-two-line stories of the wrecks, council and school board meetings, and cancellations when it snowed. I was, of course, terrible at this, and terrible on the air. I tried to affect a booming bass radio voice of authority that came out as a stammering, stuttering monotone, then one day heard myself on tape and was embarrassed. So I taught myself to relax, to relate to and invest my consciousness in what I was reading, and the stammer and the stutter went away in a matter of a day, a simple act of confidence. Decades later I was a student of Peter Matthiessen's in a week-long writing workshop, and he delivered the best writing advice I have heard: never publish a word you have not read out loud. This self-corrective is automatic for broadcasters, and works. In time, my sentences began cleaning themselves up as a consequence of the stumbles I made on air. Bill Moyers once said, "A journalist, it is said, enjoys a license to be educated in public." This is true now and this was true for me then.

———

Don Parteka was a weekend DJ at WATZ, and mostly hung around so he could do the Polka Hour, his pride and passion. So when he called me at home that weekend, I couldn't imagine why; I had nothing to do with the Polka Hour. I had forgotten for a moment that Parteka was also an addicted police scanner nerd. On that morning of September 26, 1976, he had heard something about a plane crash. Maybe I should go, he said. I drove to a spot where a section-line road dead-ended against a tangled, third-growth cedar swamp twelve and a half miles southwest of Alpena, left my car, grabbed my portable tape recorder, and started slogging through the scrub and brush, headed west. It was rough cover, and no sign to indicate anything of a plane crash in the direction I was going, but these were the coordinates Don had given me. I covered about a half mile of unbroken brush and scrub, and then all of a sudden I was standing in a clearing, a quiet break in the woods that signaled easier going, a silent spot that looked like somebody had logged off a half-mile-long strip worth of pulpwood. Still no sign of anything resembling an aircraft, but there were bits of trash. A dump maybe? Then I could see the trash was spread everywhere, thin shards of aluminum, pieces strewn like confetti, most of the pieces the size of a Post-it note. Then I saw the first of what looked to be a black mannequin tossed in the turf, a naked, hairless copy of a human form, but near an overturned airplane seat. Then another black mannequin, but this one spewed intestines. Now the diverse snippets of image came together to a realization that corrected the mental image I had carried into the woods. I was expecting some weekend pilot's Cessna, crash-landed in a farmer's field, but here I was standing all alone, no one and nothing around, amid something terrible enough to clear-cut acres of forest in a few seconds and smash a jetliner to bits not recognizable as anything built, and litter a forest floor with charred bodies. My tape recorder was useless here. There was no one left to talk to, and I was speechless.

It turned out there had been living people on the scene only moments before, and some of them had been passengers in this aircraft, an Air Force KC-135, which is a military version of the Boeing 707. Of the twenty men on board, five had survived, one, Airman Dale J. Solon of Lakewood, Ohio, had done well enough to walk away, largely because of his low rank. The rest on board were officers and so seated ahead of him on the plane. The energy of an aircraft that crashes nose-first gets absorbed progressively from front to rear, meaning much of it is dissipated by the time it works its way back. The five had been helicoptered out before I made it onto the scene. The remaining fifteen were the black mannequins.

I do not know how long I stumbled around that clearing, not nearly as long as a good reporter would have. Later, I would get used to scenes like this and would have stayed to confront and question until someone threw me out, but then I was a twenty-five-year-old kid who thought reporting involved mostly bowling scores. I made my way back through the swamp before anyone arrived, found my car, and then came cops and helicopters. An Air Force officer spotted my tape recorder and asked me if he could borrow it. He wanted to record an interview with a witness. Maybe sometime during the walk back to my car, I had realized that what I had seen in the past half hour of human vulnerability had somehow made me into a reporter, but something did change me, and I told him no. I would need my recorder to do a job. And I did, got the information I needed, drove back to the station, and went on the air, then filed a story for the wire service, then recorded a voicer, and my story in my voice went national. Through the following weeks I tried to learn to sleep again.

I must have finally learned to do something right during my two years in radio, because shortly after the plane crash, I got a call from Betty Werth, a reporter at the *Alpena News,* the local paper. She was the younger sister of my high school friend David Werth. She and I had played saxophone in marching band together, and we became friends in our own right when I began doing radio news. There was an opening at the paper. Would I like to apply? Even then, I knew of status differential in the print-broadcast divide and knew I was on the wrong side. So I crossed.

Then covering Alpena County and the three adjacent counties, the *News* was the biggest paper in northeast Michigan, which is not saying all that much. It had a daily circulation of about 13,000. Besides me and Betty, there were six other full-time staffers in the newsroom and a couple of correspondents. Lew Sowa was the managing editor, Bob Westrope the city editor, Frank Przykucki another reporter, Dick Higgs did sports, a photographer, and a woman working what was then called "socs," short for the society page, the rundown on weddings and engagements that would later be universally re-christened "lifestyles." The five of us that worked hard news sat around the horseshoe, then the near-universal core geometry of newsrooms, large and small. It was a big U-shaped desk. The spot on the inside of the U was called "slot" and re-served for the editor, the guy in charge of assembling the daily paper from copy that flowed from reporters to copy editors on the rim. There was more or less constant chatter and banter, always through a haze. Those who had quit smoking smoked pipes, a sentence that for some curious reason was thought to have meaning then.

Sowa had started working at the paper in 1943 when he was fifteen years old. He became managing editor in 1955 and held the job until he retired in 1989. The first day on the job, he told me it would be my duty to pound out enough copy to fill the space between brassiere ads, and so I learned to write. The journalist A. J. Liebling said, "The only way to write is well and how you do that is your own damned business."

You begin by jamming the skinny notebook in the hip pocket of your khakis and cruise the cop shops before dawn, knowing full well the quality of the day's stories is largely a matter of chance: who hit whom at which bar and which cop has desk duty: the surly wannabe Nazi who hates reporters or the guy who likes your jokes. You check the pile of reports of wrecks for fatals, usually high school kids piled up against a tamarack tree on the two-lane out behind the cement plant in the early hours after a case of beer and the driver putting his foot way too far into the four-barrel carburetor of his GTO. Fatals have special rules, and if there is one, you will have a bad day. Sowa requires that you will go to the victim's house and knock on the door and ask the kid's mother for his gradu-ation photo. A mug shot with every dead kid, that's the rule, so you go, and you get it. Then you'll hit the newsroom and may call the mayor with a few more questions about last night's council meeting. Then peel off your share of the obits from the pile the undertakers walked in. In March of 1979, I peeled my Grandmother Mayo's vitals off that same pile and I wrote up her obit.

You pull yourself around to address the ancient Underwood, roll in a slice of newsprint, and—it being near midday—unwind the red strip that tears the cellophane top off the day's second pack of Camels. Deadline is at eleven. Soon, all this becomes more a matter of rhythm and touch. The Underwood requires a heavy hand, a confident snap that seems to dictate simple, declarative sentences, and after a while, the feedback that says you've got it right is the snap of sound, like playing piano. Get your brain out of the way and let it flow from the fingers. Time passes and this rhythm embeds in your brain to the point it is no longer a style of writing so much as it is a way of life: I have something to say, not much time to say it, so let's do get to the point.

Single pieces of newsprint get glued together so that each story is one continuous sheet. A fatal is maybe a foot long, enough to wind down a kid's life. The council meeting gets two or three feet of paper. Anything longer, and you'll cause Sowa to loom over your desk.

"Izatta, Izzata, Izzata . . ." Sowa had a crippling stutter and would begin all animated conversations thusly. Sometimes the stammer would loop for thirty seconds while you wondered if you were being fired or being praised. Then he would finally take his pipe out of his mouth, and it wouldn't make all that much difference. He'd finally get it out: "Izzata izzata, is that a fucking bedsheet or what, and what am I supposed to do with it." A bedsheet was any story longer than he was, and he would stand over me and unfurl it just to make the point. Cut it. Then a couple days later, the bra ads would indeed be in danger of bumping, and he would tell you to write long.

The copy came out of my typewriter, and then I'd make the first run through with a copy pencil, a series of hieroglyphics meant to correct typos, move words. Paragraphs got moved by cutting and pasting, like now, but with a glue pen and scissors, not a mouse. Then I'd hand it to Bob Westrope, who would either edit it or occasionally set it on fire accidentally with ashes from his pipe. Bob taught you that the First Amendment was not so much exercised with robust speech as it was with the *Associated Press Stylebook,* that it mattered as much that you spelled it right, capitalized, spelled out numbers or used numerals as the occasion demanded. "FBI" allowed, even on first reference, even "pope" and "president" lowercase standing alone. You learned early on that every single soul sitting around the horseshoe knew this stuff cold, and you would too if you meant to stay and collect a paycheck every week.

You learned that all was won or lost on your lede, the nut graf, which was then always the first paragraph, the short straight sentence or two that nailed the story, all five Ws. And you could figure you were getting somewhere when the day finally came when Sowa stood over your desk and after the usual minute of stammers, complimented you on your lede, then ordered you to write a new one so he could steal it for his headline.

Deadline came. All copy in. Then everybody read proof for a half hour or so, strips of type returned from the backshop ready to be trimmed and pasted on pages. Reading proof was meant to catch any typos introduced by typesetters, and we keenly understood it mattered. Once, one of us had written a cutline—a photo caption—about a small town's basketball team that had advanced to the state finals. The copy noted that during the weekend, "Onaway, where half the town was gathered in pubs," to watch the game. Only the typesetter hit an "f" instead of a "g" in "gathered," and a proofreader missed it. It happened that Onaway's papers came off early in the press run, so the truck had left before someone caught the typo. The staff was polled to see who had the fastest car, which was dispatched to catch the truck.

Then off to the Taproom for a beer and a burger, off to the commissioners' meeting at the courthouse for the afternoon, and then do all again the next morning. As these heady days ran to months it occurred to me that I was living a life of great privilege, but more to the point, I could do this thing. Understand, it was relatively easy then for a small-town reporter to inflate the estimate of his importance. This was the mid-1970s, just after Bob Woodward and Carl Bernstein had brought down a sitting president, and an evil bastard at that. Many young reporters wanted to do that and began looking for excuses to add the superfluous modifier "investigative" to the simple act of reporting. Never mind that we only had part-time mayors and county commissioners who were also our uncles to work with. Kids with skinny notebooks and Underwoods were then the lone guardians of the public's right to know. My personal version of the Watergate Complex happened to be the Alpena County jail and a perennial prisoner named Edmond "Beaky" Tadajewski.

Beaky was the compliant sort of miscreant who would not necessarily wait to be arrested as the occasion demanded, but would simply check himself into jail from time to time. Nothing serious, but occasionally the guy needed a stay, usually for passing bad checks, and life at the county jail seemed to agree with him. But then a source of mine explained why Beaky was so welcome behind bars: he was not staying behind bars. The sheriff, Tom Male, who happened to be a friend of mine, was in the process of remodeling his house and Beaky was a carpenter. So every day, a deputy drove Beaky to Male's house, then back to jail at the end of day for wages of room and board. I confronted Male about this, and he did what targets of such stories almost always do: he confirmed it. He explained this practice was simply good therapy for inmates, allowing them honest labor. I asked Male if any other citizen in need of a day laborer might be issued a slave on request. Then I wrote the story. I filed it. Westrope and Sowa read it, then each looked as if I had delivered a dead body to the copy basket. This was not done in their world. There was no point in pissing off the sheriff, a guy whose help we needed all the time. These were old-school newspapermen in a small town, and the people they wrote about were the same people they bowled with and saw at Mass every Sunday. What would Phil think about this?

Phil Richards was the only guy on the second floor with an actual office, which he had inherited. He was the owner and publisher of the paper, as had been his father, which meant I got my start at what is today the rarest of institutions, the family-owned paper. Richards was patrician, well educated, eccentric, and taciturn. He was a devout Catholic. In fact, I think I was then the only person on newsroom staff who was not a Catholic. The sole consequence of my minority was that every time a local church needed to raise money for religious equipment like new bowling shirts or bingo cards, I would be required to buy a raffle ticket for something like a deer rifle, usually from Sowa, who would take my five bucks and my ticket stub, then announce without a hint of stutter: "I'll see that this gets put straight into the Protestant box."

Richards was always a looming presence, never seemed to take much of a day-to-day role at the newspaper, but when people in power needed something, they went to Richards. I found myself seated in his office in short order while Westrope and Sowa fidgeted outside. He read my story as I noted a placard pinned to his wall and it said, "The duty of a newspaper is to print the news and raise hell." The story ran.

Events such as these are rare in small-town newspapering, and in the end, not our reason for being. We did learn to raise hell, but mostly we learned to print the news: to know the difference between an assessed and market value and how to calculate the cost of a bond issue for the average taxpayer, to learn the difference between an arraignment and a trial, a temporary restraining order and a writ of mandamus. That states don't have borders, only nations have borders and it's only "half mast" on ship; on land the proper term is "half staff." "Attorneys general" not "attorney generals." What a bargaining unit is. There is a technical difference between a snowstorm and a blizzard, a strike and a lockout.

One day you take a dictated story over the phone from a rural correspondent—our woman in the town of Greenbush—who reports the winter has been easy on wildlife, hand it off to Westrope, who takes the opportunity to teach you what it means to be the Zen master of the mundane. He tags it with an immortal headline: "Rabbits Eating Well in Greenbush."

You learn that government is mostly about sending clean water up one set of pipes and sewage back down another in a reliable manner, about keeping the streets plowed, the buses filled with gas, the drunks in jail, and teachers paid. Beneath all this there was a steady and daily stream reporting births, deaths, and marriages, not the whole story of a town's life, but a pretty good outline of it. That's mostly what we wrote about, and it was worth some dedication.

In one case, even mindless dedication. Alpena wraps around the head of Thunder Bay, a large inlet in Lake Huron. My house then, in fact, faced a large park that fronted the bay, two doors down State Street from where my great-great-grandfather A. R. Richardson had built his house in the glory days of timber. The lake view, however, came with a cost. Northern Michigan could get slammed with epic snowstorms, and lake effect could pound Alpena even harder. I had grown up with this and remember well being snowed in for days on end. But the worst I and anyone else I knew of had ever seen came in the last week of January in 1978. The barometer dropped to a record low, the onshore winds set to howling, and the skies dumped two feet of snow in a single night. It overwhelmed snowplows and all other measures; the National Guard was summoned.

I lived only a couple of blocks from the paper, so skied to work, joined by a few others who lived close by. We had big news, and set to working the phones, finding out that all of the county and all of the surrounding counties were in similar straits, a storm of a century. We shot some photos, wrote main stories and sidebars, and informed our public of prospects of weeks of paralyzed roads. People needed to know. A skeleton crew in the backshop set it all into type, pasted it up. A skeleton crew in the pressroom let it roll.

Then we piled up 13,000 papers against the loading dock doors buried under four feet of snow, and there they would sit until twenty-four hours had rendered them as useless as yesterday's newspaper. Funny how none of us saw that coming. So we skied two blocks to downtown, which was filled and drifted with snow over the awnings. Someone had cut a sort of rabbit hole under the awning of the Owl Café, a true act of mercy, and we squeezed in to find a bar full of people drinking as if it were July 4.

Mostly my job was cops and courts, which meant I had to learn to sleep with a police scanner. The paper was too small for a night staff, so I kept a scanner at home and learned to sleep through the routine chatter of the night, but when something bad happened, the pace and tone both notched up enough to awaken me, as they did one morning near daybreak in January of 1979. A woman was dead in her car in her garage in a normal residential section of town. I went there. Sheriff's deputies stood around while a detective interviewed the dead woman's husband inside. No, I could not talk to him, not even to request a mug shot that I knew Sowa would send me back for later. Then a deputy I knew took me aside and talked, but not for attribution. There'd been some sort of spat, and the woman had stomped off and shut herself away in the car, started it, who knows why, and then she was dead. So I filed my story that way, and that's how it ran.

That night, after the paper came out, I got a phone call from the grieving widower, who told me he was at that moment standing before his wife's casket at the funeral home and would I care to hear what she looked like dead. There had been no argument, he said. They had, in fact, made love, and after she had gone to sit in the car for a cigarette or some other postcoital ritual, maybe they had both been in the car, and she simply started it to stay warm, then fell asleep. But my story had turned an act of love into shame. The onus accrued from the Catholicism of the town, the particular shame the church places on suicide. My story suggested that possibility, and nothing I could write by way of correction or apology would make that go away. Nothing can be unsaid. The man sobbed through our conversation, then again described what his wife looked like in the casket, then hung up. I went straight to Phil Richards's office the next morning and offered my resignation. He declined it, then spent the next hour or so shut in his glassed-in office with the grieving widower.

In the context of events, in the daily body count that is our world's news, this seems trivial and quaint, but it affected me, maybe even more than the fieldful of charred bodies I had found a couple of years before. I was not the same reporter after; I had fully exercised my license to learn in public. Seventeen years later, I was on a journalism fellowship at Stanford University, and I got a telephone call from this same man. He had taken the trouble to track me down and apologize for what he had done. Some sort of atonement, I guess, so he could go on, that he finally understood he needed to remove me from the crosshairs of his anger. I told him no apology was necessary, that he was in a large part responsible for making me the reporter I had become.

In June of 1978, my wife, my longtime friend from high school David Werth, by then a practicing lawyer, and I headed west on vacation. None of us had spent much time at all outside Michigan and then only in the Midwest. I had never seen mountains but knew something of their mystique, and the pull of Montana had been planted in me by my old friend from Ann Arbor, Peter Bowen. We threw our three backpacks in the back of my Dodge pickup and drove straight through the night, taking turns driving, twenty-four hours or so across Michigan's Upper Peninsula, then Wisconsin, Minnesota, North Dakota on U.S. 2, a highway known in Montana as the hi-line, a parallel of Jim Hill's Great Northern railway line that brought the settlers into the high plains. It takes a good eight or nine hours to drive across the plains in Montana, not flat land, but rolling hills, cattle country, a great wheat desert in a few places with fallow-stripped wheat fields seeming to stretch for miles, because they do. We crossed a couple of Indian reservations, one with a powwow in progress, hundreds of Plains Indians gathered in full dress to dance. Then suddenly ghostly snow triangles appeared on the western horizon and we drove toward them for what seemed hours before they became the mountains of Glacier National Park. We hiked the mountains for a week.

Suddenly, there were possibilities. Mountain wilderness does nothing so much as prove the existence of infinity. It lifts the lid and blows down all the walls and suddenly life is enormous and unbounded. I knew almost nothing about what I was seeing, could not name a single tree or flower. No one I knew, not a single one of my relatives or friends, had ever been here. I knew I was sharing the place right then with grizzly bears and so for the first time in my life was a part of the food chain. All the better. But I knew for sure that this was where I belonged. I moved west forever the following spring.

8
PUBLIC
IDAHO

I didn't know then that Idaho was such a strange place. In fact I didn't know anything about Idaho, other than I could find it on a map, trace the spine of the Rockies from where I had backpacked in Montana southward, and could see the cordillera extended well into that neighboring state. Mountains? Good enough for me. So I sent the résumé and clips as suggested in the *Editor & Publisher* ad for a journeyman reporter, *Editor & Publisher* then being the magazine of record for job seekers in the newspaper business. I did a telephone interview, got the offer, and took the job as cops and court reporter at the *Idaho Falls Post Register* in the early spring of 1979. When word of this spread among my friends in Ann Arbor, Peter Bowen, the former Montanan said, "My God, doesn't he know about Mormons." I didn't know about Mormons.

I jammed my family's each and every possession into a U-Haul, tethered my pickup truck behind on a tow bar, perched my wife and son, then four years old, on the high bench seat of the big truck, and we three lit out for the territories, leaving Michigan before dawn one April morning. A day later I was crawling under the U-Haul after a country gas station in northern Minnesota—the heart of Keillor country—had failed to protect its gasoline storage tanks from spring runoff and sold me half a tank of water. Freezing rain falling sideways. I tore out gas lines, sucking them dry, disassembling the delicate carburetor float chamber, then coaxed the U-Haul back to life. A day later, we hit a blizzard in North Dakota and holed up in a motel, still stuck in the Great Plains, but heartened: with weather this bad, we had to be getting close to the West. We hung with I-90 across Montana, and the weather slowly improved until we left the interstate and cut south into Idaho across Yellowstone National Park, my strange little caravan threading its way on winding mountain two-lane switchbacks among winter-weary herds of elk and bison. Then south and down out of the mountains to the sunny, brown high desert of the Snake River plain and on to Idaho Falls, a city of about fifty thousand centered by a gleaming, white-spired Mormon temple on the banks of the Snake River. From city's edge, I could see the peaks of the Tetons poking up on the eastern horizon, real mountains visible while I was standing flat-footed in my new town. Mountains? Good enough for me. What I did not know, however, what would, in fact, take me decades to realize, is I had not, despite appearances, signed on for duty in some remote backwater of the nation's body politic. I had arrived at a thriving little theocracy that was then incubating a virulent strain of know-nothing politics, a proto–Tea Party republic. I was getting a preview of the present.

Idaho is at least two very different places, which is why it is constantly at odds with itself. On the one hand, it holds, especially in the skinny north half of the state, in the panhandle, some of the world's most spectacular and pristine rivers, mountain ranges, and wilderness, formally designated. We generally use the term "wilderness" loosely, but in the West it has a legal definition, large tracts of federal lands "untrammeled by man" to use the language of the 1964 Wilderness Act. There are no roads, no mechanized travel of any sort. Not even bicycles are allowed. The nation holds 109 million acres of such places, most of it in the Rockies and Alaska.

Idaho has much of it, almost five million acres, and so has all the amenities that elsewhere create chic mountain towns like Boulder, Vail, and Santa Fe. One of these meccas of the fleece-clad is Jackson Hole, Wyoming, a short drive over a pass from Idaho Falls, its closest city. Sun Valley and Ketchum, Idaho, stand like islands of retreat for the rich, the famous, and ski bums in the center of the state. But Sun Valley and Ketchum have almost nothing to do with Idaho, and smugly preserve separation.

The real center of gravity is the Snake River plain—flat, volcanic lands arrayed like an inverted rainbow that spans the southern half of the state. At its edges, the plain is a high desert of lava flows and sagebrush, but closer to the river the lava has broken down to a crumbly, mineral soil that, if irrigated, grows potatoes, spuds on millions of acres, sprouting in obsessively straight rows under center-pivot irrigation lines. The tractors that work these fields are big as houses. There are no small farms; this is industrial ag, factory ag, dependent on incoming streams of capital, water, cheap nitrogen fertilizers, pesticides, and Hispanics. It is the best place I know for learning the driving aphorism of the arid West: water runs uphill toward money.

Yet one large corner of the Snake River plain has been saved from potatoes, if only because it is even more arid and remote than the rest. These factors caused early-day nuclear scientists, then experimenting with crude reactors at Fermi labs in Chicago, to seek someplace less populous, in the event that something really does go wrong. These initial experiments led to first one reactor, then another, at what was to become the Idaho National Engineering Laboratory, sprawled across the desert just west of Idaho Falls. Most of the scientists and lab workers live in Idaho Falls, which bifurcates the population between Mormons and educated. Nonetheless, the dominant force is indeed Mormon, especially in surrounding areas.

The *Post Register*, however, was not. It was an independent paper owned by a Catholic family. When I was there, the publisher was a genteel, soft-spoken man, J. Robb Brady, and he ran an honest operation. Yet for that newspaper to continue, we at the paper had to understand a fundamental fact: that our readership was 80 percent Mormon, and it was widely believed among both Mormons and gentiles (Mormons in the West routinely refer to non-Mormons as "gentiles," apparently unaware the term has been taken) that it was true what they said, that Mormons too conservative to live in Utah move to southeast Idaho.

It turned out my courts and cops job was short-lived. My first week there, the guy who was training me said he had already taken another job, so the city editor moved me to covering the county commissioners and county schools, a much more interesting assignment, more interesting than I expected. All three county commissioners were former Mormon bishops, as were the key members of the school board and the superintendent of schools. Mormons famously operate with a lay ministry, meaning that after the local insurance agent completes his mission (one-and-a-half- to two-year proselytizing trips taken by young men in pairs, and he wouldn't have gotten a job at the insurance agency had he not completed his mission) he ensures his temple recommends, is sealed in a temple marriage, advances in church hierarchy and then gets to lead a flock. Bishops lead wards, which is not so much a church as a political subdivision. Wards aggregate as stakes, led by stake presidents, and a certain number of stakes attach to a temple, such as the one at the center of Idaho Falls. Once the insurance agent has served as a bishop, he is considered qualified to become a county commissioner. The church hierarchy superimposes on the political.

Individuals attach to a certain ward according to geography, meaning one does not choose a church because he happened to like a particular bishop or the architecture of a particular building. It was and is a seamless and unbroken imposition of church organization on a given piece of geography, every inch covered, the geometry of a theocracy. The overlay with the political emerged in odd ways. For instance, during my first few days in Idaho Falls, I was amused to watch a television interview in which the county civil defense director explained his new emergency plan. The county had decided that, in the event of an emergency, each resident of the county would be obliged to report to his assigned ward building. The interviewer reminded this man that some residents of the county were not, in fact, Mormon and so were not assigned a ward. His response was that may be, but everyone, Mormon and otherwise, certainly knows where his ward is. Then he looked into the camera with what I would come to call the sweet, blank stare of bliss. I would see it often.

Mind you, all of this could be terribly entertaining, and as I made friends—all of them gentiles or jack Mormons (the term for a lapsed Mormon)—I discovered there was an instant bond among those of us in opposition. Cocktail party and dinner chatter tended to center on revelations of Mormon eccentricities: that the saints all wore funny underwear, that the reason they were so interested in genealogy was so they could identify and retroactively baptize all their ancestors, that temple weddings featured very funny hats and anointing of genitals, and that after Jesus died he came to North America to live with Indians who were really lost tribes of Israel so that he could leave some tablets that an angel named Moroni could show to Joseph Smith, who saw them only long enough to remember enough for the Book of Mormon, then Moroni made them disappear, but trust us on that last one, and that the Garden of Eden was not in fact in the Middle East, but in Missouri. Today these wonderful little factoids are widely available in everything from Jon Krakauer's book *Under the Banner of Heaven* to the television series *Big Love* (although you will likely not hear this information from people like Mitt Romney), but then, most of this was closely held. Some of it had been spelled out in Fawn Brodie's 1945 exposé, *No Man Knows My History*, but the book was even in the 1970s only available at bookstores under the counter, literally. In fact, everyone realized the first order of business on moving into a place like Idaho Falls was to make friends with a jack Mormon. These people are easily identified. For instance, in a bar the jack Mormons are the ones drinking the most. Knowing one is a benefit because, in their cups, they are the people most willing to disclose the esoterica of blood atonement, celestial marriage, and the exclusion of black people from the full rights of church membership until 1978.

All of this can seem terribly goofy, but it needs perspective. The saints have only been among us for not yet two centuries, so it seems silly, because the history is recent and well documented. Doctrines such as the virgin birth and papal infallibility have had millennia to be obscured in dust. In matters religious, one should remember the difference between a cult and a true religion is about five hundred years. But it seems less silly and more threatening in light of the fact that Mormon fundamentalism has a long history of violence, child abuse, and systematic rape.

Transparent absurdity, however, leaves the Mormons with something of a greater burden of avoiding uncomfortable questions, hence the prominence of the sweet, blank stare. As a reporter, I learned to provoke it with a diligence approaching glee. I'd check in with the three county commissioners several times a day, and the first thing you need to know about them is they were genuinely nice guys. I was always welcomed into the room like a relative come to call, and we'd talk about the weather and fishing. No, I mean it. Nice guys. I landed in the hospital after an odd accident one time (nothing serious) and these three commissioners came to see me before my friends did. We had open and informed discussions about millage rates, zoning, and snowplows.

But every once in a while, I'd have a chance to push them to an edge of contradiction. For instance, there arose in one school district a few complaints about "primary school," the quote marks necessary because the term referred to a particular institution of Mormonism. It did not mean elementary school, but rather a religious school for indoctrinating Mormon kids held daily after regular school ended. The public school buses delivered the Mormon kids to primary, in those odd cases when the primary was not adjacent to the public school parking lot. Yet by some oversight or understandable error, who knows, gentile parents would periodically notice that their kids, even fundamentalist Baptist kids, were being delivered to primary by public school buses so that they too might benefit.

And then parents complained to the paper, and I'd ask the school administration about this, and I'd ask the commissioners, and I'd get something like this for a response: "Well it gives those other kids something else to do after school and what's wrong with primary?" Then I'd duly point out the rights of gentiles to raise their kids as they damned well please, that there were, in fact, other religions or atheists, and then would come the sweet, blank stare. To a man (and they were all men), they would turn their heads ever so slightly, smile a bit, and go blank. It was not an act of defiance or even anger. It was just a learned response: shutting down rational processes that might lead one to the edge of conflict and questioning. The process playing in their head is "This does not compute. Reboot," and it doesn't compute, not in their world. It's not at all unique to Mormons, but I got my search image for it because it is so prevalent in their world. That hard edge of conflict is so much closer and available for disruption by the plain facts of everyday life.

In retrospect, I remembered I knew it well. My mother had that same blank stare. So did her mother. And now I genuinely wonder what it is like to inhabit such a brain. It's like being a whitewater rafter and seeing someone who beaches his boat before the rapids. Why would you do that? You're on the edge of the most interesting part, the most exhilarating part. When tossed about by contradiction, we learn. Why would you avoid that?

Oddly, though, there was no antipathy in my relationship with these Mormons, although maybe there should have been. I had a friend then who was a clinical psychologist, and every once in a while I would notice him having at the wine bottle with a bit more determination than usual. It generally revolved around the same story, that he had been counseling a woman, a Mormon woman, who was suicidal. Typically she had married in her late teens as soon as her husband returned from his mission, spent her twenties turning out eight kids and raising them according to the dictates of her husband, and then she hit thirty having no sense of self-worth whatever, and she went into therapy. But then she would be torn, and she and her husband would have a talk with the bishop, whose trainings in the darker intricacies of the human mind came from his experience of owning the local auto parts store. And the bishop would advise the young woman that she did not need counseling and medication and could be healed by the loving arms of her brothers and sisters guided by the heavenly father. She would take that advice, then came the suicide.

But I experienced no real antipathy in my contact with the saints. That would come later.

I learned the trade at a much smaller paper in Michigan; the *Post Register* had about triple the circulation of the *Alpena News,* and in a far less populous state, so had a great deal more influence. It was the second largest paper in the state and covered a vast area stretched across the southeast quarter of Idaho, from Montana south to Utah. This situation gave me much better access to statewide politicians than I had in Michigan, and every once in a while I got to interview Frank Church. By then he had been in the U.S. Senate for more than twenty years. Like Eugene McCarthy and George McGovern, I knew him as a lion of the antiwar movement. He had been the sponsor of key legislation to end the war and as chairman of the Foreign Relations Committee had mounted direct challenges to the excesses of the CIA's and FBI's surveillance techniques. He had been the floor sponsor of the Wilderness Act, one of the best things our nation has ever done. He had a long record of support of wilderness to the point that the largest piece of wilderness in the nation outside of Alaska today bears his name. I was then a twenty-eight-year-old kid with a couple of years experience at hick papers covering drunks and sewer bond issues. There wasn't much I could ask a genuine statesman and render in my skinny notebook that would add to the body of knowledge on these matters. But I had the only skinny notebook in the room, so license to challenge Frank Church on the issues of the day.

He was soft-spoken, polite, and engaged. The second time I met him, he was with his wife, Bethine, at a public event. She looked in my direction, whispered to him, and he walked up to me and greeted me by name. I was new enough to the job to be impressed by this. It was a different sort of time, when dealings with the most liberal of Democrats in a rock-ribbed Republican state were still genteel and handled in first names and a handshake. The name I did not know that day, but that Church probably did, was NCPAC, but I was soon to learn.

Church stood for election in 1980, the year after I first met him, during the coming of the Reagan revolution. His opponent was an empty-suit golden boy, who felt some entitlement to the Senate seat by virtue of his father's money. Steve Symms, however, was largely irrelevant in the race. NCPAC, the National Conservative Political Action Committee, was a right-wing hit squad that beta-tested the technique that today dominates American politics. It was a third party political group ostensibly not affiliated with either candidate, but existed to produce and air attack ads against Democrats, in this case, Church. It is the same technique given almost unlimited sway in the 2010 Supreme Court decision in the case of *Citizens United v. Federal Election Commission,* which is to say, it has been in play as a tool of movement conservatism for thirty years.

NCPAC, founded by well-known movement conservatives Terry Dolan, Roger Stone, and Charles Black, actually first appeared in one race in 1978, but in 1980 it came into its own and beat Church, McGovern, John Culver of Iowa, and Birch Bayh of Indiana. NCPAC's emergence in Idaho gave us a preview of the politics that were to expand and dominate the nation thirty years later. The campaign was first and foremost overwhelmingly negative—the shouted, lurid ads were a novelty, but we all know them so well now. *The Washington Post* much later quoted Dolan as saying, "A group like ours could lie through its teeth, and the candidate it helps stays clean." Something like that happened.

But more to the point, the campaign was built around a second crucial technique of modern movement conservatives, the wedge issue. The idea is to boil down all of the complexity and nuance of all of public policy to one central, emotional threat that is generally irrelevant to the lives of voters, then wave the bloody shirt and rouse the rabble into believing they are victims. Gun control issues work great for this, especially in the West, as does abortion and even the current birther issue. In 1980 in the case of Idaho and Frank Church, it was the Panama Canal. NCPAC alleged Church was leading the effort to give it away. The United States subsequently did indeed cede control of the canal to the Panamanians, and the world did not end, but then in Idaho you could be forgiven for believing that every ounce of irrigation water for Idaho's potatoes somehow flowed through the canal, so vital was its continued control to the vested interests of our state. Come election night, Church lost by less than one percent, and a lot of reporters, not just the new kid from Michigan, but people who had observed for a long time, scratched their heads and wondered what just happened here.

For some curious reason, my boss at the *Post Register* decided that, with three years experience as a newspaper reporter under my belt, I was of sufficient skill to serve as city editor, so he promoted me to supervise a half dozen reporters and a copy editor. It worked well enough and I liked the job, which had more moving parts to entertain me. I did not, however, get along all that well with my boss, so in another year took a job running a failing small-town weekly in Hailey, Idaho, a few miles down the road from Sun Valley's glittering ski resort. It was where the servants lived and an odd place. The Hemingway girls would occasionally walk into the local bar and Bruce Willis later took over most of the town. The allure for me was the prospect of running the whole show, but I had not considered that a weekly paper would have no resources, so mostly I and a few others worked like galley slaves and made some modest gains in the paper. The work got noticed by the editor of the daily paper in the region and he hired me as a news editor a couple years later, the slot position, meaning I daily sieved the fire hose stream of a couple of hundred stories, everything from what our reporters generated to the flow of a couple of wire services worldwide, the analyses, commentary, cartoons, and horoscopes, and assembled all of this to minimize entropy and keep the girdle ads from bumping, then go home at 1 A.M., sleep it off, then do the daily miracle again.

It was interesting work, but the editor who hired me, a

quirky guy named Steve Hartgen, had other things in mind. A year or so in, I was a city editor again, running a half dozen reporters, and haggling with photographers (no one supervises photographers; they are to a person artistes and unsupervisable). It was one of the better jobs I had ever had for several reasons. One was location. The paper was the *Twin Falls Times-News,* centered in a flat grid of an ag town in south-central Idaho, at the southern nadir of the bow of the Snake River. The Mormon coefficient was somewhat less than southeast Idaho's, but spuds and irrigation were still the rule of the land. Nonetheless, our coverage area, both as residents and as a newspaper, ranged north into central Idaho wilderness, stunning high desert, and to some of the best trout fishing and pheasant hunting in the world, all of which interested me and drove our coverage at the paper.

The two bigger benefits, however, were the fact that Hartgen was known in the West for hiring young, talented, aggressive first-year reporters, and, second, that somehow we were blessed with a sizable population of hard-core nutcases, including one particular congressman who supplied these young reporters with red meat to chew on. I subsequently saw a wildlife film in which a wolf mother teaches pups to hunt by exposing them to targets of opportunity, and I had a strong sense of déjà vu.

The nutcases were not randomly sorted, but were bellicose right-wingers. Through the years, these guys have taken on a variety of causes, from the anti-Communism of the John Birchers that my father favored to the white supremacists, the theocrats, antiabortionists, and constitutionalists in the mix. Running through all of this—including my father, from the time I was a kid until the day he died—were the tax protesters, generally expressing their outrage as blind hatred of the Internal Revenue Service. My father could never accept the very simple notion that the highway he drove on and the schools my grandfather built would somehow need to be paid for, and he was not alone.

This sort of sentiment was generally on the rise in southern Idaho, in particular in the early 1980s, spurred by an ultra-right-wing Mormon crank named W. Cleon Skousen, and his organization, the Freeman Institute. Skousen had strong ties to the Birch Society, but had discovered a new brand that worked well in the West, at least in pockets. He had the ear of the Republican congressman, George Hansen, also a Mormon, and not of the gentle, ex-bishop variety I had gotten to know on county commissions and school boards through the region. Hansen was a bellowing conservative who had the bloody shirt flapping in the air most of the time.

We at the newspaper largely considered ourselves fortunate to have such people as Hansen around. The Freemen and tax protesters didn't make much of a difference to the day-to-day operation of the place. Further, unlike other right-wing groups elsewhere in the nation then—the Posse Comitatus in the plains, the white supremacists in north Idaho, and the militias in Michigan—they weren't violent. Instead, they authored dense tracts exposing the perfidy of the federal government headed by Ronald Reagan. There weren't enough of them to dominate local politics, so the streets got paved and school buses had full tanks of gas. Every reporter knew that the tax protest movement was a sort of genetically mutated species certainly doomed to extinction. We had watched the process work in microcosm many times in our careers: A fiscal conservative complains about high taxes and on that basis gets elected to the school board as a maverick tax cutter. Then the fiscal conservative gets to know the realities of the budget, state and federal law, and comes to accept that teachers need to get paid, votes for the millage increase, and changes his label to fiscally responsible. Tax protesters cannot govern. Take this to its absurd extreme: imagine a Congress dominated by tax protesters. What could they possibly do? Shut down the government? Then, this was the absurd and unimaginable extreme.

True enough, Hansen was in Congress, but ineffective and isolated, largely considered a buffoon and of zero consequence nationally. He may have been ineffective, but he did give us something to write about. One reporter in particular, Rick Shaughnessey, did exemplary investigative reporting and Hansen did a stretch in prison. That latter outcome was not the result of our reporting, but of a federal investigation of his failure to file full financial disclosure forms. But Shaughnessey's subsequent work on Hansen was perhaps even more damning. The congressman was then touting an anti-IRS diatribe of a book he had written, the title of which speaks much about his mind-set: *To Harass Our People: The IRS and Government Abuse of Power*. It was aimed at his base, the conservative Mormon acolytes of Skousen's Freeman Institute, but Shaughnessey learned and confirmed that the project had been bankrolled by an arm of the Reverend Sun Myung Moon's Unification Church. An alliance with the Moonies was not what the Freemen had in mind, despite the fact that Moon's church had its own problems with the IRS. We printed the story.

Subsequent stories exposed a pattern very different from Hansen's self-proclaimed role of "dragonslayer" out to protect the saints from government harassment. His troubles always seemed to stem from sleazy ways to raise cash. Shaughnessey learned and documented that Hansen was using a check-kiting scheme, writing a cycle of bad checks from bank to bank, then using the float to pay for his campaign. That story ran too. Then Shaughnessey started interviewing a series of state-level conservative politicians and found many of them had made personal loans to Hansen on the order of $5,000 each and, no, he hadn't repaid and some time had passed and, no, they did not expect to see repayment.

A dinky hick-town newspaper in the middle of Idaho's spud desert is not the sort one would expect to do this quality of work, but on the other hand, who else was there to do it? Our isolation became our necessity. In fact, we did not have the money to send Shaughnessey digging for months on end, but the editor, Hartgen, hustled up a grant to pay for the work. Had he not, I think we would have done it anyway. It was our job. Then, a newsroom could consider something other than the bottom line. At the end of this series of stories, Hansen got beat in the 1984 election, granted by fewer than two hundred votes, but beat.

The paper came under fire from the right for an alleged liberal bias, an allegation not new but unusual then, now, a stock-in-trade of movement conservatives. I got a chance to address it when I was a guest on a conservative radio talk show and gave a seemingly flippant but not-so-flippant answer: "Sure we're liberals. Show me someone with a solid college education and willing to work for $25,000 a year and I'll show you a liberal."

Through the years, I've not shied away from the charge. Most journalists I know vote Democratic, if they vote at all, and some don't. Most are liberal. Thirty years ago we didn't go into the business thinking of ourselves as liberals, nor did we convert. But the tenor of American politics has left no center ground. This, in fact, became obvious in southern Idaho in 1980 when NCPAC used, as would the rest of the Reagan machine, the big-lie technique. It became acceptable practice to say a false thing repeatedly in service of election. One cannot believe in openness, rationality, and honesty—as journalists must—and find this acceptable. One cannot believe in rationality and still believe the tax protesters had a legitimate place at the table, or that people like the birthers do today. The political landscape shifted and left us standing on the left.

The apotheosis of this evolution came in 2004 in Ron Suskind's famous interview with *The New York Times Magazine,* when a then unidentified aide to George W. Bush, later identified as Karl Rove, criticized Suskind for belonging to "the reality-based community." Yes we do. And if that makes us liberal that's not an assessment of what we journalists have become; it is a measure of what national politics has become.

We thought of Cleon Skousen as our own little private Idaho eccentric. In 2010, he emerged as the patron saint of Fox News demagogue Glenn Beck.

I'd had very little contact with my family in the early 1980s. I had heard that a couple of my brothers had left Michigan's rust-belt decay and depression to take up work in and around Denver. One still works and lives there, another settled in

Yakima, Washington. A third, Paul, disappeared. During one phone call, however, my father began recommending a book to me by a congressman from southern Idaho, allowed as to how he considered this congressmen to be a hell of a guy, and suggested my paper give some press to him and his revealing book about the IRS. I told him we were doing just that and, in the process, also looking into a whole series of right-wing groups. I mentioned that I worked with this guy who had good sources on right-wing and religious-right militias around the nation. I meant this as a goad, but my parents didn't get angry; they instead started asking questions. Did we know anything about an armed group in Texas, called something like "the sword, the cross and covenant?" I'd check. My brother Paul had gone to Texas to become a Baptist preacher, but then dropped from sight. Or at least my parents said he disappeared, and he, in fact, contacted no other members of the family. But through those years, my mother seemed to know some things that she left buried behind her flat, blank face.

Somewhere in the early 1980s, work dried up for older men in Michigan too. My father was still humping power poles, but power-line construction only happens in booming economies or after storms, so the union sent him west to Pasco, Washington. The nearby government nuclear site, Hanford, was undergoing some retooling, and there was work. I got a call from him one night, and he had been drinking, a new development as far as I knew, and he told me it was over between him and my mother, and there was someone else. My reaction to this was "about time," but there was likely nothing new about this development, and it explained his periodic and regular needs to find work somewhere other than where my mother was living. It turned out my parents were not through with each other. Soon enough my mother moved west to Pasco, and my dad built her a house, a geodesic dome. Pasco was about an eight-hour drive from where I lived in Idaho, way too close, I figured, and I found myself wishing they had stayed on their side of the Mississippi River. All of my siblings were emancipated but one, Joe, the youngest, and the now total religious rule of the household did not sit well with him. He conspired with my sister, the only one of my siblings still living in Michigan, and she sent him a one-way airline ticket that allowed him to quietly disappear from the new home. He finished high school in Michigan, put himself through undergraduate work at Michigan State, then veterinarian school and has since done well.

Hartgen, my boss in Twin Falls, took me aside one day and told me I was doing well as a city editor, that the small family chain that owned us, Howard Publications, had some other papers looking for editors, some in upstate New York. He'd put me in for a job, then told me I would succeed in management as soon as I got some of my "rough edges knocked off." He did indeed use the phrase. It was a jolting bit of advice. I had always thought that rough edges were what made a newspaperman good and had planned to keep mine. Still, his advice was a subtle signal of what was to come. Little newspaper chains like ours were becoming the exception. Larger corporate chains were taking over, and in fact, Hartgen had already sent me to a management training seminar run by an executive of Gannett, the monster gobbling up little papers by the dozen and running them the same way an accountant would run a chain of shoe stores. MBAs were slithering into publisher's chairs, replacing those grizzled old cusses who thought the duty of a newspaper was to print the news and raise hell.

So I began asking around. All of us knew there were three papers in the Pacific Northwest that still did good work and valued reporters enough to pay them well. They were the *Register-Guard* in Eugene, Oregon; the *Spokesman-Review* at Spokane, Washington; and the *Missoulian* at Missoula, Montana. Montana. Wasn't that what brought me west in the first place?

9
CONTEXT

One day in 1985, I drove north from Idaho into Montana on U.S. 93 over Lost Trail Pass, then downstream, winding along in circuitous parallel to the Bitterroot River. As the valley broadened, the ponderosa pine became my totem tree. I had, of course, seen ponderosa before. They have a free run of the Rockies south to Arizona and north into British Columbia. But I never really considered them fully until that day I was driving into Montana. They seem to grow best here. Idaho is mostly desert and dry, and even its mountains seem to favor lodgepole pine and, on wetter slopes, Douglas fir. Plenty of places like this in Montana are given to fir and lodgepole, as well, but at low altitude, in the broad, arid intermontane valleys, ponderosa prosper, often not as forest but in grassy, parklike savannas, five or ten trees to the acre, monumental trees, producing boles two people hand-to-hand cannot reach around, towering trunks of deeply fissured rust-red bark running skyward fifty, sixty, seventy feet without a limb, then a steep conical crown of long, deep green needles. Monarchs like these can be three hundred years old and suggest permanence, which was what I was looking for in that day of driving in 1985. I was driving a twenty-four-foot U-Haul truck, with the same copper-colored Dodge half-ton pickup truck I had dragged out from Michigan seven years earlier on the tow bar behind. By then, I was making the thirteenth move to a new house in the sixteen years since my dad's Ford Fairlane had delivered me, a portable stereo, and two suitcases to the University of Michigan's dorm. In the later years of that period, a twenty-four-foot U-Haul was just about right, load a day, drive a day, unload a day, and you're done. I'd moved enough, and this time I was looking for more than a quick unload and another slot at a newspaper; I was looking for a home. Thirteen houses in sixteen years.

A few years ago, the British geneticist Brian Sykes told a story most convincingly as a proof of sorts that we who wander are lost. Better still, he did this with a subset of humanity that I understand to be my people, the notherners, more precisely, those insular northerners of the British Isles, where all my traceable DNA traces. The long story we tell ourselves about these people is one like mine, of a peripatetic people. In deep history, my ancestors are the Celts, Angles, Saxons, Frissons, Vikings, and Normans, the successive waves of invasion that supposedly wiped out Ice Age people and founded a wandering breed of imperialists. In more recent history, these are the people—they and their very closely European allies—who conquered the globe, left a stamp of imperialism on every square inch of it, and left most of its temperate regions—North and South America, South Africa, New Zealand, Australia—aflood with European surnames and languages. My father fit with this story, people who did not know home when they saw it. Wandering is the rule; there are legions of U-Haul trucks in the collective history of northern European people, or so the story goes.

Yet Sykes drilled a hole into a 12,000 year-old tooth taken from the remains of an Ice Age man preserved in Cheddar George in Somerset, England. Twelve thousand years is sufficient scale to matter, sufficient to span history both deep and shallow. Sykes compared his caveman sample with cheek swabs gathered from the people living on the caveman's ground today, in walking distance of ancient bones. About 80 percent of those people were directly related to the caveman, descendants. The wanderers may write the stories and the histories, but most of us have a sense of home written in our genes.

My drive that day took me almost straight north, north across the 45th parallel. Today, twenty-six years later, I'm still living in Missoula, Montana, the town I found at the end of that drive. This was not my doing. Throughout my life here, circumstances roiled and periodically promised to send me packing, but nonetheless, I am still here.

My decision to abandon anything that looked like a management track in newspapers was a good one, although at first it didn't look that way. By the time I went to Missoula, I hadn't worked as a reporter for six or so years, and had lost some of my chops. Right away I made some silly mistakes that stood out sharply in my new context. The *Missoulian* was and is the daily newspaper of western Montana, but because Missoula is widely held as a good place to live and because the paper was then paying salaries above average, it had attracted a core that was competent. This had the upside of some increased professionalism; the downside of organizational complexity, turbulence, and not a small amount of ambition, meaning it harbored a few who would cheerfully slip a knife into a colleague's back. But I learned to avoid them and, more importantly, remembered how to work a story. The latter accomplishment meant addressing what I had long and secretly realized was my biggest shortcoming as a journalist: people saw me as outspoken and aggressive, but this was a front. The truth is, I was never comfortable in dealing with people. I was and am shy. I could never engage people as successfully as my colleagues and so developed an abrupt and sketchy style of interviewing people. Other reporters I had worked with might ask twenty questions where I would ask five.

When I was in school in the late 1960s studying the explosive political issues of those days, one of my political science professors had castigated the whole of journalism as being unreliable and shallow, but we students pressed him about what we might read, and he finally allowed there was one exception: I. F. Stone, an independent gadfly and one-man news organization who published a four-page quarter-fold newspaper, *I. F. Stone's Weekly*. I left class, looked up a copy of the weekly at the library, and sent off my subscription, then bought a three-ring binder. When the weekly came, I read it cover to cover, punched holes and stacked it in the binder. I accumulated a small collection by the time the *Weekly* ceased publication in 1971.

Only years later did I hear that Stone's strength as a reporter was based in a weakness. Unlike me, he was gregarious and perfectly happy to be around people, but he was so deaf through most of his career that he had some difficulty hearing what was said at press conferences and even in interviews. He compensated by reading transcripts, often catching things other reporters missed, but also by learning to navigate the written record, to work paper. I learned to work the record because I liked and trusted paper better than people. For a while, this tactic served my narrow purposes, which was to get stories.

And sometimes it was just embarrassing. I drew an assignment of covering Jesse Jackson for a day when he was gearing up to run in the 1988 presidential campaign. I wangled a seat on his leased Citation jet out of Missoula to follow him at several campaign whistle-stops around the state. This was a fairly intimidating assignment for any hick-town newspaper reporter, let alone one who is shy, but there he sat next to me, all six plus feet of him, staring out the window while I tried to explain to him the breadth of the Bob Marshall Wilderness below. His press aide strongly hinted I should begin asking him the standard list of questions, so he might rattle off his talking points to be duly recorded in yet one more skinny notebook. I sat and watched him instead, which everyone on board must have thought truly strange. I am an observer and perfectly happy to watch in silence, but then later in the day, as we arrived at a dairy farm for a visit, two yellow school buses pulled up and discharged full loads of stern men with

Abe Lincoln beards, straw porkpie hats, and suspenders. I recognized these people immediately as Hutterites, a deeply conservative religious sect closely related in theology, history, and practice to Amish and Mennonites, all German Anabaptists. They live on very large communal farms in eastern Montana, and a busload of Huts were the last thing I expected to see at a Jackson rally.

But their leader announced, "Yeah we want to see him. We're Americans too, by God." Jackson's rainbow seemed to have a broader spectrum than anyone could have imagined, so I had a story, developed by keeping my mouth shut and watching.

Later that day, Jackson appeared at a packed high school gymnasium for a rally that was headlined by a gospel group, and he said he didn't expect to find a town in Montana with enough African Americans "to start a choir." A competitor reporter heard this phrase as "to start a riot," and directly quoted it that way in the following day's edition. I was glad I was not him. Getting it on paper is more reliable.

For instance, early in my career at the *Missoulian* (I was assigned then to cover the county commissioners and keep an eye on state politics), a Republican operative stopped by to introduce his client of the moment, then Secretary of State Jim Waltermire, and bluntly stated Waltermire was using his current office to run for governor. This sort of conversation happens routinely with reporters and is just as routinely expected to remain unreported. I had then and still have the rather naive notion that secretaries of state ought to use their office to be secretary of state. I talked to no one, but thought for a while about what sort of record might reflect that a guy was spending all his time on the public dime running for office. In the days before e-mail and private cell phones, the clear indicator of how one spent his day was how he used his office phone, so I made a couple of calls and found a bureau-crat in some obscure cubicle who was responsible for all of the state's telephone bills. Could I have Waltermire's? No, I could not. The problem was the whole business was comput-erized and aggregated, and he had no way to sort out one phone. My only option would be to take a copy of records for all phones in state government, every single one, and sort it out myself. You mean like boxes of computer printouts? Nope. They're on microfiche, single sheets of plastic with microscopic lettering. Every phone in the state. Waltermire. The governor. The governor's mansion. All the cops. The legislators. All of them. How much might this cost? Copying costs, it turned out, a few hundred bucks, so I drove the two hours to Helena, the state capital, and took delivery. Our newsroom library had a microfiche reader.

I assumed Waltermire's phone was a needle in a very large haystack, but it turned out to be a well-ordered haystack and I found it. There was no reverse telephone directory in the state, so I started calling numbers, listening for identifying answers or simply asking whom I had reached. I began look-ing up campaign contributors and their phone numbers, then cross-matching to my list. More paper came to me, and I learned he had a paid political consultant in Seattle, a man who had already called me and challenged me for what I was doing. Then I found a particularly frequent number in the records, called it, and got that consultant's private, unpub-lished number, and we had a very different conversation than that earlier phone call. I was eventually able to show that Waltermire did little else as secretary of state except manage his gubernatorial campaign. I wrote it up, we ran it. There's no way of knowing what effect this had on his political fortunes; Waltermire died in a plane crash while campaigning for the Republican primary.

But the initial story led to tips on other phones in the state, including that of the commissioner of political practices, whose phone was pretty much connected nine to five, five days a week to her sister in Billings. She resigned. Similarly, a long bipartisan list of state legislators who spent a lot of time talking with relatives in other states and places like the corporate offices of Burlington Northern Railroad. More stories.

Slowly, I learned of Montana: that the small mountains that hem the city's edge—Sentinel, Jumbo, the Rattlesnakes—are webbed with trails. That a brilliant yellow flower balsamroot lights the slopes late May, that the flower's name "larkspur" is simply a synonym for the deepest blue the human eye can register. That there are elk and sometimes bighorn sheep at ridgetop, and black bear wander in my front yard well inside the city limits. Take the right trail and you can walk north from my house all the way to Canada, a couple hundred miles, in wilderness and mountains all the way. Mission Mountains, Bob Marshall, Glacier National Park. It's seventy miles across the Bob Marshall Wilderness the short way, west to east from Holland Lake to Gibson Reservoir, and takes ten silent days if you do it right. That there's a ridge near White Mountain Pass that on the right afternoon can harbor three grizzlies snarfing huckleberries. A half day's drive from Missoula will land you at trailheads for Scapegoat, Badger Two-Medicine, Cabinets, Bitterroot-Selway, Sapphires, Pintlers, Great Bear, Absorka, or Beartooth, wilderness all, three and a half million acres of wilderness, roadless, motorless silence.

I learned that there is a stream, Rock Creek, and when spring runoff wanes just enough to wade it, just barely wade it, salmonflies nearly as big as hummingbirds hatch and flutter in clouds and large trout go mad with gluttony, and if you can learn to stand center stream in gale force current and cast just under the limbs of the ozier dogwood and willows that hug the banks, you can take good advantage of their madness. Or the Big Blackfoot on a silent faultless blue July afternoon. Follow your rod tip to the apogee of backcast and notice a bald eagle soaring just beyond.

That there is a stretch of white water just downstream of Missoula on the Clark Fork with suck holes, washing machines, haystacks, rollers, and back eddies circling infinite. Cliffside, Tumbleweed, Fang, and Boat Eater, everyone knows the names of the rapids. Mind your oars, and your raft stays righted.

A Hellgate wind means trouble in January, that an ocean's worth of the Arctic's cold air has plummeted south through Alberta, topped the Great Divide, and now comes sliding down the west-slope canyons and valleys in miles deep, roaring rivers of angry air. All of a sudden it is forty below and the gusts are clocking fifty-five. For a week or so you will be cold no matter how many sweaters you layer.

Downtown Missoula there is a bridge across the Clark Fork River, and at summer solstice, make a point to be there.

Everyone else does, all facing mostly straight downstream to the horizon line opened by the river and to the perfect snow-tipped tit of Squaw Peak lit in sun glow to nearly 10 P.M. A block away, there's a shotgun shack of a bar lit in full fluorescent burn at all hours where you get a decent pepperjack burger and a beer after a softball game. Another bar up the street has no front door key, always open, where Mike Mansfield used to pick up constituent mail when he was Senate majority leader. There's a live poker game in the back most of the time, breakfast all the time, and they'll make you brains and eggs.

The current psychological wisdom suggests that kids with sketchy upbringings have problems attaching to other people as adults. Thus they are condemned to wander, to divorce, to load U-Haul trucks. Maybe so. And maybe if you can't attach to people, a place will do.

As a reporter who favored the written record, I always held to the possibility that someday a life-changing story might emerge with the simple act of opening a single file folder. I did not, however, believe I would find such a folder in my own desk drawer. Almost three years into my work at the *Missoulian,* I had settled into the pace of the job, when there came a chance for a new assignment. I had been covering politics and local government, but western Montana's unique setting made for an unusual beat at the paper. The readership cared deeply for issues like wilderness, water quality, wildlife habitat, and the environment. Meantime, then more than now, a great deal of the region's economy rested on timber and mining, much of which is done on public lands, the same land we count on for sheltering wildlife and raising clean rivers. More than in most towns, our biggest fights were about protecting the environment, so much more that the *Missoulian* needed an environmental reporter. The guy doing that job when I came got a promotion, opening what was my dream beat. I asked for the assignment and got it, and my predecessor's files in the bargain.

Most reporters know more than they report and would be better reporters by simply closing that gap. Often, however, the difference lies in whether you know it well enough to print it. And just as often, failure to report fully can be blamed on accommodation of sources to maintain access, or cowering before controversy, or simple sloth. Often to an unsortable combination of these. What my predecessor had in his file was not solid enough to print, but it was sure as hell worth looking into. It was two parts: a dot matrix printout that was a transcript of an interview he had done with the state forester, the guy nominally in charge of timber on state lands, but also in charge of monitoring how loggers were behaving on federal and private lands. It was not much of a responsibility, because then as now the state has no laws governing logging on private land. Like pre–Civil War plantation owners, timber corporations were free to beat their slaves as they wished.

At the time, two corporations—Champion International and Plum Creek Timber—owned about 1.5 million acres of their own timber lands and also bought most of the logs coming off state and federal lands. All of this fed the massive plywood and lumber mills that were the basis of the regional economy. In public, these corporations claimed two important things: that they were using logging practices that did not harm the environment, in fact "improved" the forests, and that they were harvesting a sustainable volume, which means cutting at a rate that equals regrowth. The latter ensures a stable economy.

The interview my predecessor had done with the state forester was off the record and quoted him clearly as contradicting both of these points. He said that the companies were, in fact, lying on a massive scale. Meantime, on the record, this same guy was backing the lie.

The second element in the file folder were plastic sleeves of 35 millimeter slides shot by a Missoulian staff photographer. The photos were clear evidence that the loggers were using egregious practices that silted up streams, punched roads into virgin territory, and wiped out wildlife habitat, the equivalent of not just beating their slaves, but beating them to death. They were placing both the environment and the economy of an area half the size of California in jeopardy. I went to work. I found sources to confirm all this, but it wasn't enough. The corporations would simply disagree, and I didn't want the story to turn into a pissing match between sources.

I hooked up with a *Missoulian* photographer, my friend Michael Gallacher, and we flogged my Jeep Cherokee for weeks up and down two-track logging roads, following log trucks and listening for bulldozers and chainsaws. We watched dozers slide straight down mountain slopes, their blades dug in as brakes, raking a foot of topsoil off skid trails, leaving a skein of fiercely eroded sluices on slopes. We found city-sized valleys clear-cut and abandoned to a luxurious regrowth of noxious weeds. We talked to loggers who we thought might beat us up and abandon us up some forgotten logging trail and instead they openly confessed embarrassment for what they had done, for doing their jobs as their bosses told them.

And still it wasn't enough. The corporations could claim we had only seen an exception. Their operations were vast and no way could we photograph every square inch. Then I had an idea. Timber corporations in Montana are taxed not on acreage they own, but rather on inventory, the amount of standing timber. Thus, it is in their interest to report the accurate amount of "harvested" land to reduce their tax rate. I called a guy, and he gave me the proper state records, what amounted to a book, pages on pages of county-by-county, parcel-by-parcel reporting, and none of it totaled up, raw, unsorted data. Unsorted by design; the authorities had no interest whatever in a readable accounting of what the corporations had done.

There were no personal computers in newsrooms in those days, only mainframes dedicated to specialized word processing software that eliminated typesetters. My bosses were of no mind to stretch the budget with what appeared to be my harebrained idea. So I maxed out my own credit card and ordered up a Mac Plus, state-of-the-art for the day. I bought a simple spreadsheet program and set to work straining the Mac's whopping 512 kilobytes of memory. It only took a couple of days for me to punch it all in and a couple of minutes for the Mac to spit it out: the corporations had indeed been lying. They had clear-cut virtually all of their timber, according to their own reports of inventory.

I printed out the spreadsheets and made an appointment

to toss them on an executive's desk at the Champion Mill at Bonner, one of the most entertaining target interviews I've ever done. His choice was to admit the corporation was lying to the public and Champion's own workers about a sustained yield harvest, or lying to the state about its taxes. He tacitly admitted to the former. Then over the course of a week or so, I pieced together a rationale for what it turns out was a conscious decision by timber companies throughout the Northwest that even had a name, the "accelerated harvest." Corporation bean counters had figured out that there was no future in the sustained yield, because timber grows slower than the then prevailing interest rates caused money to grow, and what's worse, timber is susceptible to bugs, fires, and revised public sentiment on the beating of slaves. Better to cut all your logs as rapidly as possible and put the money in the bank or the stock market or the Japanese economy. Further, once this realization became general knowledge in the industry, corporations that resisted the accelerated harvest were vulnerable to hostile takeover, then all the rage throughout corporate America. The logic was cut or be cut, both for individual executives and companies as a whole. Further, this logic prevailed not just in Montana, but throughout the nation's most important timber region, the Pacific Northwest, and no one anywhere had reported it. I had my story. I wrote it in May of 1988. Then began a five-month battle with my editors to get it printed.

Most people today blame the Internet for killing newspaper journalism, but this rationale forgets that the heart of the business already had petered out. The earlier problem was that newspapers could be terribly profitable. By the end of the 1980s, in fact, industry observers were citing newspapers as the most profitable legal business in the country. Then publishers routinely expected 20 to 40 percent profit on net revenues while some chains could reap as much as 59 percent on net revenues. At the same time, corporations like General Motors, Exxon, and IBM were reporting margins half that large. That profitability was journalism's poison pill.

Newspapermen like my first publisher, the publisher of the family-owned *Alpena News*, were better newspapermen than they were businessmen. They settled on a comfortable profit margin below 20 percent and spent more on their newsrooms, on labor-intensive investigative projects, and on discharging their duty to the community, discharging the responsibility that pays for the rights given by the First Amendment. It did not have to be so, and the leader in demonstrating otherwise was the Gannett chain with its flagship, *USA Today.* By stripping down newsrooms, pumping up the volume of breathy features, and dialing down the ratio of news to advertising—known in the business as the "news hole"—they learned they could pump profits. This knowledge precipitated a corporate takeover of the industry.

In 1960, corporations controlled 32 percent of the nation's newspapers. By 1986, their share had jumped to 70 percent and by 1990, 80 percent. The ten largest chains controlled 43 percent of all papers in 1986. The profitability drove the takeover, which is to say, if you were a publisher of the old school, you left your paper vulnerable to takeover. Some publishers did indeed resist predation, but even small-town family papers were generally presided over by a board, generally composed of second- or third-generation owners, not all of whom were solely interested in the First Amendment and some of whom who could be tempted by the inflated prices on offer. That is, you could gut your own paper, or have somebody else do it for you. If you just now noticed how this parallels what was happening in the timber industry at the same time, you are quicker than I was. It took me a few months to realize that the story I was covering outside the newsroom was the same one at work inside.

The *Missoulian* was already a corporate paper when I arrived in 1985, owned then and now by Lee Enterprises. Lee was then a small chain of nineteen papers, mostly in the Midwest, but had big ideas. Lee executives, in fact, consciously modeled operations after Gannett and set about gutting newsrooms as the model demanded. The *Missoulian* had remained something of a maverick among Lee's holdings; we were conscious of this and it was a matter of pride. But corporate would not tolerate this long, and eventually parachuted in a planeload of executives to bring us to heel. I would learn that I no longer worked at a newspaper but at a "media property" and a "profit center." There was a conscious shift in culture that was not subtle.

Doug Underwood, a former reporter for *The Seattle Times* and for Gannett, wrote about this in an important piece in 1988 in *Columbia Journalism Review*. "Many of the people I talked to say they feel increasingly unwelcome in the business that once was a haven for the independent, irreverent, creative spirits who have traditionally given newspapers their personalities." That's just how it felt.

The former newspaperman with *The Baltimore Sun* and now a screenwriter, David Simon, summarized his experiences in an essay in *Esquire*:

> And worse still, in the newsroom where I grew up—a semi-intellectual environment where everyone once seemed to be arguing about everything all the time without actually impairing their careers—dissent will become problematic.
>
> This is the personal part.
>
> Because the new way of doing business apparently leaves no place in the newsroom for fundamental disagreements about content, about reportage, about the substance of what we are doing or not doing. Arguments over quotidian matters such as the slant of Mideast coverage, or an ethical debate over attribution, or the use and overuse of a stylistic device will soon bring transfers and demotions until, finally, an exodus begins.

The exodus, however, was not total. Some journalists were perfectly willing to make their peace with the new order, especially in that the new deal often meant incentive bonuses for those editors willing to go along and get along. Brad Hurd, my boss at the *Missoulian,* happened to be one of them. Underwood also wrote in his *CJR* piece: "Do you see a corporation that is in the business of making money going out and investigating another corporation?" It would have been easier if I had considered that question before my story landed on Hurd's desk.

The newsroom at the *Missoulian* was like most newsrooms,

a gymnasium-sized expanse of desks and computer terminals unbroken by so much as a cubicle. But off to one side was a glassed-in office that was Hurd's. From May until October, there were meetings after meetings in that office between Hurd and my city editor, Brian Howell. Marked-up copies of my series of stories were spread on the desk. Never once was I allowed in to defend what I had done, but after such a meeting, Howell would take me aside and detail the litany of my sins and demand some sort of rewrite. None of it was substantive. Hurd was simply gutless and stalling. I rewrote, then there were more meetings, and one more round with Howell. In the end, nothing they could do would change the fact that I had an irrefutable database and Gallacher had shot irrefutable photos. We would not back down, and I was determined those stories would see the light of day, one way or another. I think Hurd finally realized this. The stories ran in October of 1988.

The response from the timber industry was organized, sophisticated, and targeted straight at me. The overt part was a series of letters to the editor, and that was to be expected, but more importantly, there were corporation-to-corporation discussions. In all of the controversy, however, the *Missoulian* was never once forced to eat a single one of my words. We ran no corrections or clarifications on anything I had written in the series and on any of the follow-up. No one said I was wrong, because I wasn't.

I learned later I had seen only the tip of the corporate machinations and did indeed confirm that the industry wanted me fired. That didn't happen, but almost a year after the timber series ran and the outcry had not yet subsided, Hurd pulled me into that fish tank that was his office and announced I could no longer cover the environment. He was pulling me off the beat. I quit on the spot, cleaned my desk, and hit the door in less than a half hour. My days as newspaperman were over.

Those who heard the discussion that day, or later, heard a familiar story of the time: a reporter quitting as a matter of principle when his bosses caved in to corporate control. Surely this was the case, but there was a subtext that day that no one else but I could hear: the sound of a roaring pickup truck and towering rage when my grandfather smashed his year's worth of potatoes in a ditch, that defining parable from my childhood. He had been told his work was worthless, and for some of us, towering and unparalleled rage is the proper born, bred, and learned response. Many people thought I had done something extraordinary that day, but among the people who raised me, it was a normal and expected response to abused authority. Sons-o'-bitches.

The truth is, this response has not always been a matter of pride in my life. Just as often, my near-pathological inability to submit to authority has done me damage and done damage to those around me. Worse, on those occasions it has never been the result of a considered choice. My response is always instinctive and impulsive. I can claim no credit for having made a choice to do the right thing, and besides, in so many cases, my instincts drove me to do the wrong thing. But not that day in Hurd's office. I did what needed to be done.

Hurd, meantime, continued to do as he was told, went on to become publisher at Lee's paper on Helena, the state capital, then Lee gobbled up the Howard chain, the group that had owned that gutsy little paper in Twin Falls, Idaho. Hurd became publisher of that paper where talented young reporters had once been audacious enough to do good work. Lee itself is today one of the nation's largest newspaper chains and as a result has been in and out of bankruptcy.

It would be easy to wrap this all up now as simply a classic case from the journalism of the day. There were plenty of examples of guys like me who no longer fit in. Like many people in the business, I had mostly existed to fly in the face of power. Some of us were trained as attack dogs and were forgiven the occasional growl and snarl at our own people. But as the MBAs asserted themselves, we faced a new sort of power and that was that. True enough, but not really the interesting part of my story.

We called the late 1980s the period of the timber wars, because sometimes it felt just that way. They were characterized by a long series of pitched battles between environmentalists and loggers that played out in packed auditoriums of public hearings, street theater, demonstrations, protests, actions, tree spikings, and long convoys of logging trucks painted with slogans and honking air horns. Every reporter worth his pay knows how to cover this sort of theater, in fact, is often happy to see it erupt. This is the sort of circus that generates copy that editors love. Just scamper on out and write down what he said and then write down what she said and string together the quotes, file it by deadline, and do it again tomorrow. I was new to the environmental beat, but this was not so much about the environment as it was about politics, and I damned sure knew how to cover politics, and I did. For a while. Until I got sick of it and at the same time had a sickening feeling I was missing most of the story. This hunch only continued to grow after my timber series ran. Even as the controversy over my tenure erupted, I missed a good deal of the detail of that controversy, simply because my attention was elsewhere. I was onto a new trail.

It began with frustration that everything I was hearing began to sound alike, that it didn't matter whether I was in a public hearing or a phone interview, and it didn't matter whether I interviewed left or right, logger or tree hugger, people simply read me their bumper stickers. There was a precast set of notions and tenets that set terms of debate, or rather no real debate, no discourse that furthered understanding. In the case of run-of-the-mill politics, I suppose we can get by like this, a lot of chatter and beneath all that, a few plodding bureaucrats who see that the streets are plowed and the sewers run. But I was now writing about the environment, about nature, and this was a far bigger matter. Science derives from the laws of nature; science ought not exist to simply rehash talking points, but to arrive at answers, and nothing I was seeing in the public debate was taking advantage of those answers. Everyone talked about what they believed; no one talked about what they knew. I took this to be my fault, but then luckily the fires came along.

In the northern Rockies, forest fires do indeed happen, generally in decades-long cycles driven by drought. Predictably in western Montana, it rains most of May and June, our wettest months, but sometimes it's more drizzle than rain. And just as predictably, July arrives in faultless blue, daily high temperatures creeping slowly upward into the eighties then nineties, then August, nineties and hundreds even, then come a few afternoons when thunderheads build in the west and sweep across the peaks, but deliver no rain—just lightning, hundreds of bolts an hour flashing in tindered timber.

The summer of 1988 was like that and a welcome distraction from my battles over the timber series. It was a particularly good time to be a reporter, especially in Missoula, which is the center of forest fire fighting for all of Montana and northern Idaho. School buses by the hundreds flow in and out of town, each one packed with the yellow-shirted, hard-hatted foot soldiers of forest fire. The skies are palled with smoke, and every day begins in a constant drone of slurry bombers, the lumbering Korean War vintage prop planes that drop loads of red retardant on active fires. My job was to measure this pulse every day, then head to the lines of the biggest blowups and describe what I could, to account for the daily acreages, hot spots, and millions on millions of dollars spent. My job was to find the one guy breathless from just having fled a blowup where a rushing wall of flames nearly overtook his speeding pickup truck. In 1988 we were getting more stories like that than we'd ever heard before, and there was a dawning realization among firefighters with decades of experience that something unprecedented was happening.

Yellowstone National Park was the center. The park blew up that summer like never before, which drew national attention owing to its iconic status. Part of the cause of the fires derives from the history of management. Most of fire history in the northern Rockies has been governed by the Smokey Bear mentality that spawned something called the "10 A.M.

rule." It meant simply that a ranger's job was to attack any fire that started and extinguish it by ten the next morning. The problem with this notion was the lightning. It and tinder-dry forests had existed long before Yale-trained, East Coast–raised foresters arrived on the scene to begin making up rules. Before white settlement, the forests had burned. Fire suppression removed fire from its historical role, so allowed an unnatural accumulation of trees. An unusually dry set of summers rendered those trees to fuel, then that fuel exploded with sufficient fury to chase men driving pickup trucks. Some fire scientists and foresters were beginning to understand this scenario. Yet no one foresaw how it would play out in the early days of September of 1988.

Part of the reason Yellowstone burned was a change in Park Service policy: a new protocol that recognized the natural role of fire in wilderness and let those areas burn. The Forest Service had the same policy in effect in wilderness areas on National Forest lands, so when lightning triggered a small fire on the south edge of the Bob Marshall Wilderness in June, no one thought much of it. It was still fairly wet then and so the fire fizzled and fussed over a few acres into July and maybe over a few hundred acres into August. No big deal, especially because there were big deals elsewhere to attract everyone's attention.

Then on September 6, rangers got a weird warning from weather watchers near Spokane, a four-hour drive to the northwest, of what was then called the Canyon Creek fire. A weather balloon had shot straight sideways and had done so at an unusually low level. This strange behavior meant the jet stream, normally a high-altitude phenomenon, had dropped low and appeared to be aimed straight at Canyon Creek. It was, and when it hit the fire that night, it pushed it straight east about forty miles in a matter of a few hours. Those firefighters who could not flee deployed the aluminum foil pup tents, fire shelters they carry and call "shake and bakes." The idea is to climb inside the pup tent and stick your nose down close to the ground and colder air, as close as you can get it, when the towering flames roar over you. Canyon Creek wound up covering 250,000 acres, the biggest fire anyone had seen in the nation in seventy-eight years.

Of course there was controversy. The fire spilled out of the mountains onto the plains and wiped out ranch buildings, fences, and barns. The smoke plume was clearly visible at the governor's mansion about eighty miles to the southeast. It was a creature of the Forest Service's controversial let-it-burn policy. Ranchers view fire as they do wolves: nasty predators to be extinguished. As I said, by then I had heard it all before and paid not much attention to the uproar. What I did notice, however, was that some thoughtful people, career foresters, biologists, and ecologists, were quietly asking some questions and questioning assumptions. I got to know a few of them, and they let me in on their thinking, on process. Almost immediately I noticed among these people the very thing that was missing from the more vocal public debate: self-doubt and humility. Indeed, before 1988, firefighters and ecologists had an almost Disney-like model for the role of fire in natural systems. They believed that, left to their own devices, fires, meek little Bambis of fire, would burn and sputter to what they called then a "mosaic," a blackened bit of slope here, some saplings incinerated there but leaving lots of green.

Natural fires, they believed, would mostly prune the forest to favor old-growth monarchs, especially ponderosa pine. They even backed this assumption with cross sections of these very old trees that showed fire scars on the order of about every seven years. That is, fire had been a frequent visitor in these forests, and yet the forests survive, even thrive in the periodic flames.

Canyon Creek threw that model out the window. Much of the area it covered was solid black, every single tree incinerated. That was undeniable. And it was indeed humbling, but for scientists not so much a frustration as an opportunity. Their model had been proven wrong, and this was an opportunity to learn. It was this humility and inquisitiveness that I would eventually come to recognize as the scientific habit of mind, and I felt almost immediately comfortable in it, so much so that I took this trail. I decided I was through with bumper stickers and talking points. There are, after all, facts and knowledge about the world we live in, and I was far more interested in thinking about those.

When I packed up my desk in the *Missoulian*, I and everyone else who knows my story thought it was about my clash with corporate power, and it was. But it was also true that in the year leading up to that denouement, I had learned to ask larger questions, in fact, had become convinced that the vast chaos and wilderness that is the natural world was announcing our hubris had met its match. The context of the human enterprise is nature, yet we had somehow come to believe that by taming nature, we magically transcend that context, that we can go on forever putting out the fires and killing the wolves and face no consequences. Much of journalism is accomplice to this denial of context. Journalism is an account of the day's discussion and is deeply convinced that the sum total of human chatter is the sum total. Journalism is anthropocentric. A year of hanging out with ecologists and conservation biologists had convinced me there were larger questions not answered by what he said and what she said. The answers to those larger questions would not fit in twenty column inches filed on deadline to keep the bra ads from bumping. I left newspapering because it was time for me to go.

The night I left the *Missoulian* I went to that bar, the fluorescent lit tunnel with cheap beer and decent burgers. News of my quick departure from newspapering took no time to spread, so my table was full of reporters, several of whom were close friends, but there would be tension in the coming months over their sense that I expected them to do what I had done. Also present was a woman, not a reporter, one I was just getting to know after a few conversations at this very table. I was divorced; my marriage broke up the year before. The young woman had gotten to know me by reading my work in the paper, came to understand I sometimes haunted this bar for a burger, and had, by her admission, "stalked" me. At first, I had not paid much attention, but then her most salient feature, a full halo of rich, red curls, came to seem like the rising sun on my horizon. Tall, smart, and poised, she seemed strong, especially as I grew to understand the sun effect came from a warmth within. She was a graduate student in environmental studies. I was blindsided by charm. "Wait," I said. "How old are you?" "Twenty-three." This was a lie, but she figured by adding a year, I wouldn't recoil at the age difference. Re-coil? Smart she might be, but clearly naive on the workings of the male mind approaching middle age. She had heard about my leaving the *Missoulian* and so joined us that night in the bar. As the pitchers of cheap beer emptied, she decided to haul me away from that tableful of reporters and friends to a cabin she knew of in the mountains. Twenty-one years later, this young woman, Tracy Stone, my wife, is still the most impor-tant thing in my life. The result of that day I left newspapering was a net gain beyond my imagination. Attaching to a place saved my life, but finally learning to attach to a human was a good bit better. At bottom, this book is a love story.

One of the last stories I wrote for the *Missoulian* was a quick, slapped-together deal that required no real reporting. It was, in fact, based on a press release about some research at the University of Idaho. A professor there had taken a close look at ponderosa pine and concluded that, despite the fact this species grows in a broad range of climatic conditions from Arizona to British Columbia, its genetics are finely tuned to local conditions. A ponderosa transplanted from Arizona or even Colorado likely would not survive in Montana; trees too have a genetic fidelity to latitude. The importance of this re-lated to global warming, a term not in general use in 1988. I was an environmental reporter and had not yet encountered the term in a story; only had some vague notion of some theo-retical work on carbon dioxide. Nonetheless, this scientist concluded that should global warming occur, all the ponder-osa pine would die. At first, I took this as one might read a science fiction story, a sort of botanical Armageddon. But then I thought this is what science is for, to project what we know today onto the future, to allow us to adjust behavior and avoid dire consequences. And as a journalist, I had a role in this process. I could not imagine a consequence so dire as a vast landscape of dead pine trees. So I wrote up the story knowing that the public knowledge would translate to policy, and we as an enlightened and rational society would take the necessary steps to prevent global warming, take them now so as to not face such a horrible consequence thirty, forty years hence.

As I write this today, I can look out my study window to the hills that hold Missoula and see the ponderosa pine at ridgetop, notice the red spots in their otherwise green crowns. With UV sunglasses, the image is even more defined, and I have learned that those trees that look red in sunglasses this year will be full-on stone-dead, red-needled pine in a year or so. To the east, near Helena, entire ridgelines, entire forests, entire vistas that take in areas the size of an eastern state are red and dead. Same south to Colorado, north well into British Columbia. Not just ponderosa, but lodgepole and whitebark pine. Not just pine, but fir. Scientists agree this is a consequence of global warming.

People told me then the upheaval in my life was my growth beyond journalism, yet the context suggested otherwise. Like most reporters, I had begun by learning to write obituaries. I was not moving on so much as I was returning to first principles.

10
AS I LAY DYING

Through the late 1980s and on into the 1990s, I had as little contact with my parents as possible, but a couple of times I did visit their geodesic dome in Pasco, Washington. The dome itself began to seem oddly appropriate, a demi-globe, a five eighths of a planar approximation of a sphere that allowed them to retreat into an increasingly eccentric world of their own. The way they ate, for instance. They seemed to spend a lot of time on trips here and there in the Northwest, collecting whatever odd processed food was on offer and squirreling it in overflowing cupboards and freezers. Then at mealtime, various jars, boxes, trays, and tins would come out in ever weirder combinations and concoctions of sauces, spreads, dips, things like pickled fish and Roquefort cheese spread made special by an out-of-the-way truck stop in Yakima. Both my mother and father had become obese. My mother especially looked gray and old, but she was not even sixty.

On one visit, my dad had gotten up early to go to work, and I could hear a long series of groans and sighs as he labored to straighten the kinks and sore spots from the day before. He was about sixty then and had taken work wiring high-voltage connections in a factory. Once he would have called this sort of job working as a "narrowback," a power pole lineman's derogatory term for a mere electrician. Even narrowback work was causing him pain, but he didn't have enough money to quit, and it was the work he could get.

A couple of years later I saw them again. My father had built an addition onto the dome to house a small swimming pool. No idea why they thought they needed a swimming pool, but there it was. I walked a set of stair steps he had framed leading up to the thing and was horrified, because I realized their construction delivered a diagnosis of a mind losing touch. The steps were uneven, tilted, a fun-house form. The laws of carpentry are clear and crisp, demanding evenness, above all, in stairs: corners square, surfaces level or plumb. Any sort of unevenness in steps literally trips people up. These are the rules, and once my old man knew them. Once he built houses that looked like other houses with flat floor joists, studs on sixteen-inch centers, two-by-twelve headers over windows and doors, rafters angled to precise pitch guided by a steel framing square. He no longer respected the bubble on his level and thought that an inch and five eighths was as good as an inch and a half, and I took this as a sign that his lifelong struggle to protect his faith by denying reality was succeeding. Even the rules of carpentry no longer applied.

The front door of the demi-globe house had warped and was stuck closed. He didn't seem able to fix it, so I found what was left of his tools in the garage, not much really, useless odds and ends from garage sales or what he had stolen from job sites. Everything rusted and mismatched, not a sharp, straight saw in the place. I found a derelict cold chisel meant for breaking rock and whetted it on the concrete floor to raise an edge of sorts, then used it to shave his sticking door.

In the fall of 1994, my wife and I loaded everything we could into our Honda Civic and drove to Stanford University, where we would spend a year on a Knight Fellowship I had won. It was an important pivot point in my career and came at an important pivot point for journalism in general. I recall, for instance, a seminar with the rest of the fellows—nineteen of us from papers and broadcast organizations from around the country—with the futurist Paul Saffo. He logically laid out the broad outlines of our business, then predicted that anyone there from *The New York Times*—there was one—would be able to enjoy her pension. The rest of us would face tough sledding. The *Times* had enough momentum to weather the worst of the coming storm, but his basic message to us journalists was that the Internet was going to eat our lunch, and no one in newspapering had yet come up with a business model to reverse that simple fact. Nearly twenty years later, no one has.

Ninety-four was, of course, a watershed election year. All of us on that fellowship would normally have been working election night, but lacking nothing better to do on our paid year off, we gathered to watch returns and drink, a gathering that resembled nothing so much as a wake. We watched as Newt Gingrich and company took back control of Congress in order to prosecute movement conservatism's Contract with America. All of us had reported on the resurgent right in one form or another, and there was no neutrality in that room full of reporters. We knew what we were dealing with, a campaign of distortion and deception, and knew just as well that the troubles of our own craft were somehow wound up in the election outcome that night. My own life meant I could trace the lines not just to Gingrich and the Christian Coalition (a force that year) but to the Moral Majority, the culture wars, Jerry Falwell, and my old man, and from him on back to tax protesters, George Hansen, and the John Birch Society. Paperwork, flyers, and donor cards I had spotted during a visit to my parents' house revealed they were in fact card-carrying Christian Coalition.

The resurgence of the fundamentalist right was that year news to my colleagues, people who worked at the pinnacle of journalism. What was happening in places like Twin Falls, Idaho, events I knew well and had lived all my life, were only just then becoming visible in the national papers of record. It was news to them. Not to me.

The next day I got a phone call, a rare phone call indeed, from my old man. He had tracked me down at Stanford; I don't recall ever giving him the number, so he must have gone through some trouble to find me. He had called to gloat over the results of the election, that Christians had taken back the country and now things would be different. He was calling to count coup on me, to announce that what he had lost in his personal battle with me his people had gained in their efforts to control all of their rebellious sons and daughters in theocracy. He told me then that there is only one book any person will ever need, which is the Good Book, and now it will govern our country. I didn't really think it would go that far, but in 1994 it was impossible to harbor an accurate premonition of the rule of George W. Bush.

About this time my parents visited my father's brother and his wife. My aunt chose to make conversation by remarking how confusing she found the upcoming election, and was having a hard time deciding how to vote. My mother told her she had no such problem. "Pastor just tells us how to vote, and that's what we do."

There was another seminar at Stanford, this one with the great conservation biologist Paul Ehrlich. He was thinking a great deal about scientific literacy and public policy, as were most conservation biologists. Their research more than any other field warned of impending catastrophe. Biologists were already recording a body count of the planet's species. Ehrlich told us his single greatest wish to transform public policy was that the American public gain a simple understanding of exponential growth curves. It's not a hard concept, the same one that drives growth in savings accounts. It comes into play when instead of adding a fixed increment, a unit, to each successive step of growth, you add a percentage of the base. This is how populations grow, for instance. Plot any such growth pattern as a graph and they all look the same: nothing changes dramatically from year to year as the curve begins to arc slowly upward, but then momentum builds and the arc swings upward all of sudden, driven by nothing more than inexorable and simple mathematics. His point was the world's problems will unwind like this and are easy to ignore in the first few decades, which is when it is possible to do something about them. Then we will cross a point, a tipping point. Crashes are exponential.

We are back now in Montana and years pass. Then comes another telephone call from my parents, the sort of perfunctory contact we manage once a year or so. We make the usual reports, talk about the weather and any other topic we can think of to keep us from religion and politics. Oddly and without preface, my mother announces she has a lump on her breast. It showed up in a mammogram, so I ask her about the biopsy. Malignant? What type? What treatment and prognosis? She can answer none of these questions. You mean you haven't decided what to do about this with your doctor? No, she has not. Her sister had died only the year before from breast cancer and so maybe this sort of outcome is fate, she says. And besides, her sister had been treated, had the surgery and everything, and look what good it did her. So my mother had decided to pray instead, to place her fate in the hands of the Lord and, it turns out, the various quacks who are the Lord's minions, one of which was my brother.

A year or so passes, and I hear nothing of this, then one day, a very large, new pickup truck straddles the hundred-yard-long footpath directly across the field of native grasses I am attempting to restore. The truck drives all the way up the path, then parks in a clattering diesel idle directly in front of the earth-friendly, passive solar house, which I had built with my own hands. My old man alights, walks around the cab of the pickup, and helps my mother out the other door. I had not been expecting them. They are en route to Michigan to visit relatives, still midwestern enough to not consider for a moment flying. People from the Upper Midwest, assigned a trip to Calcutta, would simply change the oil in the Buick and then head west, hoping for a Motel 6 somewhere in the Gulf of Alaska.

But then I notice the backseat of the extended cab truck is piled high with jugs of black liquid, maybe fifteen or twenty gallons, too much cargo to fly with. This is where my brother came in. He had a hand in getting this stuff from Jamaica. Can't get it in the United States, because it is a surefire cure for cancer, which of course means the government and the AMA won't allow it to be sold, or so I am told.

The brother in question I knew as Paul while he was growing up, the same one who disappeared in Texas while in the process of becoming a Baptist preacher. He surfaced years later as a naturopath, allegedly trained in Germany with a thriving practice in Florida, later upstate New York. Only he is no longer "Paul." He has changed his name to "Bear Walker" to reflect his deep spirituality and intimate connections to his Native American heritage. To quote his website current in 2011:

Bear Walker is a Native American Healer and Spiritualist, who has dedicated himself to his medical practice as well as to preserving the traditions and stories of his tribe, the Anishinabe. In his professional life as a practitioner of natural therapies, using herbs, homeopathy and all things natural, Bear has an extensive private practice, where he treats many individuals, including luminaries like Alan Arkin, and Demi Moore. He also consults with traditional doctors on alternative approaches to healing, in some cases helping to avoid surgery. Bear was trained in the ancient Medicine Man ways by his Grandfather, himself a Medicine Man. He also applies "state of the art" medical practices, having been trained in modern diagnostic tools and methods by NASA.

Bear has been telling Native American stories, The Sacred Tales, to groups of children and adults most of his life, as his Grandfather told them to him. The stories are thousands of years old. How the Dragonfly Learned to Fly is one of a series of Sacred Tales that has been passed down from generation to generation via the Native American oral tradition of story telling, of which Bear Walker is very much a part.

The business about training as a medicine man is, of course, bullshit. Another version of his website claimed his grandfather was a "full-blooded Anishinabe elder." This is simply a lie. Nonetheless, my parents refer to him as "Bear" that day, and my mother, who would not hear of conventional treatment by a medical doctor, is drinking vile black stuff by the gallon.

We talk around the issues for a few hours, mostly about who they would see in Michigan, then it comes time for them to hit the road. My mother takes her leave by exposing one breast to reveal a grapefruit size tumor erupted from it. I say goodbye and know it is goodbye.

———

Even in Montana I shared the sense of numbness and uncertainty that gripped the nation in late September of 2001. Given that, I was glad for the chance of a drive, especially what I knew to be one of the most beautiful drives extant. My route took me east across the Continental Divide and out onto the plains near Augusta, then north along the Rocky Mountain Front, across the Blackfeet Reservation, then north along the east side of Glacier National Park. I drove directly past that same trailhead I had hiked in 1978, the trip that changed my life and brought me west. The east edge of the park is a series of tilted, sweeping plateaus frizzed in quaking aspen, Day-Glo yellow in late September at that elevation, a few ridges of deep green limber pine lining the base of craggy rock faces. Overhead, a cloudless blue sky. The border crossing into Canada was more tense than I had ever seen it, my first sign of what we would become, a nation of cowering, shoeless travelers submitting to full body scans. Somehow, camouflage clothing and automatic rifles seem even more incongruous against a backdrop of wilderness.

My destination was the Canadian side of the park at Waterton, a town named for a large lake scooped by glaciers, seemingly only a couple of days before. It shone clear and cold against the mountains as if untouched since laid down at the creation. I was there on business, set to speak the following day to a group of Canadian writers. But I never made the appearance. My wife called to relay a phone call from my father, who had been sobbing and didn't make much sense. Could I come? So I reversed the route and went, six hours back home to Missoula, a night's sleep, then Tracy and I made the six-hour trip to the geodesic dome at Pasco.

We found the place a mess, mud and dirt caked on floors, dishes and debris stacked on all the counters, no food in the house, the old man looking as if he had worn the same clothes for a month and he probably had. My mother was in her bed in a coma, looking like nothing I had ever seen human. She had taken on a brown-gray pall and her head bobbed side to side, her mouth in steady reciprocation, making her look like nothing so much as a helpless, begging baby bird. I took this to be a sign of some pain and hoped something more than jugs of black slurry were at hand to deal with it. I asked my dad about hospice and, yes, they had been and, yes, there had been morphine. I suggested hospice return with more morphine, and he agreed. They did, then my mother seemed to calm. My dad and I went to the undertaker's shop the next day to make arrangements. After, my dad talked about how my mother had been only a few weeks before, glued to the television like everyone else the day of September 11. She watched the twin towers fall, then said to him, "Now I know the Lord is coming." My parents' preacher and his wife came by, which I thought would be good for my dad; they might know some of the code language to ease his grief. But instead, the preacher's wife took Tracy aside and tried to convert her. "Have you been saved?" she asked. They left.

Tracy had cleaned the house while we were at the undertaker's. Then she roasted a chicken, and we ate it. After dinner, my mother died.

There was a funeral in Pasco for church people, and I did not go, but my mother had wanted to be buried in Michigan. When my brother died in the car wreck, my parents had bought space at the graveyard big enough for three. Family would come to that funeral so I would need to go back to Michigan. My sister had made arrangements and decided there would be no graveside service, so I stole a few minutes before the funeral to drive the section line roads across Saginaw Valley farm country to the little cemetery southwest of Freeland, and found the spot I remembered in a grove of old oaks at the back, my first visit to my brother's grave since he was laid there thirty years before. A backhoe was parked and had already opened my mother's grave, so I looked in to see the exposed side of my brother's concrete burial vault. They would be close again.

My sister had made an odd request, that I bring a guitar to the funeral, which was to be in the same funeral home, the same room, as my brother's. I suppose my sister had some sense there would need to be music, and the only musical types around were church people, and she wanted to avoid that, so I brought a guitar, carried it into the chapel, greeted brothers I had not seen in years, took a seat. This was to be my private joke. I had started to play the guitar in high school and finally used the money I had earned butchering beef to buy my very own electric bass guitar and amp from Alvin Ash's music store. My mother became enraged and shrieked at me that I would by God take that devil's instrument back to Alvin Ash. She believed a guitar was the first slippery-sloped step to a life of sex, drugs, and rock 'n' roll, which was, of course, exactly the career path I imagined. Her preachers were then identifying rock 'n' roll as "wild African jungle music," a direct quote of a phrase that made it all the more attractive. I pointed out the simple logic of the fact that the money spent was my own. She deployed my father in the battle and he trumped this logic with the simple law that nothing was my own as long as I lived in his house. I'm sure he said it then, because he said it often: "I am your father, and I do not have to be fair." Alvin Ash took the guitar back.

I did learn to play guitar as an adult and over the years spent a small fortune bringing home vintage instruments I would not have to return. I eventually learned blues and folk music, an elaborate style of fingerpicking that gave me access to one song in particular, a song out of New Orleans called "Just a Little While to Stay Here." It is, in fact, a funeral song, but the jazz tradition of New Orleans divides funeral songs into two categories. The solemn, grieving tunes are reserved for the march to the graveyard, the first line, but en route back the music shifts to joyous, up-tempo marches that celebrate the fact you are among those returning in the second line, not staying behind in a box. The song I played and sang at my mother's funeral was a second line song.

Just two months after my mother's funeral, my extended family found itself assembled again, this time in a suburb of Denver, Colorado. My brother's three boys had been headed home from school, one of the eldest, a high school kid, driving the family Suburban. There had been a wreck, and two of the boys were uninjured, but the youngest, Rory, eleven, took a freak blow to the head from a window and died. This brother happens to be the remaining evangelical in the family, so the funeral was in a shopping mall megachurch, which was packed with little kids. The preacher, of course, warmed to the occasion with the usual set of stories of how little kids can die suddenly and without warning and therefore little kids ought to come to Jesus sooner rather than later, best to come to Jesus right now. I suppose with an audience like that, he could not resist. Kids scare easier. Nonetheless, he was talking to an auditorium mostly full of Little League uniforms, which made the discordance more striking.

A small group of us, of course, were at that moment in our heads at a parallel funeral forty years before. I was back in Freeland listening to a guy who thought the best way to honor my grief and my brother's life was to use fear to sell one more pint of snake oil. The Denver preacher's parallel tastelessness fueled my anger, which was good. I was counting on anger to get me through the event and the memories it triggered. This worked for me, but not for my father. I found him in the church's foyer after the funeral weeping and shaking, lost in his grief. Then I said to him one of the worst things I have ever said to anyone and instantly regretted it. I told him to buck up. People were counting on him. My brother was counting on him. He could lose it later.

In the years since that event, I learned to excuse myself for that moment by telling myself what I had said to him was what he would have said to me, were the situation reversed. I can even hear his voice saying it, that my command to him was a gift back to him, a sign he had somehow raised me right to forgo my own grief or pain or vulnerability, to shield up and boot up, to protect and defend. He had taught me to be a man, a Manning. I can hear his voice saying these things to me, and it is that voice I echoed back to him. But this is a rationalization. I was letting myself off way too easy. After years of rehashing my awful charge to him, I finally realized he never said anything comparable to me when I was a child. Not once. That as a child I had carved out my own little stick image of "man," somehow drawn on a distorted image I had of him. I created a mythical character that was uninhabitable, then taught myself to inhabit him.

Thanksgiving the following year, and my dad accepted an invitation to join us for our big-deal holiday. Tracy loves the feast, loves to cook and loves people, so annually fills our house with food and friends. My dad was relaxed and even genial. He had a couple of glasses of wine with dinner, something I had never seen him do, nor would he have done so if my mother were still around. There is an old western joke that says you should always take two Mormons fishing with you, because if you only take one, he will drink all your beer. Apparently this applies to Baptists as well. My dad was then in the process of cleaning out and selling the geodesic dome and he had brought me three items that are to be the sum total of my legacy: the antique .38-55 Winchester rifle that was my great-grandfather's, the same single-shot 20-gauge shotgun I had used to botch the killing of my first deer, and a black-and-white photo mounted on plywood backing and cut to a silhouette by the photographer in about 1960. Both subjects of the photo are in the Little League uniforms of the mighty Eagles. I am kneeling with a catcher's mitt artfully slung across my right knee. My brother, Mike, is standing with his right hand on my shoulder, a bat handle in his left hand. That Thanksgiving, he gave me just these three things.

But that same day creates a new photo. My son, Josh, has

come for the occasion with his wife and son. So we pose—my dad, me, my son, my grandson—pose like a real family. A bit of sanity and calm before three men in the photo would slip off into a world of increasing madness.

My son until then had been beginning a career as, of all things, a reporter. He had, in fact, gotten his first job at the *Idaho Falls Post Register,* the same paper where I had been city editor, the paper that brought me west from Michigan. A reporter who had his first job working for me at another paper had hired Josh. But it hadn't worked out, as I knew full well it wouldn't, journalism being well into its death throes. Yet it turned out his skills at handling information opened a niche for him in what would be a growth industry through the rest of that decade and well into the next. He joined the Army and trained in intelligence gathering. That Thanksgiving, he was headed for a tour of duty in Kosovo, then two postings to Iraq while he was in the Army and a third tour in Iraq of six months as a civilian intelligence analyst for a defense contractor. The irony in this is that his skills in handling information accurately were no longer in demand in American life, but were very much in demand in a war that began with criminal distortion of information.

George W. Bush's decision to send my son and a bunch of other sons and daughters to a quagmire war came only after the Christer-in-chief sought the counsel of his heavenly father, so my own father would be fine with the war, as he would have been with much that went on in that decade. His people were in charge. He did sell the house and everything in it, then loaded what he had left into his pickup truck, always a pickup truck, and began to wander, a man in his early seventies hitting the road. I admit to feeling some worry about this, but then as that decade unfolded, it began to make sense. My worry was based on my membership in the "reality-based community," and clearly he was not so limited. My father was of the same habits of mind that were then ascendant as national madness. He would fit right in. Now and again I would get a report from a relative that he had been sighted, landed for a few weeks, then moved on, mostly between Michigan and Florida. He would have felt smug and secure as the Cheneys, Limbaughs, and Roves of the world reduced us to oligarchy, and open embrace of torture, banishment of science, an economy run by con men, and denial of nature's terms of engagement. To employ an old-country simile, my old man went off for a good wallow in the madness rampant sea to sea, and should have been happy as a pig in shit.

Meantime, I was out of the country for much of that time taking full advantage of my license to be educated in public. While I had been at Stanford in the mid-1990s, I made some contact with Paul Ehrlich's circle of conservation biologists and developed a solid friendship with an agricultural economist in that orbit, Rosamond Naylor. I tagged along on a couple of her field projects, then she had an idea that I write about an extensive project of the Minneapolis-based McKnight Foundation. The foundation had recruited a board of about a dozen first-string food scientists, geneticists, agronomists, and economists to figure out ways crop science might alleviate poverty in the developing world. My job was to visit a dozen such projects spread around the world and write a book about the work. It took a couple of years, then led almost immediately to a similar project with the Rockefeller Foundation, then another with the Rome-based Food and Agriculture Organization of the United Nations. Altogether, I spent about ten years during that period of my life carrying a skinny notebook through about thirty different countries, most of them poor beyond American imagination.

The word "poverty" outside the United States requires a different frame of reference. We do not have significant pockets of starvation in this country, at least not yet. Much of the world does. There are about a million cases a year of childhood blindness from vitamin A deficiency worldwide. In India, I got used to looking straight into the inquiring faces of children with unrepaired cleft palates and to seeing bodies on the street. About a fifth of humanity—about 1.5 billion of us—lives on less than a dollar a day.

One day, my wife and I spent about four hours bouncing in a compact car, trying to make forty kilometers on Ethiopia's main highway. All along the way, the road's edges were lined by tin huts, with elegant, hollow-eyed, high-cheek-boned faces staring out at us. Every few kilometers we'd see an overturned truck of some sort lying like a giant wounded animal along the road. An ant line of humans streamed from the wreckage, looting first cargo, then parts for scrap. We saw a child hit by a car and naively asked our host, an Ethiopian man trained as a plant geneticist at Texas A&M, when an ambulance would come to help the child. He told us there was no ambulance and even if there was, no place to take her, no doctors or hospital around. He seem puzzled and a bit vexed with us for not knowing this. He told us she would die, and she did.

My travels took me down back roads in pickup trucks, through canals and klongs in canoes, in cattle-car-like trains across India and up mountain pathways in the Andes to re-mote villages few tourists would ever see. Yet the rule was al-ways the same, that no matter how poor the village or farmers, they would invite me into their homes and offer the best they had, flower wreaths in India, chicha and guinea pig in Peru, maize beer in Zimbabwe, deep fried sparrow in China. I shared boiled greens and warm conversation in Vietnam with Ph.D. plant breeders who had been Vietcong soldiers.

Somewhere along the line I learned the paradox of African laughter. Africa is the worst. While much of Latin America and South and Southeast Asia have eased their poverty, Africa is worse off than it was twenty years ago. HIV-AIDS, violence, corruption, and chaos have made life untenable in an increasing number of places. Yet in African villages people still invited me in and offered the best, and then the room would invariably ring with the deep rolling lilt of a laugh that I came to think of as the signature of the place. I came to love the extended vowels and delicate consonants that Anglo-phone Africans use to turn everyday spoken English into song. How do these people find a place for song? How deep is this reservoir of human spirit?

In India, I saw a blue-tarped pile of bagged surplus rice the size of a domed football stadium and a couple of kilometers away an extemporaneous, blue-tarp village of people begging for rice. India now produces enough grain to feed itself, but because it uses some modern and costly methods, it also has a significant population of poor who cannot afford the food. This at the same time Bangalore was becoming flush with dot-com millionaires.

In the decade I worked on this project, the population

clock ticked one full notch, from just shy of six to just shy of seven billion. China and India hold fully a third of these people. Gradually it dawned on me this is the weight of the world, and we ought to be paying more attention to China and India.

I interviewed Chinese scientists who had survived the persecutions of the Cultural Revolution, but more importantly, the deprivations of the Great Leap Forward. In the latter event, Mao's delusional—by this I mean he lost touch with reality, which is to say, ignored science—farm policies caused massive crop failures that starved to death 60 million Chinese. Stop. Go back. Take a second to comprehend that number, 60 million. Cannibalism was common. People who have gone hungry will do anything to never go hungry again. Anything. Bring up the subject of persecution of Tibetans, and the Chinese will bluntly say, "What's the big deal? You Americans killed the Indians when you needed to industrialize." Which is, of course, exactly correct. Bring up their nation's contribution to global warming by its insatiable appetite for coal-generated energy, and you'll get a similar response with the added facts that a) we Americans are selling them the coal and b) they are using the energy to make our sneakers and our iPads. Exactly correct.

The Chinese, however, were then trying to figure out what to do about water pollution. They had to. Canal water on the lower Yangtze Basin had become so polluted that using it for irrigation, as they must, was killing their rice crop.

Hang out with the world's leading ag economists in Rome or at the better conferences, say at a nice hotel in Brisbane, Australia, in the early part of the last decade, and you would have heard a relatively sanguine view of the world. The economists had their data charted nicely. Sure there were trouble spots like Africa and sure population was nipping at the heels of increased food production, but the curves matched up. The Green Revolution will triumph and look how many people have moved above the poverty line in the last decade, which is true enough. But I could never seem to swallow it. I had been on the ground and what the economists were calling alleviated poverty did not look like all that good of a life. This is when I finally concluded that too many of the world's decisions are made by people who think reality is what they see in their data sets and from the window of the town car en route from the airport to their five-star hotel.

Once I had tried to explain the concept of wilderness, vast tracts of trackless, untrammeled mountain forests, to a small group of graduate students in India. They couldn't get it. Couldn't conceive of it. Why would we choose to leave land unused? People need it. This was their norm: overpopulated, polluted, crowded, noisy. This is the norm for much of the world, the extremes people tolerate. It is finally this tolerance that is the most deeply unsettling and salient fact of the world. The adaptability of humans to ever-worsening conditions forecasts how far humanity is willing to go.

And we have gone there. In 2008, a series of climatic upsets spawned by global warming caused a radical spike in food prices worldwide. Today, that is the only way things happen—worldwide. The commodity system is so intertwined that a flood on the Mississippi creates malnutrition in Kenya and bonuses for long-positioned futures traders in Chicago all at once. None of the sanguine ag economists saw this spike coming, because they had not factored in global warming upsets, nor had they factored in the fact that Americans were funneling their corn crop into the gas tanks of their SUVs as ethanol. A soccer mom's run to the mall now competes for grain with a kid under a blue tarp in India. Highest bidder wins.

Likewise, the ag economists did not see the same thing happening again in 2011, as I write this. Drought in China's grain belt, catastrophic flooding in the Mississippi Basin, all global warming's doing. Overpopulation, climate change, environmental degradation, have all made our life supports systems brittle to the point of breaking. The food supply has a tipping point driven by global warming. In America, our official position as a nation is denial.

I was back in Missoula for the summer of 2007, so could watch it unfold from close up. On July 6 of that summer, the temperature in our town reached 107, the highest ever recorded here. The daily average high for the month was 96.5 degrees, 12.9 degrees above normal. Throughout western Montana, July 2007 was the hottest month on record. Total rainfall was 0.03 inch. The first half of August was almost as bad, leaving live trees holding less moisture than kiln-dried lumber.

By late July, we were ablaze, early for fire season, but there was no precedent for the weather. One could climb one of the hills surrounding our valley of about 100,000 people and have in sight at once six or seven active fires, most bigger than ten thousand acres. Given a proper series of winds, any one of these could blow up and inhale a town. In fact, it took a proper series of winds just to see the hills surrounding the towns. From July on into September, most days were shrouded in smoke, with visibility at a few hundred yards.

But it was the clear days we feared the most, high pressure and winds that cleared smoke, but fanned flames. On one such day I was walking out of my house at the edge of Missoula and saw most of the northern horizon line was not a pall, but a white-hot towering column of smoke ten, maybe fifteen miles wide, like a mushroom cloud or ash from a volcano. The signature formation meant a fire had blown up, the term firefighters use to describe their version of a perfect storm. A blowup comes late afternoon when humidity has dropped to the daily low and doesn't require all that much wind, just enough to start a positive feedback loop and exponential growth. If the slope of the hill and fuels are right, this becomes a fire no longer restrained by weather. It has enough power to make and sustain its own weather. Firefighters can't do a thing about such a fire but flee, and flee they did, downslope and to a highway in the Seeley-Swan Valley about fifty miles northeast of Missoula. The town has a permanent population of about two thousand, four thousand in the summer, and firefighters admitted there was not much they could do to protect it. There were evacuations, as there were all over Montana that summer, a battle that lasted for weeks, and in the end firefighters got a lucky break. Seeley was saved.

All told, more than 600,000 acres of Montana burned that summer of 2007, two million acres in Idaho, eight million overall in the West. All of these were fierce conflagrations bigger, faster, and hotter than anyone had seen. Veteran firefighters who had been stunned by fires like Canyon Creek in

1988, the fire that was pivotal in my own education in this matter, now saw that one as not even a worthy precedent. Something bigger was happening; the northern Rockies were getting a glimpse of the planet's future; we were beginning to live global warming. As I write this in 2011, a single fire of 500,000 acres is burning uncontrolled in ponderosa pine in Arizona. Canyon Creek was a single fire of 250,000 acres, with no precedent in modern times. Since 1988, there have been at least thirty fires larger than this in the West.

The last I had heard anything about my dad, it was an unsettling and almost unbelievable rumor that he had somehow made it to upstate New York and used every dime he had made from selling everything he had to leverage purchase of an organic dairy farm. I tracked him down and this turned out to be true. Why this madness? Wait a minute. Did the shaman formerly known as Paul Manning have anything to do with this? Something, I think, but one way or another, my father became convinced he could make a killing in organic milk. My assumption was he planned to do so by shortcutting organic certification standards. Rules were for suckers.

It was no surprise when I heard a year or so later that he had indeed gone broke, lost it all in this venture. Then he had showed up at my sister's place in Michigan in a cheap, compact Japanese car. He'd lost his prized pickup truck in the dairy deal and the box was all he could afford. He stayed awhile with my sister, but that grew uncomfortable. He began mistaking my sister for my mother. He was slipping.

Nonetheless, the shaman had a plan and hooked my old

man up with a lawyer near Atlanta, Georgia, who was developing a sort of spa or resort in Panama. My old man could earn his keep there supervising construction. So he left, but not before the shaman advised my father that he really wouldn't need his last $30,000 he managed to pull together after the dairy deal. The shaman would borrow it and put it to good use.

Then my father disappeared after a year or so. I tracked him down through the lawyer in Atlanta, who was helpful, although his deal with my dad hadn't worked out, probably no fault of the lawyer's. I filed that information away, along with the reluctant realization I would have to go to Panama and find him, sooner or later.

Meantime, in the fall of 2008, while first the banking industry, then the American economy collapsed, I had my own problems to attend to. The manifest failure of journalism told me I needed to come up with a Plan B to pay the bills, so I started a little retail business with the idea of letting it grow and provide a nice side stream of income. It did not. My business failed at the height of the 2008 recession, and I went broke. Meanwhile, it was an election year, so the nation did one more epic battle with movement conservatives to regain rational government. I thought I had my father safely forgotten in some jungle in Panama, but he kept popping up in various incarnations wherever I turned. Somehow, the whole nation had become trapped in what looked awfully like the personal history I spent my whole life and intellect trying to escape.

11
BURIED IN THE FAMILY

It was beginning to look like we would do this alone, but at least I knew for sure it was the last time I would have to see this piece of ground, the little cemetery near Freeland, Michigan. So we gathered on July 4, 2009, my wife and I, my son, his wife, his two children, my sister and her husband. None of my other brothers was there, but then I didn't blame them, my family's history being what it is. It had taken some time to get the little plastic box of ashes back from Panama, so we put off burying it in the cemetery until the weather was decent and people could travel. And they did. As I was resigning myself to a quiet event, a line of midsized American-made sedans and minivans—domestic cars are the emblem of loyal Michiganders—pulled into the cemetery and discharged elements of an even more extended family, uncles and aunts I had not seen since my mother's funeral. Cousins I had not seen since I was a child.

The only photo I have of my father's family when he was young was also taken on July 4, but in 1942. It shows my grandfather in work clothes and my grandmother in church clothes standing in front of their brown Insulbrick house on Manning Hill, and next to them, arrayed in perfect stair-step order, my dad and his three brothers. Each male wears a fedora and suspenders. Neither sister is in the photo; one was in Flint working in a defense plant, and the other took the photo. Both now are dead. The lone survivor from that group is my Uncle Dale, and I was glad to see him at the cemetery that day. I had a copy of the 1942 photo with me and passed it around.

My sister had asked me to do the talking, but there was not a lot to say. I knew more of the story of my father's last few years than anyone there, save my sister, but did not feel like telling a bit of it. Most everybody there knew the rest. Not much to say, so I delivered a eulogy of sorts that lasted maybe a minute. I said that the plastic box in my hands held my dad's remains, which was an odd word in the context of his life. Never once did he seem able to remain, not anywhere. So it was our task, those of us gathered this day, this fragment of family, to finally ensure that he remained, no small charge, I said, and most everyone nodded. But then I said I had a shovel and from where I stood I could see a number of Mannings assembled, including my son and my grandson, and whenever there were a sufficient number of Mannings and a shovel on hand, things tended to get done. So I dug a hole.

Then my Uncle Dale spoke up, the elder in the group. He had noticed something about the shovel I was using. "I thought I taught you to clean the concrete off your shovel when you're done work," he said. He was right. There was hardened concrete on the shovel and he, in fact, had taught me that very lesson when I was no more than eleven. "Sorry, Dale," I said. "That's what happens when you have to borrow tools from the in-laws. It's not my shovel." He laughed. Then I finished burying my old man.

Then I invited all to join us at a café nearby for lunch and what would have been known to all of them in earlier days as "a visit." But before we could leave, there was an interruption, as I knew there would be. My mother's sister was there, one of the religious relatives, and as if on cue, she said, "Wait a minute, Dick. Didn't you forget something?"

I knew she meant prayer, and, no, I had not forgotten. Not a single solitary word did I forget. Forgetting is difficult when one is standing on the remains of his father, mother, and brother. Were there such a thing as souls then surely those of the three beneath my feet that day had suffered enough from Baptist bilge, but have at it, Auntie. The First Amendment applies even in graveyards. Go ahead. Say a prayer. These three are dead and beyond the reach of Jesus now.

Then we're leaving the graveyard, and I greet a few people, even the aunt who prayed. And then I get it. Suddenly and for the first time in my life, I understand. In a flash, it comes to me. Something snaps into focus, and I know enough to unravel this whole story. There's a pattern I have missed all my life, because I have simply sorted the two sides of my extended family along religious lines, and that's true enough as far as it goes. But there is something more to this story. The praying aunt, for instance. I happen to know that she herself was a teenage mother, one of her daughters is terribly alcoholic, that the state of Michigan took away the daughter's children because of neglect, and that one of those kids is in prison as a result of a random shooting. At the graveyard, I learn that one aunt from my mother's side didn't come to the graveyard this day because she was tired of funerals. Her husband had died, but he was old so that was okay, but so had four of her five children, all my age or younger. This was the most religious branch of my mother's family, yet my cousins had died of things like suicide and alcoholism. All of this sort of sadness accrued on my mother's side of the family, but not my father's. This simple fact was not an answer, but it did give me the right question.

I happened to be in Atlanta for a conference and knew the town to be headquarters for the Centers for Disease Control and so the place where Robert Anda lives and works. Anda is an epidemiologist and responsible for a landmark piece of research, so his time is in great demand, but nonetheless he agreed to meet me for an interview at a downtown hotel. As a scientist, Anda has earned the arrogance that others of his stature sometimes claim, but he doesn't. He's easygoing, plainspoken, and affable. He nonetheless was a key player in assembling a body of evidence that is one of the more important findings of our time. The original study, first published in the early 1990s, produced more than fifty publications in places such as *The Journal of the American Medical Association*. Yet little of this work has penetrated public consciousness and policy. This is not because it is unimportant; it has much to say about the nation's leading social and economic problems, in fact, suggests we rethink our most cherished assumptions about the human condition. It has failed to penetrate public consciousness because it demands we rewrite our story, and we are simply not willing to do so. Like a lot of good science, this research did not begin with such sweeping ambitions; researchers simply wanted to know why people are fat.

In the mid-1980s, the California health insurer Kaiser Permanente was interested in trimming the health care costs of obese people by trimming obese people, so conducted what turned out to be highly successful clinics to help people lose weight. The only problem was that the most successful patients were dropping out and regaining hundreds of pounds in a matter of months, and no one could figure out why. So researchers began intensive interviews of the dropouts, asking shot-in-the-dark, almost random questions in an attempt to tease out a common thread. They found a couple. First, the dropouts had histories of some sort of drug, alcohol, or tobacco abuse, other than food. Second, there was a common history of abuse or neglect when these same people were children, especially sexual abuse. Learning this, Vincent Felitti, who was heading the research for Kaiser Permanente, sought out Anda, who, as a CDC epidemiologist, had studied such problems as cholesterol and heart disease. Anda brought a public health spin to what on the surface appeared to be some sort of psychological problem. Felitti was looking for some way to disentangle the various factors—obesity, childhood abuse, and substance abuse—into some sort of causal chain. But Anda had another idea, to lump the whole business together in a complex array of factors and see what sort of mosaic emerged.

The two researchers devised a questionnaire to deliver to not just fat people but to a cross section of about 17,000 people insured by Kaiser Permanente in California. They called it the ACE study, an acronym for "Adverse Childhood Experiences," and asked these now middle-aged, middle-class people common questions about their childhood: Were they physically abused, sexually abused, neglected? Was there an alcoholic in the household? A drug user? Someone mentally ill? Someone in prison? Anyone institutionalized? Was your mother treated violently? Had one parent been absent? For each yes answer, a respondent was given one point. The results were totaled as what is still known as the ACE score.

Less than half of the sample had a score of zero; about 14 percent had a score of four or more, an interesting result in its own right. Remember these are employed, middle-class educated people, and yet more than one in seven people had childhoods filled with multiple abuses. Still, the more interesting result came because Felitti and Anda decided to look at ACE scores arrayed against such factors as drug and alcohol abuse, suicide attempts, depression, and smoking, but also against simple issues of physical health such as heart and lung disease. What they found was almost a complete correlation in every one of these cases, and it was not simply true that abused kids had more problems. It's even more refined than that. For instance, if you graph child abuse against alcohol abuse later in life, there is a clean, stair-stepped graph as the ACE score increases from zero to one to two and so forth, not just in alcoholism, but a dose-specific response. As the ACE score rises, so does daily alcohol dosage. That same stair-stepped graph holds for issues like promiscuity and teen pregnancy, and also for heart disease and lung disease. We assume the common history of smoking and obesity might explain those health issues, but the researchers normalized their data to subtract the effects of smoking on lung disease. They found that abuse, in and of itself, had an effect on disease, we now know, because it suppresses the immune system. Felitti and Anda continue to mine that data set, and their most recent publication says people with a high ACE score die, on average, twenty years earlier than everyone else.

Felitti, in one paper, offered a summary of the findings that at the same time explains some of the resistance in accepting them:

In our detailed study of over 17,000 middle-class American adults of diverse ethnicity, we found that the compulsive use of nicotine, alcohol, and injected street drugs increases proportionally in a strong, graded, dose-response manner that closely parallels the intensity of adverse life experiences during childhood. This of course supports old psychoanalytic views and is at odds with current concepts, including those of biological psychiatry, drug-treatment programs, and drug-eradication programs. Our findings are disturbing to some because they imply that the basic causes of addiction lie within us and the way we treat each other, not in drug dealers or dangerous chemicals. They suggest that billions of dollars have been spent everywhere except where the answer is to be found.

It occurred to me in that Atlanta hotel bar that there had to have been a Eureka moment when Anda saw these numbers roll out on a computer screen. It had come at his home office one day as he sat working alone.

"I said 'No way. You gotta be kidding me.' It didn't seem like it could be real that the level of exposure to toxic stressors to abuse and neglect and households that are filled with substance abuse and mental illness and violence are almost the norm. But unless I'm an idiot and designed it improperly, it must be true," he told me. "I was devastated. I was an emotional wreck. I wept. This is not how I want it to be for people. . . . I was seeing the sum total of 17,000 lives. . . . It was hard to deal with. It was really hard to deal with. . . . [So I went] driving back and forth in my community and I started looking at my neighbors' houses. . . . It's gotta be here too. I found myself driving, gazing at houses. I know it's here but which one? Which houses is it in, and which things are happening in these houses?"

Anda then made what is an odd admission for a scientist, that he continued to doubt his findings, to recalculate and rejigger for years, and his doubt continued until findings by others, especially the expanding abilities in neuroscience, explained why what he saw was true. There are, in fact, two large bodies of science on the issue—the ACE study housed at CDC and a national network sanctioned by Congress and begun in 2001. That is, much of this research that fails to penetrate public policy and consciousness is, in fact, government-sponsored public science. The latter effort—called the National Childhood Traumatic Stress Network—was founded by a Harvard-trained psychiatrist now widely acknowledged as the world's leading authority on the effects of child abuse and neglect, Bessel van der Kolk. It so happened he was in that same hotel in Atlanta that day and agreed to join Anda and me for a drink. Van der Kolk and Anda knew each other, but hadn't really talked in years, so I sat and listened to Anda explain how his doubts about his work evaporated as he got to know the other half of the puzzle as assembled by van der Kolk and a network of researchers the latter had founded.

As a young man, van der Kolk left the Netherlands and a fundamentalist Christian upbringing to be educated in the United States. He retains a Dutch accent, which can give him a leg up in status at conference halls swollen with shrinks, and he has seen plenty of those. He is, for instance, a past president of the International Society for Traumatic Stress Studies, the world's foremost body dealing with post-traumatic stress disorder. Yet he often levels the playing field by inserting sentences mid-lecture like: "I couldn't fucking believe it," or one of his favorites: "After forty years as a psychotherapist, I no longer practice psychotherapy."

One of his first postings was with the Veterans Administration working with the psychological wreckage of the Vietnam War, just as it was occurring to some that these guys were bringing a set of serious problems home from the war: depression, suicide, flashbacks, nightmares, terror—problems the government would just as soon sweep under the rug, or failing that, blame on psychological failings unrelated to the war. Nonetheless, van der Kolk knew something about what had been called "battle fatigue" or "shell shock" in earlier wars, so joined the effort to formulate what he now calls a "political diagnosis." Sickness does not exist unless it gets a mention in the *DSM*, the *Diagnostic and Statistical Manual of Mental Disorders* of the American Psychiatric Association. In fact, some things that aren't diseases, like homosexuality, can become disease by making it into the *DSM,* as it once did. So van der Kolk and some colleagues came up with the diagnosis of posttraumatic stress disorder, and PTSD made it into the *DSM.* The important and political word in this was "trauma," not some organic failing of brain chemistry, but a clear statement that something dramatic and awful had happened to these people that reduced them to an almost permanent state of deep terror. Then, that's about all we knew.

Van der Kolk was and is not the sort to suffer bureaucracy well, so he and the VA parted, and he set up his own shop intended to treat people with PTSD, who he assumed would be not just veterans, but victims of terrible events like natural disasters and car crashes. There were a few, but he quickly learned almost all of his patients were victims of domestic violence. The statistical fact of the matter is the actual terrorists in our society are our own family members, and domestic violence was triggering a mechanism in our bodies meant to protect us.

If you lock in your mind's eye for a second the standard anatomy chart picture of a human brain, you will not see the seat of the problem. What is visible from the exterior image of a whole brain is the outer cortex, by far the largest volume of the brain and where most of us live. This is what we think about when we consider brains, because this outer cortex is the seat of learning and intelligence. It processes language, thought, rationality, logic, exercises self-control, plays music, sees, and hears. In humans, it is exceptional and exceptionally large, even compared to close relatives like chimpanzees. This is the tool that gave us the world.

Yet the cortex wraps around a fist-sized knot of complicated little structures that make up the limbic system, a reptilian brain we share with all other animals, the inner brain. It guides automatic responses like breathing, yet it communicates with the higher brain in all sorts of complicated ways, especially in guiding emotions and memories. This is also where terror lives, in the inner, primitive brain, the limbic system.

Confronted with an immediate threat like an overpowering predator, not just humans, but all animals have the same response, and the first is to shut down that logical processing portion of the brain, an evolved reaction that is adaptive and necessary. No time for thought now. Thought, self-doubt, debate, and analysis take time, and delay will get you eaten. Response to an overwhelming threat is immediate and automatic, and immediate response is handled by the limbic system. Terror makes us go limbic, which triggers one of three overt responses, fight, flight, or freeze, depending on a species or an individual's status in the pecking order, the situation, or the animal's abilities. Yet this response is exquisitely tuned and refined by evolution, just as are responses to food and sex. These are the big three. Eat, reproduce, and avoid getting killed. Neurologists like to joke that all the brain's work, every single thought from hamster to human, distills to only three questions: Will it eat me? Can I eat it? Can I fuck it?

Each of these is visceral, but the terror response is literally so. Sometimes our language knows more than we do. The vagus nerve—it shares the same root word with "vagabond" because of the way it wanders—is the only nerve attached to the limbic system and it enervates everything in your guts from throat to gonads, your viscera. It comes alive during moments of terror to automatically increase heart rate and respiration and tense muscles, obvious and necessary measures as the body prepares for fight or flight. But there are less obvious steps and just as necessary, such as shutting off digestion and shutting off the immune system. Both are energetically expensive systems, so it would waste precious energy to run them during an emergency.

All of this is normal and necessary to our survival, which is to say, mindless terror is a normal response to an abnormal situation, not a mental disease. It triggers through a complex cascade of biochemistry that includes in the mix chemicals for turning this response off when the emergency abates. When the crisis passes, logic, thought, analysis all resume. But what if the abnormal threat is so persistent it becomes normal, as it does in domestic violence or in war? Over time, the mechanism for turning off terror atrophies, and some people begin living in a permanent state of what psychologists call "arousal," a permanent state of fight, flight, or freeze. Wrapped in this is a short circuit in the limbic system between short-term and long-term memory. Under normal circumstances, we face a frightening situation and then it goes away, so we file it as a memory to learn from, file it in a limbic structure called the hippocampus, but there is an adjacent structure called the amygdala, which is an emotional hot spot and the very center of terror. There are no memories in the amygdala; everything it contains is in the here and now. In a repeatedly traumatized person, memories do not move from amygdala to hippocampus. This explains flashbacks in the washed-out waste of a Vietnam vet living on the street in your town. He is not experiencing a memory, but is in that terrifying moment still stuck in his amygdala. The event is here and now.

Yet as difficult as all of this is for adults in our troubled world, the work of van der Kolk and others eventually caused us to understand there was an even more important dynamic in children, realizations that suddenly explained the great power of child abuse revealed in the ACE study, the effects that linger forty and fifty years.

The past decade has seen great advances in neuroscience that have upended some cherished assumptions. Chief among these are the concepts of neuroplasticity and neurogenesis. The first says the brain is malleable and changeable, so that various parts of it can learn new tasks. The old assumption was parts of the brain are hardwired to functions, so damage to a structure—from a stroke, for instance—meant the loss of that function. Not necessarily true. The second new concept—neurogenesis—says we can grow new neural pathways and cells as needed. These two ideas are the foundation of an important realization: the physical development of the brain is not a preordained process locked in place by genes and nutrition; it is a function of how an individual is treated.

Sometimes in lectures van der Kolk shows footage of World War I veterans with what was then called shell shock. A couple of them simply sit on beds and tremble in what is obviously excruciating terror. A couple of them try to walk assisted by others, and they cannot. They all look pretty much alike and yet van der Kolk says he has seen ten thousand cases of PTSD after Vietnam and not a single victim looked anything like the World War I vets suffering exactly the same condition. Same problem, whole different set of symptoms. In the lecture, he left it at that, but I got a chance later to ask him why different wars produced different symptoms. It was not the war; it was culture. The brain, he said, is a social organ. Its very physical structure—its chosen neural pathways and its pruned neural pathways—are functions of our relationships.

Much of this can be explained by the fact our brains are big, which places on humans an enormous burden, compared to all other species. Our brains are so big that infants' heads would not fit through the birth canal if they were born with a fully developed but small brain, as they are with fully developed but small feet, fingers, toes, and arms. An infant is, in fact, born with only the primitive, limbic, inner reptilian brain. The rest, the outer reasoning, logical, talking, singing, laughing human brain, only forms later, a process like building a ship in a bottle, over the course of about twenty years. Before maturity, a child's brain is a work in progress, meaning human infants are relatively helpless for much longer than any other species. This is the great burden of our species that dictates the imperative of family.

In the beginning the process of brain development is driven by the mother, the single most important relationship an individual will have or will not have. Infants have no intelligence, but they do have perceptions and mimicry and use them to form their brains. Mimicry of a smile builds the ability to smile;

they become what they see and feel. A colleague of van der Kolk's is particularly fond of a photo he has, a classic shot of an infant staring admiringly into a mother's eyes. Only he points out that the infant is staring into a particular eye with an opposite eye, left eye to left eye, right brain to right brain. The infant is downloading software, almost literally.

Given the importance of this relationship, we can begin to understand the importance of its absence or disruption, effects we need not imagine, but now can see. Abused and neglected kids have brains that are physically different from those of normal children. This we know now through magnetic resonance imaging and functional magnetic resonance imaging, MRI and fMRI. These sophisticated tools have revealed that, specifically, the prefrontal cortex of abused kids is smaller than that of normal kids, the area that processes language, logic, and self-control. The corpus callosum, that all-important structure that balances between right and left brain, is also smaller. A set of fMRIs done at Stanford University compares the brain response of a normal adolescent with one from a child with a known history of abuse. In each case, researchers showed the subject a generic photo of a friendly, smiling face, then recorded their brain's reaction to the photos. The normal kid's brain lights up, processing an emotional response. The traumatized kid's brain is dark, unlit, fails to even register a potential friend. Shown an angry face and a fearful face, the traumatized kid's brain lights up just as the normal child's does. He has learned to recognize anger and fear; he had to in order to survive.

The most critical difference, however, is that traumatized kids have a hypercharged limbic response, their adaptation to living in a house where a drunken stepfather might beat them night after night, or in a boarding school where a priest might sodomize them, or simply seeing their mother beaten—which, it turns out, is one of the worst things that can happen to a kid. Slowly they lose their ability to turn off the terror response. The pathway from logic to limbic becomes well worn, and they begin to live permanently in their terror-seized animal brains.

That habit of mind becomes their norm, and they take it into adulthood. The kind of psychic pain terror engenders builds as constant anger or arousal that needs to be shut down with alcohol or opiates, or it becomes a permanent numbness that has to be jolted with nicotine or cocaine. These are simply medications that work for the moment. So are the prescription drugs that are now eclipsing street versions as the drug of choice. Typically, abused children enter adulthood with bodies locked in terror mode, meaning compromised immune and digestive systems, and all of these problems begin to snowball to the tangled knot of difficulties teased out by the ACE study. These same people enter adulthood knowing nothing about relationships, other than what they were shown to be the norm, so the abused become abusers, another turn of the cycle. The brain is a social organ. These things run in families. They also can be fixed.

On assignment one time as a reporter, I began hearing about the pharmaceutical industry's influence on medical practice and so began asking a few MDs who were friends what they knew about overprescription of drugs. The story, they told me, was just the opposite, that finally medication had emerged that showed real promise for one of the most common problems they saw in their practices. This was in the late 1980s, when the medical model of psychiatric problems came to the fore; this is when we began to learn about SSRIs, selective serotonin reuptake inhibitors, a class of antidepressants. The thinking was, the neurotransmitter serotonin was greatly involved in what was then called clinical depression, so tweaking its presence in the brain was a cure for depression. I did some more interviews and wound up writing a story, not so much about drugs, but about depression. Finally I had a name for it, the thing I had been calling the "black hand" since I dropped out of the University of Michigan. A lot of people I knew in town came up to me after the story appeared and said, Thanks. Good to know.

Then I forgot about the whole deal. I had ridden out my own troubles for so long it had become a way of life, an ebb and flow that was my rhythm. But as I aged, I learned that what was true for many people was true for me, that the troughs between waves deepened and lengthened, and the depression was no longer bearable. So I became a solid citizen of the Prozac nation and remained one for about a dozen years. The good thing about antidepressants is they work for a lot of people, give some relief. So do nicotine and alcohol, the drugs of choice in self-medication, but nicotine and alcohol have side effects, your doctor will tell you. And besides, we have established a priesthood in the Prozac nation that sanctions the actions of guys in white coats or with couches and ample supplies of Kleenex. Their good offices provide the dispensation that removes the stain of self-medication and renders it simply as medication, just as a scoundrel can become a statesman by announcing he is "in treatment." And yes indeed, antidepressants do have side effects, judged to be more tolerable than those of street drugs of choice, but your physician will cheerfully prescribe yet another antidepressant to take the edge off the unwanted effects of the first.

Opium has been with us forever, but morphine, a natural component of opium, appeared in the nineteenth century and became the drug of choice of the Civil War. Remember, the fiddle tune, "Soldier's Joy," derived its name from the nineteenth-century euphemism for morphine. Wounded soldiers became addicted to morphine, likely even those suffering the invisible wounds we would come to call PTSD a century later. But the problem at the time was addiction, so a German company developed a synthetic version of morphine, heroin, and Bayer began marketing it in the United States as a cure for morphine addiction. Then another German company developed methadone. Remember methadone clinics, the cure for heroin addiction? Now methadone is a widely abused drug.

We know where this is headed. In June of 2011, *The New York Times* reported:

> The toll from soaring rates of prescription drug abuse, including both psychiatric medications and drugs for pain, has begun to dwarf that of the usual illegal culprits. Hospitalizations related to prescription drugs are up fivefold in the last decade, and overdose deaths up fourfold. More high school seniors report recreational use of tranquilizers or prescription narcotics, like Oxy-Contin and Vicodin, than heroin and cocaine combined.

The ACE study did indeed look at the relationship between abuse of illegal street drugs, as it did alcohol and tobacco, but also prescription antidepressants. In all cases, it found exactly the same stair-stepped, dose-specific response trending ever up with the severity of childhood troubles. If there is such a vast difference in medication and self-medication, why do they look so much the same on these stark graphs? I first saw these graphs in 2009, realized what I was seeing, and I resigned from the Prozac nation.

The network van der Kolk started, the National Child Traumatic Stress Network, has developed about forty "evidence-based" practices to treat kids with problems related to abuse. None of them involves medication and part of the research the network has published shows that kids with histories of abuse are often misdiagnosed with depression, anxiety, bipolar disorder, attention deficit disorder—often multiples thereof—and they are medicated. This is a particularly vexing problem for a couple of reasons. First, many of the medications in common use are not appropriate for kids, not tested on kids, and they have side effects that suppress their responses to the normal pleasures of life. That is, they insulate the kids from relationships that drive healthy social development and learning.

But second, the problems of abuse run with poverty. Note, for instance, that the ACE study showed about 14 percent of its middle-class, employed sample had ACE scores higher than four. Someone repeated this study on a group of Indian reservations, where poverty is epidemic and beyond the imagination of most non–Native Americans, and found about 35 percent had scores higher than four. Child abuse does occur in wealthy places, but it is rampant in the growing pockets of poverty across the nation. There is some assumption in the national discussion that poor people among us live pretty much like everybody else, they just have less money. But poverty for a kid means being raised by a single mother (one ACE point), who is stressed out and depressed (another), maybe self-medicates with the street drug she can get (another), and so neglects the kids (another), and from time to time in desperation makes a bad choice about a partner who beats the kids when she's not looking (one more).

Low-income kids who are diagnosed with psychological problems are eligible for Medicaid treatment, and a study completed by Rutgers University in 2010 showed Medicaid-eligible kids are four times as likely to be medicated with antipsychotics than other children are. That is to say, we deal with the manifest problems of their poverty with chemical restraints. This is where the medical model has brought us.

The alternatives are much easier and cheaper and seek to unwind the effects of trauma by understanding its visceral nature. There is indeed a long list, forty "evidence-based practices," but mostly this is a long list because psychologists are overfond of making up their own method, giving it a catchy, cutesy acronym, and detailing results in PowerPoint presentations at conferences. This is how careers advance. The simple fact is, all of these practices have some common elements. First, they are physical, that is, generally involve teaching kids basic steps like deep breathing and relaxation techniques. They must address the visceral root of the trauma response. As the children become proficient in these techniques, the therapist then ramps up the emotional level and teaches the kids to use the relaxation techniques to modulate arousal. Many kids who have been severely abused have a trauma trigger, a specific sight, sound, or smell that will trigger something that looks and acts like the flashback in Vietnam vets. As a kid gains skills in self-control, the therapist will often trip that trigger, then help the kids use the skills to confront the terror and calm down.

This all sounds simple enough, but on the neurological level, these approaches work the key divide in human behavior. These methods talk a kid out of going limbic, out of retreating into the fear of the reptilian brain. The successful therapies are using a growing understanding and skill in a kid's mind to talk her off the limbic ledge of her brain and into the logic and light of day of the frontal cortex. They are talking her into a place where she can live with the rest of us. This is how the mainstream therapists operate, but van der Kolk has departed from the mainstream in some significant ways. He, in fact, labels much of this work "yakking," his derisive term for talk therapy. His work has gone far more physical. He experiments with such ancient methods as qigong and yoga, practices of body movement that are thousands of years old. His reasoning is that war and suffering have always been with us, and societies have evolved time-tested ways to deal with them. He is fond of theater therapy, not just acting, but theater in the sense the ancient Greeks used it, chanting, public gathering, and venting of grief, anything, he says, that gets people together and moving together rhythmically.

I once saw a Shakespearean actor, Tina Packer, demonstrate

how she turns around the lives of juvenile delinquents with theater therapy. She uses Shakespeare because the language is powered with hard, blunt words that strike at the core of the human condition. In the demonstration, she used the murder scene from *Macbeth* and had two actors (one of them van der Kolk) face each other at agonizingly close range and repeat each word of each line maybe ten times, primal, blunt words like "father" and "murder," and then after each repetition she would interrupt with a question designed to evoke every possible connotation and association with the word. "Whose father? Your father? Why do you want to murder your father?" Not talk therapy, but an evocation of the deep emotional punch of words. She evokes this language of ours, the thing that holds us together.

A colleague of van der Kolk's, John Ratey, a neuroscientist at Harvard, says that dealing with many of the issues that plague children is simpler still, a matter of exercise. His prescription involves having kids exercise at levels that provoke about 75 percent of maximum heart rate for something like forty minutes a day, and he has demonstrated how this changes brain chemistry, including serotonin levels, but also dopamine, the neurotransmitter intimately wound up in addiction. Humans evolved to move. Humans evolved as the finest long-distance runners of any species on the planet, and we ignore the conditions of our making at great peril.

Van der Kolk especially likes a promising method of treatment called "neurofeedback," what he calls "rewiring the brain." The process looks about as simple as a video game, because it sort of is. A video game is used to reward the patient for activating neglected neural pathways, as measured by an electroencephalogram, electrodes on certain and varying parts of the patient's brain. As the patient turns on the desired circuits, the game on the video monitor goes well. There is no real connection to the brain other than the visual feedback of success, but somehow the patient learns to manipulate his own neural pathways. No one really knows how. Neural pathways are the technical term for habits of mind, and neglected ones can atrophy like unused muscles. This was the technique that got me off Prozac. I did a course of neurofeedback, and it helped.

Van der Kolk's group has distilled all of this to a simple set of principles to guide treatment, and everything they do fits within that framework. The first principle is attachment, a psychologist's term for our bond to one another. Kids raised by depressed or anxious or emotionally absent mothers do not learn that fundamental human skill of close connection with another human, and they go through life as angry little islands, but over time this can be gradually unwound.

The whole list of approved therapies go by the label of "evidence-based practices," but when I finally heard what van der Kolk was really saying about all this, it was because he distilled it down to a simple human interaction: "*The* evidence-based practice is relationship," he said.

The second principle is regulation, by which they mean teaching kids to not retreat to that limbic part of the brain, but to practice the habit of mind that allows logic. After a while all of this appears not so much as therapy, but as socialization, of learning the basic human skills that allow us to live together. Nor is there a bright line between the troubled and the well, those who need this sort of education and those who do not.

All of us are capable of going to the rage and irrationality of limbic life from time to time. Fight, flight, and freeze are deeply ingrained normal responses to abnormal situations, and we seem to live in abnormal times. The real question is, can we talk ourselves out of it when we need clear thought and foresight, the ability not to flee from a problem but to solve it.

In 2011, some researchers in the U.K. published results that concluded they could predict about 70 percent of the time whether a person was politically liberal or conservative using simple brain scans. This is truly a political diagnosis. The difference was simple, that the conservatives were more likely to go limbic when presented with a challenge; the liberals were more likely to apply reason and sort out a solution. My upbringing among fundamentalists, my long and close-up experience with the religious right and movement conservatism, says this is exactly right. These are the separate habits of mind that divide us.

This is not to say all conservatives were abused kids; there are other ways into this habit of mind. Nor is this to say that all conservatives are illogical; clearly some are not, and that is even more upsetting, because the logical ones must be deeply cynical. I would guess that the work of these researchers in the U.K. would come as no surprise to Karl Rove, Grover Norquist, or the Koch brothers. I think they figured it out by trial and error, and it explains the tone of discussion from the right: the lurid, screaming television advertising framed in the language of victimization, fear, and wedge issues. All of this is meant to trigger a limbic response and visceral reaction. They have learned that an atmosphere of permanent warfare and terror pushes more people into the limbic end of the world, where they are easily manipulated.

All of this is particularly vexing if we understand the limbic response evolved especially to allow us to address short-term threats. The grizzly bear was there and then he was not, and we were safe again. Through the deep history of time, through evolution, these were the only sorts of threats we faced, because we did not yet have the power to radically alter our world. Yet if we continue to inhabit our reptilian brain as a society and continue to yield to terror, we will remain a limbic society. Logic and science will not be available to us to solve long-term threats like global warming and overpopulation. We will not come out into the daylight of relationship and bonding that allows us to realize we are all in this together.

The day I buried my father's remains I learned there had indeed been physical abuse of children in the house I grew up in. My mother did it. I did not see it; it occurred when I was gone, usually when my brother and I were off with my father, specifically in the case of one terrible incident my sister remembers, when we boys and our dad left on those summer days to play Little League, maybe on the very day my brother and I mugged like men for the camera to record the image that sits on my office shelf today, my memento photo of two boys being boys. At the same time, my sister was mugging like a woman. She had, as little girls will do, sneaked into my mother's dresser, stolen makeup, and painted her face. She would have been about seven years old. My mother caught her, flew into a rage, and removed the makeup with scalding water as a way of punishing my sister for the sin of being a girl, the only girl in our family. It was not an isolated event.

Would it have stopped at this, I perhaps could even muster a rage and vented it on my mother more than fifty years later, but I know these things run in families. Blaming it on my mother would not explain all the absences that day at the graveyard of dead and imprisoned cousins, nor the clusters of alcoholism, suicides, isolation, and sadness in her own family. I suspected there was more to the story, so I asked more questions. There had, in fact, been sexual abuse in my mother's family, chronic sexual abuse. My grandfather did it. I don't know whether she was a direct or an indirect victim, but that terror, and the poverty she knew in the Great Depression, all would have helped explain her lifetime of fear and isolation, unable to bond with anyone around her, left to self-medicate on her family's drug of choice, the loving arms of Jesus.

One need not be a victim of child abuse and neglect to feel its effects. I couldn't explain my lifelong depression with anything other than some unresolved grief over the death of my brother and the sense of uselessness that derives from watching journalism, the work I loved, collapse in a lifeless heap. When you are a writer it's easy to believe that depression and high-functioning alcoholism pretty much go with the territory. I am not sure knowledge of what had happened in my family made this any easier to bear, but the truth is, I had not suffered a direct hit, just a glancing blow. I was raised among the walking wounded. As a child, I didn't have the tools to figure out what had happened to them, but I was smart enough to detach when it became necessary. Since then, however, Tracy, my wife, has taught me about attachment, which is to say love, so I'll be okay. I got lucky. It happens.

12

FIRE

My world will burn. This prophesy is not apocalyptic, merely a fact. I did not learn this from a hallucinatory revelation recorded by a band of illiterate shepherds a couple of millennia ago. I get this from people who have caught a glimpse of the coming Armageddon in rushing walls of fire real as rock. This is the reality of the twenty-first century, and I have a deep sense of satisfaction in knowing it is true.

Not this year, but soon. This year, here in the northern Rockies, we get water, floods this time. In fact, fire is, as I write this in late 2011, the furthest thing from our minds. The Pacific Northwest is at the tail end of a La Niña cycle, the wide swing in ocean currents that is a normal event and brings abnormally high amounts of rain and snow to this region. Only this time it wasn't normal, but epic, snow like we have never seen. Too soon to tell, but the best bet is we humans have already altered the planet enough with carbon dioxide to make the swing of normal cycles wider, deeper, longer. A warmer atmosphere holds more moisture, and it did this year, and dumped it on our mountains. More moisture, more clouds, so we did not see much of the sun from October through June. Normally, snow holds in the mountains only until the last week of May, first week of June, but it is July and most of it is still there, now coming off in a rush that has flooded not just the upper Columbia, but much of the Missouri Basin from here to Iowa, well into July.

The mirror image of this at the moment is a strip of the longest, most intense drought ever recorded in a swath of land from Georgia into Arizona. The Southwest normally dries during La Niña, but never like this. Global warming is not simply warming, but ever larger swings of normal cycles. Hurricanes more frequent. Stronger tornadoes that take out whole cities, as one did in Joplin, Missouri, this year. Ever fiercer floods and fires.

We of the northern Rockies are on the wet end of the cycle, but oscillation will bring us back to the bizarre summers of the last decade that we came to think of as normal. Soon, there will be little snow in the mountains in midwinter and shirt-sleeve days in February, welcome at first, but alien to those of us whose ancestry tracks through 35,000 years above the 45th parallel. Then comes summer, no rain all of July and record highs, and we will burn, not just in fires of a few thousand acres, but the whole end of a state. Whole towns inhaled. Maybe even cities. It's happened before, and it is going to happen again. The setup is the red trees, not just the ponderosa pine, but lodgepole and whitebark pine, and even the Douglas fir, all the trees. Global warming set this up by enabling pine beetles in all of the Rockies from Colorado to British Columbia, the red trees I spoke of earlier. Red trees burn like bombs. For the past few years, I have watched these forces align not with dread, but with anticipation. This is near-continental-scale upheaval at hand, grand and glorious retribution by nature. Odd now that I find myself only a half step removed from the fire-and-brimstone preachers of my childhood, people who, if they couldn't convince me at least tried to scare the hell out of me by invoking an angry God willing to burn me up if I did not repent my evil ways.

The deal is, we had a chance to repent. For more than twenty years solid, credible basic science told us increasing carbon dioxide in the atmosphere would yield catastrophic results. Now we are further from consensus and further from mending our ways than we were when science first realized this. We are in denial deepened by the willed ignorance of people like my parents and deliberately manipulated by the interests vested in preserving the status quo of an energy society.

The irony in this is that the deniers are at bottom not unscientific; they are insisting we do a science experiment, that we do science. Global warming is not a theory but a hypothesis, a reasonable conjecture based on observation and modeling. Science moves beyond hypotheses by testing them with experiments. But for three decades, climate scientists have been doing nothing so much as urging us not to run this experiment, not to test the hypothesis. For a couple of good reasons. First, we don't have another planet to serve as a control, so it's not a valid experiment, and second, we don't have another planet. But the deniers have insisted. Very well. The discussion is over. Inaction has decided we will run the experiment, and we will get a result. No point in arguing about this anymore.

Do I take some satisfaction now in seeing the deniers punished with hellfire? Yes I do. But not much. The oil barons, investment bankers, and conservative propagandists are not likely to suffer all that much in the coming plague. That's precisely the point of their manipulation, that they can hog enough wealth in a world of diminishing resources and increasing misery to ensure that fire does not touch their multimillion-dollar mansions at the ski resort and flood and hunger do not take their children. The rich will escape the judgment of fire. I am not expecting justice in this new world. I welcome the judgment of fire for more complicated reasons. The truth is, there is something more in this setup for fire than global warming.

In the summer of 2007 when my place was besieged by fire, the people here talked a lot about 1910. It was our best precedent. In the early part of the twentieth century, the northern Rockies saw the first real attempt to domesticate the landscape, when timber barons threaded railroads up tight mountain canyons, across jury-rigged trestles, and through narrow tunnels punched through mountain rock with sledgehammers and dynamite. The goal of all of this activity was logging off the forests, which created a weird set of conditions, including piles of tree limbs—dead limbs loggers call "red needle slash." Then came trains drawn by sparking, screeching locomotives. The combination set a series of fires that no one paid much attention to until later summer drought and wind fanned them to join as an almost continuous wall of flames. In the matter of a few days, fire ran from St. Maries, Idaho, to Missoula, Montana, a distance that is today spanned by an interstate highway that takes three hours to drive at top speed. That fire burned about three million acres with an official death toll of eighty-five humans.

In 2007, I interviewed George Weldon, the official at the U.S. Forest Service responsible for firefighting in all of the northern Rockies, a man well aware of the 1910 precedent. We were then beginning to think what had been unthinkable only a decade before, that we could once again see fires of the 1910 scale in the northern Rockies. Did Weldon think it possible?

"Absolutely," he said. "It's not a question of if; it is a question of when."

It remains a question of when, and this is not simply the fault of global warming, but also the Forest Service's response to 1910, a fire that shocked the nation, sparked a politically charged debate, and demanded a response from the agency. Forestry was then a new "science" in the United States, largely fostered by the Progressive movement, specifically by Theodore Roosevelt's cocksure and combative chief of forestry, Gifford Pinchot. The Pinchot family had rooted the science in the country by founding the famous Yale School of Forestry and his response was to dispatch Yale-trained foresters to Missoula in the aftermath of the fire, foresters known as "little Pinchots." They created the 10 A.M. rule. The foresters then set to work developing the tools, techniques, and bureaucracy to carry out that rule, and for many years were successful. Fires occurred, but were kept relatively small to avoid a "timber famine." The real result was a totally unnatural landscape. Both lightning and Indians had started fires in forests long before the Yalies arrived. Most forests in the northern Rockies saw fires frequently before Europeans came. The result was more savanna than forest with a few stately ponderosa pine towering over a grassy forest floor. Young trees were snuffed by periodic fires. As a result of fire suppression, however, forests became choked with trees, meaning choked with fuel, and so readily burned. Fire suppression had stored energy in the forests, overwinding a spring that would eventually have to be unwound. This factor was as much in play in the sweeping fires of 2007 as was global warming.

That is to say, with motives that none of us would question, with education and armed with the best science of the day, the Yalies did as much to damage this environment as global warming. In complicated systems, the road to hell can indeed be paved with good intentions.

Those 1910 fires spawned a legacy beyond policy; they created a swaggering can-do culture of firefighters that I know well. This is especially true of smokejumpers, guys and now some women who to this day parachute from light aircraft directly into forest fires. They are the elite troops of firefighting, physically fit, tough, and macho, even the women. George Weldon was himself a smokejumper as a younger man and freely acknowledges adopting the swaggering hubris of his trade. But during that interview in 2007, I saw something different coming to the surface.

Once, firefighters believed they commanded nature. "We were trained that we could put out any fire," Weldon said. "All we needed was more air tankers, more smokejumpers, and more hotshot crews. . . . In the 1970s and 1980s we were able to basically exclude fires from these fire-dependent ecosystems mainly because it rained a lot. We thought it was because of us. But mainly it was because it used to rain."

Federal bureaucrats like to take credit for solving problems, especially when the problem threatens to wipe out an entire town, as fires did indeed threaten the towns during the summer of 2007. But Weldon and other firefighters did not take that credit in 2007. They openly admitted it was a matter of the sheerest of luck. Wildfire has a way of doing that, teaching a sense of humility. It's why I live where I do. Wild landscapes do not long tolerate hubris. But at bottom, all of the world is a wild landscape.

To this day, I can walk into any café or cocktail party in western Montana and provoke an informed discussion about the 1910 fire. It is a part of our common story here, a founding myth, which has always been a matter of pride to me, always left me feeling fortunate to live in a place beset by an unprecedented fire that spawned an enduring awareness of place. But the problem is 1910 is not unprecedented. Only a few years before, there had been a series of sweeping catastrophic fires in the Upper Midwest. The nation's leading fire historian, Stephen J. Pyne, summarizes: "There will be little violence done to history to construct from the various single accounts a single composite narrative. It can apply with equal verity to the Wisconsin (Peshtigo) and Michigan fires of 1871; the Michigan fires of 1881; the Minnesota (Hinckley),

Wisconsin and Michigan fires of 1894; the Minnesota, Wisconsin and Michigan (Metz) fires of 1908."

Metz? Wait. I knew that name somehow, but when I read Pyne, couldn't remember why. But Metz stood out from the composite for another reason, that it was very large and fast, in fact burned across 2.5 million acres in a matter of a day or so, and it killed a lot of people, thirty-seven. Most of them, some of them women and children, died trapped in a railroad boxcar after the fire warped the rails and the Detroit and Mackinac train jumped the track. Here was a fire that indeed provided precedent for the 1910 fire that still shapes the culture and understanding of my place. The fact is, this should not have been news to me at all. The town of Metz for which the fire was named is about ten miles from Manning Hill. The fire itself burned south to the Thunder Bay River near the village of Long Rapids, where I played as a kid. It would have been clearly visible from my grandfather's farm when he was a young man working that land. More than visible, it would have been pivotal in shaping that landscape and its people. Reading through the list of the dead, I recognized family names wound in the history of my own. Yet in growing up, I cannot ever remember hearing mention of this fire. No one told me stories about a 1908 Michigan fire of the sort that are common and regular today, here in Montana, about a 1910 fire. Certainly some of this has to be selective memory, but I fact checked this with an uncle. Did his father ever tell him about the fire that was a pivotal event in his life? My grandfather would have been fifteen at the time, my great-grandfather was still alive and running the farm. No, Dale Manning said, they hardly ever talked about it.

They would not have talked about it because the story they told themselves would not accommodate wildfire. My ancestors were farmers and had been for a very long time. Those who were not farmers were loggers, in fact, my direct ancestors, the Richardsons, were likely profiting heavily from the very logging that created the conditions that fed this fire. But they were not logging in the sense of forestry. The Northeast and the Upper Midwest were both deliberately clear-cut with no intention of creating a lasting relationship with the forest. The idea was to clear the land for farmers. It was an act of domestication, of taming the land, and it in fact succeeded, in the limited sense of a short-term conquest of nature. After 1908, the landscape I grew up in had been so radically altered by logging and fires, it was no longer sufficiently wild to support wildfires. Infernos like 1908 are no longer possible near Manning Hill nor anyplace in the Upper Midwest. It is tame.

To be sure, the original settlers in western Montana had something similar in mind. So did the little Pinchots dispatched after the 1910 fire here in Montana. They meant to tame the landscape, the driving force behind fire suppression, but also behind the extermination of the bison, grizzly bears, and wolves. And they would have tamed this place were it possible, but the land is too rugged and remote, too steep, rocky, and cold in winters to accept this story. Over time the land has taught us that its resistance to domestication has value in its own right, that we can learn something from this, accept limits, be awed, develop humility. Some of us have learned the value of wilderness for its own sake, and now, as the world changes around us, all of us need to learn this.

My story to here has been greatly preoccupied with my struggle against religion and ignorance, my mother's story, but the truth is, I have learned to distrust my father's family's story as well, the farmers and loggers who tamed the land. I can best explain this with a religious story, the story of Job.

The conservative columnist and former Nixon speech-writer William Safire was, like me, fascinated by the story of Job for similar reasons. In his book on the topic he wrote: "The Book of Job delights the irreverent, satisfies the blasphemous, and offers at least some comfort to the heretical."

As one who is cheerfully guilty of all three counts, I agree. And part of the satisfaction I draw matches Safire's, that the religious fundamentalists misread Job. Those of us used to present-day propagandists among the faithful are forever vexed by their twisting of the text, that their readings of science, or politics, or simple matters of fact enter a never-never land of babel. If you are among the people so vexed, take some comfort in their ability to do exactly the same with the King James version of the Bible. Job was taught in the Sunday Schools where I was incarcerated and preached from the pulpit of Greely Baptist Church by the Reverend Norris Beck. And the message was that God, on a bet with Satan, pretty much mercilessly abused Job as a test, and that Job passed with flying colors, refusing to curse God. Bullshit. The text reveals otherwise, that Job blasphemously called out God and challenged him in no uncertain terms. Safire, the conservative, celebrates Job as "the first dissident," the guy who would go so far as to summon God and demand justice. Job had a problem submitting to authority.

Yet the more interesting element of the story of Job is it contradicts itself. It reads like a cut-and-paste job, as indeed it probably was. The fundamentalists explicitly believe that everything in the Bible is the word of God, the indirect work of a single author. In effect, they treat it as if God hammered out all of it on his iPad in a single draft, bypassed copyediting, and set it straight to type. (Infallibility has its benefits.) Biblical scholarship, the idea of examining the layers of text and translations, is explicitly circumscribed by fundamentalists and has been since Billy Sunday preached that the Bible scholarship popular in Germany at the beginning of the twentieth century was responsible for World War I. The Reverend Sunday notwithstanding, the Bible is a palimpsest, and the layers reveal much.

For instance, the story of Job does indeed get a happy ending, that Job still thinks God is okay and all that has been taken from him is restored. Yet this ending is so inconsistent with the rest of the story that some scholars believe it was a tacked-on bowdlerization meant to redeem an otherwise blasphemous text. Christians couldn't deal with the harsher questions the story raised without a smiley-face ending. Having lived among the faithful, this explanation rings true to me, but I am more interested in the fundamental conflict of Job that offers a more profound illumination. Like *Beowulf,* the *Odyssey* of Homer, *Njal's Saga,* the Icelandic Sagas, and the tales of King Arthur, the Bible drew its text from oral tradition that preceded it by hundreds of years, and made its way to print at the same time (relative to each of the cultures) that produced those other enduring texts, as writing became possible.

Generally and in broad terms, this coincides with civilization, the advent of farming and settled society. Hunters and gatherers have very different expectations from their gods than do farmers. Hunters learn to live with the ebb and flow, learn to roll with the punches. They can coexist with the capricious gods of wilderness. Famers, however, need to be assured they will reap what they sow, as the Bible explicitly promises. They need to know that if they plant seeds, rain will come and they will harvest, that rivers will rise to provide irrigation, that there will be order and predictability to their lives. The story of Job evolved as the people of the Middle East made this transition, and it remembers capricious gods, but begins to demand a just God. This is Job's great frustration when he literally calls God out. He compiles a long list of injustices committed against him and then calls God into accounting, and it is worth here quoting Safire's setup along with Job's speech:

> The oath is Job's gauntlet thrown at God's feet, the most irreverent moment in Scripture. Job concludes his speeches with these lines, demanding a written list of charges against him and promising a ringing defense in any fair adjudication:
>
> *Let me but call a witness in my defense!*
> *Let the Almighty state his case against me!*
> *If my accuser had written out his indictment,*
> *I would not keep silent and remain indoors.*
> *No! I would flaunt it on my shoulder*

and wear it like a crown on my head;
I would plead the whole record of my life
and present that in court as my defense.

An indictment? From God? Job uses legalistic language in an attempt to draw God into a contractual relationship. Contracts are the very cornerstone of civilization, because they enable commerce. People used writing to record transactions and contracts long before using it to record stories. Contracts say, "if I give you this, then you have to give me that," a completely necessary understanding in commerce, but a terribly narrow view of the creation. Whoever wrote the Book of Job understood this contradiction and so the God that thunders back an answer to Job's blasphemy is not the God of farmers—as Job is clearly wishing him to be—but a God who has been handed down to this story by hunters. Again, it is worth quoting God along with Safire's play-by-play:

"Who is this whose ignorant words cloud my design in darkness? . . . Where were you when I laid the earth's foundations? Tell me if you know. . . ."

This is the scathing voice of a blustering God infuriated by Job's presumption. The doggedly questioning human, with his fierce courage and his inescapable oaths, has forced the divine hand; God, not Man, is now on trial and must defend the cosmic management. But God, as Job had feared, blows away the court—resists the plea to explain his purpose in torturing Job. Instead, using lofty poetic images, God flexes his muscles and mocks the man's effrontery by showing the chasm be-tween creator and created: "Have you descended to the springs of the sea or walked the unfathomable deep? Have the gates of death been revealed to you? Have you ever seen the door-keepers of the place of darkness? Have you comprehended the vast expanse of the world? Come tell me all this if you know?"

This is a snarky, mean-spirited, taunting God, and one we ought to know better, and we will, now that we have challenged the earth's foundations. We moderns and postmoderns may take some comfort in our disbelief, in knowing there is no angry, bearded old man in the sky pulling the strings of our fate, but this comfort dissolves in knowing the sky itself is angry. The God of wilderness is perfectly willing to rain down fire and chaos just to remind us we were not present when the earth's foundations were laid.

It has been said that all of the New Testament is an attempt to counter the Book of Job; certainly all of civilization and Christianity is an attempt to bring order to chaos, to tame by forcing the creation into a contract. More to the point, religion is an attempt to overcome mortality, the ultimate inconvenience forced on us by nature. The contract is explicit: "For God so loved the world, that he gave his only begotten Son, that whosoever believeth in him should not perish, but have everlasting life." Believe in the lord Jesus Christ and thou shalt be saved, granted eternal life. This contract, however, is only the reductio ad absurdum of the larger Western tradition. My father's fathers did not bargain for eternal life, but they, as farmers, implicitly engaged in the more fundamental pact of civilization, that if we plant we will reap, that if we tame a landscape, we get some protections from the capricious God willing to rain fire. Mostly they got away with it and sustained a satisfying illusion of control.

Indeed, this illusion of contract is not limited to farmers. It is precisely the impulse, for instance, that carried the Yalies to the northern Rockies to forever banish fire, an illusion of control backed by limited understanding. Not their fault; they didn't know any better. Science in its infancy—and even a lot of science now—is necessarily reductionist. It needs to weed out all of the extraneous factors in order to reduce a problem to fit within our understanding. It needs a model that fits easily within linear equations: input, process, output. The good thing about this oversimplification is it mostly works within normal circumstances. Using it, we can build steam engines, grow grain, make airplanes fly, and do heart surgery. Yet in all fields of science, as knowledge progresses, it comes up against the limits imposed by complexity. We must finally confront the fact that at the edges, all of life is complex and unpredictable, other than for a few simple facts like we live, breathe, and die.

I can't criticize reductionist thinking, because I did some of my own. The oversimplification that is input, process, and output is sometimes called the industrial model, and for most of my career, I practiced and believed in industrial model journalism, a belief that my job was to provide information as input and that a rational process would deliver an output of sound policy—straight, clean, and neat. It maybe even worked once at a simple level, say a village council. But real life is messy, capricious, and complex. Humans are capable of logic but also of willed stupidity, greed, xenophobia, intolerance, and brutality. Humans are going to do what they are going to do. That's always been true. What has changed is there are a lot more of us, we are capable of ever increasing levels of violence at ever increasing scale, and we have radically altered the conditions of life with global warming. It is the last I fear the most.

The one lingering question that vexes me in trying to unwind my story is the persistent fidelity to north, not just in my immediate family, but in every ancestor I can account for and, indeed, in my own DNA extracted in a cheek swab. The two lineages it could trace, Y chromosome and mitochondrial DNA, tracked to at least thirty thousand years ago near what is now northern Spain or southern France, what would have then been the very northern limit of human habitat, because the rest of the continent was then sheeted in ice. Why would these people have gone as far north as possible and stayed there for thousands of years until it became possible to go further north into the British Isles and then they went there and stayed there for thousands more? I can't answer this, but I can answer something about the fidelity of these genes to northern latitudes in the past six thousand or so years, the factor that kept my more immediate ancestors above the 45th parallel for almost four hundred years in North America. They were farmers; they had entered a contract with nature.

European agriculture is specifically based in wheat and beef and so evolved to exist in the temperate regions of the world. It works best in temperate grasslands and forests. In fact, if you look at the great temperate regions of the world today, not just north but antipodal, you will notice something odd, especially in the temperate grasslands.

Temperate grasslands are in northern Europe, a broad band from Siberia stretching west across Germany and France, but also in North America, in South America in the Pampas, in New Zealand and Australia, and in South Africa. These are the places where most of the world's agricultural exports come from. They grow wheat and beef. But they are also places of European surnames and European languages. It's not that European farmers didn't try to colonize places like sub-Saharan Africa or Asia. They did, but in those other places, they mostly failed. The contract with nature failed.

We farm temperate regions because it is relatively easy to do so. The winters kill off pests and make insects and disease tolerable. Rains are predictable. Soil is deep from millennia of organic investment by prairies and forests. Where these farmers run into trouble is up against the edge of these places. For instance, the last of North America's grasslands to come under the plow was here in Montana, in an arid region that gets about ten inches of rain a year. Too dry for wheat, and when we plowed up that land, we created the Dust Bowl, still the greatest environmental disaster in American history, recent oil spills notwithstanding.

Biologists and agronomists often refer to these arid, harsh environments as "brittle," meaning you can't bend them very far before they break. It's a good adjective, but so also is "chaotic." Unpredictable. Wild. Behemoth. Leviathan. Brittle landscapes resist taming, will not enter the contract of domestication. They are more important to us now than any other sort of place for this very reason. The point is: global warming is about to make much of the planet brittle, chaotic, and unpredictable. Before global warming, we could go about our business relatively confident that a given action would produce a given outcome, input, process, output. This is no longer so. All bets are off. Fire and flood will teach us humility.

This is the understanding that allows me to decode what now passes for public discussion in our nation, the echo chamber that is the habitat of the chattering classes. I hear our nation's discourse run through and through with echoes of the sort of denial that was the ruin of my parents' lives, the very thing that drove them mad, drove them to superstition and faith healers and early graves. I hear the bargaining and rationalizations, but the lessons of the wild have moved me beyond anger to bemusement. You have no idea of the earth's foundations. The gates of death are about to be revealed to you.

It may be age or it may be where I have been, but I have abandoned thinking of these matters in immediate terms. Or it may be that humanity's ignorance and irresponsibility have forced us now into catastrophe that can only be righted in geologic time. In any event, I find myself taking Aldo Leopold's advice to think like a mountain. I remember now that this was the thought that struck me when I first saw mountains on that first visit to Glacier National Park in 1978, that I sat before the sheer rock mass of the thing for a solid afternoon marveling at nothing so much as my own insignificance. This is scale. This is time. This massif is but a small piece of the earth's foundations, and against this, you and your ideas are nothing. Yet on the face of every mountain, no matter how implacable and forbidding, one almost always sees a shelf or outcrop, often with one single scrawny tree rooted in rock. Life may not be as implacable as a mountain, but at least it is stubborn.

We are entering a time of chaos, not as apocalyptic a pronouncement as it sounds. We have always lived in chaos, at least at the edges. But we are also entering a time of catastrophic upheaval, and I mean that in the biological sense. We have, in fact, been easing our way into catastrophe since we began farming and burning coal. Catastrophe is how science marks the epochs of geologic time, when some global-scale disaster like the crash of an asteroid foments mass extinction and resets the rules of life. The measure of catastrophe is simple: the number of extinctions, and by any measure we have met that measure. For all of time, only geologic time reveals how these matters work out, and this time is no different. My prophecy speaks of fire, but this is not apocalyptic, just fire, just change. We who live with fire know the flames create beginning, just as much as they create end.

This, of course, fails to predict what will happen to the human experiment, a two-million-year-long field trial of hyperintelligence, adaptability, and mobility. I have no idea. Remember, we are in chaos now, and all bets are off. Given our skills, we are probably destined to be among the last animals standing, so it seems unlikely we could unleash forces that will wipe out humanity. The science writer David Quammen gave the best assessment of the possibility of human extinction: "My quibbles with the idea are it seems ecologically improbable and seems too optimistic."

Life is stubborn.

We are, however, smarter about these things than Job was; that's the nature of science, imperfect, but progressive. We do, in fact, know something of the earth's foundations, and the rest of the universe as well. Were there a God and were he inclined to hand down stone tablets at Mount Sinai, he would understand today that he need inscribe only three immutable laws, that energy is neither created nor destroyed, that entropy increases, and that there is no such state as zero energy. These are the laws of thermodynamics. This is the holy trinity, and the greatest of these is entropy. Entropy dictates that the center will not hold. Things fall apart.

Yet it happens that there came a force, maybe just on this planet, but maybe not, for putting things together. There is a crystal that can sort the vast array of chemicals to pick and choose in order to assemble amino acids in meaningful, enduring, functioning arrays called life. Ultimately, these crystals, deoxyribonucleic acid, DNA, boot-strapped to increasing complexity enabling motion, reaction, propagation, self-protection, fear, flight, joy, thought, creation. DNA is information in the rawest sense of the word, a simple four-letter code capable of producing order and complexity beyond imagination. Given time, information too evolves in three stages in increasing degrees of complexity: from raw information, then to knowledge, then to wisdom. Given enough information and time, we can achieve knowledge. Given enough information and knowledge, wisdom is at least possible. DNA, information, raises the possibility of eternal life. Information battles the increasing disorder of entropy. This is the creative tension that will decide how all this works out. Now and forever, entropy's disorder pushing against DNA's order, the irresistible force and the immovable object.

13

26.2

Sometimes when I am traveling in the developing world, I prefer to fly. True, one misses a lot of detail from altitude, but I had already spent the week bouncing around the back roads of Panama, interviewing pineapple farmers, assessing erosion on *fincas*, mostly overwhelmed, as I have been in dozens of countries, by pervasive and wretched poverty. It's pretty much the same the world over, but in Panama the backdrop is a punch line. The Panama Canal threads through many scenes in surreal perspective. Frequently one sees a literal backdrop of a ship sliding silently behind the shacks and squalor, decks piled with cargo containers of flat screens, iPads, and SUVs headed for luxury markets.

After a couple of days of this, I had had my fill of bouncing on back roads in under-sprung pickup trucks, mostly stuck in traffic. Besides, I didn't have much time. I had wrapped up my interviews for the week's work, doing mostly what I have done my whole life: traveling with a skinny notebook in my hip pocket, withdrawing it periodically to write down what people said, then rendering it to books or magazine stories. But that work was done for this day, and now I had just the weekend to find him. I had managed to keep track of him, more or less, until about six months earlier, then his cell phone no longer worked. When I'd call, I'd hear a leave-a-message recording that was a child singing in Spanish. I'd left messages, but the callback never came.

I didn't have much to go on besides a cell phone number. His name, of course, I had that, and he was thought to be living in Los Santos Province, a lump of land on the Pacific side west of Panama City, and that he had taken up with some old German woman. This was something, and probably I could find him.

Flying to the backwaters of small countries means small aircraft, and I've learned to like this. I felt at peace for the first time in days as the DeHavilland Twin Otter lifted out of a little airport in the Canal Zone for a less than hour flight north to Chitré on August 25, 2007. The deep blue Gulf of Panama stretched below, divided by parallel lines of ships queuing for or leaving the canal. In less than an hour, I hopped off the Otter into what could have been a small-town bus station in the jungle. By the time I had grabbed my bag, the airport was mostly deserted. I found a woman closing up the ticket counter and asked about a cab. She called one, promising me a driver who spoke English. My Spanish is good enough to get a cab and order drinks, but not nearly good enough to do what I needed to do at Los Santos, so I wanted help, and anywhere you go in the world, the right cabdriver can speed you toward what needs to be done. Then I waited along a deserted parking lot for a half hour. The cab came, and the driver did not speak English, but he had begun studying English, and his English teacher was his aunt, and we could get her on the cell phone if needed, so we proceeded on to Chitré, then to the police station at the next town over, Los Santos. Police, because I had heard he had caused some trouble and the police may have heard of him, not criminal exactly, but the sort of irritants one expects from a stubborn old man who has lost his grip: bragging, rage, fanciful threats toward neighbors. Specifically, he had been threatening people on the streets by claiming to have once been a cop and to have learned a secret choke hold able to snuff people instantly. He had been a cop for a year or so almost sixty years before.

"Manning?" No, they had heard nothing of a gringo named Manning. Maybe south a few kilometers, out the macadam road to *la playa*, a small development of slapped-togther retirement homes for gringos. Out there they might know. Or at least this is how auntie's translation comes to me over the cabdriver's cell phone.

So my driver and I, we drive. We meet an American getting out of his compact pickup truck and ask him. Nope, doesn't know him. But he can make some calls. He knows people, but first we approach locals drinking Cokes under a *palapa* at a *tienda* nearby. It is beginning to rain. The American's Spanish is not all that much better than mine, but enough to tell the locals we are looking for an old man. What does he look like?

they ask in Spanish. I answer in Spanish. Like me, I say. Just like me, only older. He may have a beard. I had heard he has commanded children here to call him "Santa Claus," so he may be hiding behind a big white beard and flowing hair. I had never seen him with a beard, but maybe.

"*Muy religioso?*" one asks.

Fuck, I say to myself. They've got him. "Yeah, *muy religioso.*"

A flash of recognition surges in the locals' discussion of this, then one delivers the first Spanish words I ever remember that hurdled straight across translation to plant a pure print in my brain: "*El señor está muerto.*"

Which is, of course, pretty much what I expected, at least half expected, to find my father dead and to spend a couple of days fighting off some guilt for my negligence in the matter, despite his lifelong negligence toward me, toward my six siblings, toward reality. Instead I began thinking of logistics. There would need to be a death certificate. How did he die? What have these people done with his wasted old carcass?

"*Cuándo?*" Maybe last year. Not possible, I tell them. I talked with him by telephone only four months ago. Or did I? One's account of time grows vague in periods of negligence. But maybe this is a contradictory fact that says this story is not over.

My new gringo friend is convinced my father is dead and, like I say, he knows people. He knows a guy, Misael Banda, a Panamanian who lived half his life in the U.S. and now lives here among the retired gringos and handles details for them, like making sure Social Security checks continue to flow. Of course he could handle such a detail for an old German woman, to suppress a death certificate and such so that Social Security checks might continue to flow and deposit even though the payee is dead, and this occurs to me. And of course her best strategy would be to not answer the old man's cell phone and not return calls. My new friend says he will call Banda. It's Saturday, and there is not much more to do, so my cabdriver and I head back to Chitré where I overtip him, then check into a hotel. Overtip because I want him back first thing in the morning so we can check hospital records, city hall, round up the usual stuff.

At my hotel, there's a decent little patio restaurant and a bar that supplies the first bottle of wine to help me begin the drilling down. Then I notice my new gringo friend a few tables away. There are not all that many decent places for dinner in Chitré, and it turns out my hotel is one of them. He tells me he has called Banda. Left a message. I thank him and return to my bottle.

Then the bartender hands me a phone. "Is this Richard Manning?" a man's thin voice asks.

"It is. But who is this?"

"This is Harold Manning."

"The hell it is." I blurt this out without any forethought, because I already know for a fact my dad is dead. He assures me he is not, then puts the German woman on, and she tells me how to get to the house they live in near the village of Guararé maybe twenty-five kilometers south. She gives me a cell phone number so she might talk my driver in, as necessary.

It's mid-morning when we make the left turn off Highway 2, as instructed, at the Guararé Texaco station, accent on the second syllable of Texaco. We bump up a narrow road less than a kilometer to a gray little shack of a house, and I see my old man, sitting in a straight chair on the veranda. He does have a full white beard and shoulder-length white hair. He looks like an Old Testament prophet or a madman, if there is indeed a difference between the two. Same wild eyes, my own eyes. He is seventy-six. I'd never known him to be anything but clean-shaven, with a flat-top buzz cut. He had screamed at me and threatened me with violence when, in the 1960s, I had grown a beard and long hair. I was old enough then to tell him to go fuck himself—one of the best days of my life.

We shake hands. That's how we've always greeted. Shake hands. Smile. Fall back on the pleasantries you've heard all your life and get through this. Preserve distance.

Now I get to know Bridgette, the old German woman, and now the story my gringo friend has told me, what he learned from Banda, begins to make some sense. That's how my dad found me at the hotel, through Banda, who had indeed handled some details for him. Bridgette was a tough old skate. She had lived a missionary gig of a life with her Baptist preacher husband, and they had moved to Los Santos to live out their declining years. Her husband had died the year before (that's the death the locals were remembering) and he had looked much like my father, so when she found my father, sick, pathetic, living like a homeless bum in Guararé, raving mad and an object of ridicule, she took him in. She was the sort who took people in. All the time I was trying to talk to my father, two subteen kids were raising hell in the shack's little living room, a cheap old portable TV turned to cartoons playing full blast. Bridgette had taken them in when their mother abandoned them. Apparently she specialized in abandonment and hard cases, people whose families did not want them.

She'd straightened out my dad's Social Security checks, got them flowing again, $1,000 a month, and this financed her life and three others, if she hustled. And it was not long before I recognized her as the kind of woman I had known my whole life, saw in her bits of my aunts and grandmother, straightforward, blunt people of a certain sort: if you give her chickens she will give you eggs. I think my earlier suspicions that she was scamming the old man were unfounded.

She took great pains to tell me what a wreck my old man had been before she took him in. She told me he had gotten up that morning before dawn and had sat rigidly in that straight veranda chair looking down the road for me for four straight hours.

My old man didn't seem to have much memory left, at least not short-term. We talked some old stories, and he got those well enough, but was foggy on details of yesterday. Yes, he still had his cell phone, but couldn't figure out how to replenish the minutes and had forgotten to have one of the kids do it, and so it hadn't worked for a few weeks. Maybe it was months, he couldn't remember. I called the number to make the phone ring so he could find it in the shack.

I began making plans to bring him home, then remembered that he had never, ever held a clear idea of home, at least as long as I had known him, at least since he left Manning Hill. No matter where he was, he was always far from home, part of why I am who I am and so could begin the line of logic I would rely on to effect my escape from this scene. I remembered what nursing homes are like for poor, for old Americans in the early-twenty-first-century United States. I looked at the clear blue Panamanian sky, heard children giggle, and saw the chickens in the yard and the fresh fish neighbors had brought him. I ate some fish. I gave the old man what cash I had, then we shook hands. I called my cabdriver to start me on the first leg of a trip toward a jet airplane that would take me home. It took most of a lifetime, but I have learned what he could not. I have learned where my home is.

From that day in August of 2007 until this one I have been unable to answer the obvious and simple question of whether I did the right thing in leaving him in Panama. It is a large question, large enough to generate the story that has unwound in these chapters. This story I have told is at its heart a simple matter, an account of what transpires between a father and son, what one generation gives to and gets from another. What I got from him for sure was the ability to turn and walk away. Did I abandon him? Betray? Did I get my revenge for cold nights alone in Michigan, nothing but a boy against the winter night, no fire? Did I abandon him, or did I act from respect, knowing that neither he nor I can ever preserve any sense of dignity without self-reliance? He believed, all people in his line believed and I believe, that when you cannot take care of yourself it is time to die. And he did die. I left him there alone in a Panama jungle, and he died a year later of hepatitis, likely an infection transmitted by the filth he lived in. But I asked him, and he said no. He wanted to stay where he was. I could have lawyered up and forced him to come home against his will, had him committed, but it didn't seem right after I had asked him if he wanted to stay.

Wouldn't he have done the same for me? Done the same to me?

Years on, and I am driving across northern Michigan on a sweltering July day, a visit to relatives that most people in that place would find normal. I only later understand this is an extraordinary trip, made so because I am really there to find the last person living with the power to grant me absolution. I find my Uncle Dale, my dad's brother, doing well, working, building, a house, the sixth he finished for himself and his family in his life. By which I do not mean hiring contractors and paying bills; I mean swinging a hammer. Dale is seventy-seven. The first house he had built was on the back side of Manning Hill, and it burned, so he and his wife left that plot of land, deeded it to my dad, and we built our house on the charred foundation in 1961.

Dale, his wife, Elaine, his daughter, her husband, their children, a big, extended happy family, some I've never met, we visit. We catch up. Mostly it is family matters, the details. But in our people's way of talking least about what matters most, I manage to hear him say what I needed to hear. I do not need to ask absolution; he offers it on his own in the normal course of conversation. Dale knew my old man and where he came from better than anyone living, was himself set in the same mold of self-reliance, and he says to me simply that I had done the right thing in Panama. It's what I came to hear.

Gradually, then, in the coded quiet way both of us were

taught, we talk some about my dad and mother. I test my hypothesis on him, that the source of my dad's madness was my mother's religion, and he does not disagree.

"That," he says. "And he always was a little tetched in the head." That may be all there is to say. These days, we tend to overthink these matters.

It is the middle of the last day of 2011, and I am running. My genetics, the long-standing custom of my people, and biological adaptation all dictate that I should be spending this day as I have spent most days of deep, dark winter: dug in with a pile of split hardwood, a bottle of Jameson, dogs asleep on blankets, and books. But even the mountains around on this peculiar day are not my own, and there is no snow in the valleys. I am not at home. I have taken myself to the western edge of the Cascade Range and am running along an old interurban rail line converted to a trail that winds south through a cathedral of Douglas fir and cedar at the edge of Bellingham, Washington. Occasionally the trail attains a bit of altitude and then comes a break in the trees to give a view of the Puget Sound, ships winding toward harbor. The low-slung solstice sun occasionally burns through the coastal murk of clouds. It's forty-five degrees, no ice, and just right for running. It is silent save for my labored inspiration, my footfalls and those of 150 fellow travelers.

The organizers of this race call it the Last Chance Marathon, because it's annually held the last day of the year. The name freights a bit more meaning for me, although nothing so dire as the ultimate. I suspect there are many more miles and years in my allotment. Mostly my choice of this event is practical; it offers a chance to duck the burdens of Montana's winter. So I drive a thousand miles to run twenty-six, and I suppose there's some sense to this. None my grandfather could have seen, but I can. Besides, it is not my last chance, but my first, my first marathon ever, and I am sixty.

It would be a lot more fitting if I were to run this at home, among my home hills, along mountain trails that thread among ponderosa pine, and in a way, I am. One does not run a marathon in a day, but in the months that lead up to that day. That's where the work comes, and I have done it. The changes are made in training, and I have made them. I am thirty pounds lighter than I was five months before. My alcohol budget is zero and has been all that time. I am finding it takes almost no effort to stand upright in the day.

Nonetheless, someone has laid a line in Bellingham, Washington, and bordered it with plastic banners in primary colors, and I have come here to cross that arbitrary line. I have come here to finish, the single-minded goal of anyone who tackles a marathon. This is an article of faith, and that last phrase does not come easy. My using it is an act of synthesis necessary if I am to inhabit the life I was given, necessary to negotiate the dichotomous circumstances of my rearing. I am here to express my faith.

It's easy enough to see how this effort in Bellingham traces to my father's family. True, many of the Mannings who preceded me couldn't conceive of this, or would see it as frivolous, a waste of time, fail to see it as work. Yet more than work was at play in their lives, lives that were nothing if not real. Through all time I can account for, my ancestors directly and daily engaged the physical realities. Life was muscle and bone, and I bring nothing so much as muscle and bone to this day.

I also bring faith, but in reverse to how it channeled the lives of my mother's people. My faith is not fundamental, by which I mean the fundament. I do not begin with articles of faith as a given, then warp reason to conform. I refuse to sever the ties to reality that make a life of engagement and full living. Reason and science do not eradicate the unknown so much as they guide us to its edge and tell us how we might enter the unknown. I can say this more plainly: my mother's people believed in a creator and demanded respect for the creator's rules. That is exactly what I am doing here.

Biology has done nothing so much over the course of the past 150 years as to allow us to look full into the face of the creator. Charles Darwin first imagined and sketched the silhouette, but in unpacking the folds and layers of Darwin's wisdom, generations of biologists have given us a fully realized portrait. From cytoplasm to cell to organism to community to ecosystem to planet, the vision of evolution aligns and explains. Evolution is nothing so much as an unimaginably large number of experiments conducted over an unimaginably vast span of time, and the results of every single success and survival is recorded in DNA. Evolution is the record of what works and what fails in all possible permutations of life. It is death and survival, and survival instills a love of life. Evolution demands ethics by means of a command for social cohesion to ensure our survival. Evolution demands love of food, love of color, scent, rage, and lust.

Beheld in all its glory, evolution demands humility. A full

accounting of the scale, the complexity, tells us nothing so much as we cannot comprehend it. At any meaningful level of time and scale, predictability fails in the face of this complexity. This is not an abstraction. Each of us lives every day in a brain, yet neuroscience's greatest accomplishment in recent years has been to convincingly demonstrate that the complexity of a single brain is beyond our ken. Your brain cannot comprehend your brain. There will always be an unknown relevant to every life.

And yet, to each of our brains, each of our bodies, knowing this unknowable is what matters. Knowing is how we attend to our well-being. What good is this creator if it fails to tell each of us how we must live? None of us is so much interested in arcana that explain life so much as we are instructions for a life. Such instructions are indeed available. Evolution has written them clearly, and along with them a sobering caution. Evolution cares not a single bit about an individual. Evolution plays the odds, a long game, and in the long game individuals and even whole generations are expendable and routinely expended. The science of complexity rests on probability. In probability there are no certainties. The odds may be a million to one, but in the master game, trillions are routine, even trivial. One in a million happens a lot. This is what requires the leap of faith in translation from the general to the specific. Probability offers guidance, not guarantees.

A bedrock rule of evolution is that if a species endures for a long time across a range of conditions, then survivors are endowed with solutions to the problems posed by the conditions. Put another way, an individual of that species comes with a genetic record of those solutions, the programming, the genes, the DNA. This record is how the creator tells each of us how we should live, attend to our own well-being. Tamper with it at your own peril. This is precisely the peril we are in, and have been courting ever more deeply for at least six thousand years.

The conditions of human life, the rules of our bodies, were laid down over the course of two million years. This is more than a matter of muscle and bone. The very hormones and neurotransmitters that drive each person's sense of well-being—happiness, emotion, affection, passion—depend on motion, respiration, micronutrients, and social interactions. Yet the basic conditions of our lives today are nothing like the daily course of events that wrote the rules of our bodies. Certainly, adaptation is possible, but science has developed a clear understanding of our genetic clocks, that is, the frequency of mutations in genes required to effect adaptation. Expect a human body and mind (and by now we should know this formulation is redundant; body *is* mind) that might accommodate some of today's eccentric conditions in 12,000 years or so. Given this, it makes some sense to attempt to read the creator's instructions as to how we might live. This is my article of faith: I must obey the intent of evolution for my own well-being. I mean this literally, individually, in my daily life. It is not a guarantee to my well-being; there are no guarantees. It is how I play the odds.

Some of this is elemental. For instance, the most significant and sweeping change in human evolution was the domestication of grain six thousand or so years ago. Before then, that is, for 1.994 million years out of two million, we humans had no access to dense packages of carbohydrates that grains are. We ate fruit, leaves, and meat. Some of us did our best to return to such a diet when low-carbohydrate regimes were developed fifteen or twenty years ago. Then this was mostly a matter of faith, but the evidence on topics such as micronutrients, omega-3 fats, and a firmer understanding of the body's processing of glycogen is confirming the article of faith. So does the epidemic of obesity. Could evolution long tolerate the sort of specimens now common among us that can't fit into a seat on an airplane?

Yet this quickly extends beyond the elemental. For all that time we did not have grain, humans were hunter-gatherers, people who, by definition, did not sow nor reap, which is to say, did not attempt to manipulate the future, did not predict and scheme, the activity that today consumes most of the human brain. Instead, these people needed to be wildly observant, tuned in and reactive to surroundings, almost hardwired to their world. They had to live permanently in a state of mind we call "mindfulness," that is, the state achieved through meditation. Even mainstream science is coming to appreciate the great healing power of meditation; evolution points to the source of this power.

More directly still, I hunt. Each fall I shoot a freezerful of deer or elk fed from wild places on wild, indigenous grasses. This feeds me with the healthiest protein available rich in the micronutrients and the omega-3 fats that fed our species for two million years. More to the point, this puts me in direct touch with the forces that shape my life. I spend long days creeping among deer, constantly mindful and observant, taking more knowledge than food. I kill one or two, hundreds more I watch and leave, and they go on. More importantly, the wild places that raised them go on year after year. Evolution promised this part of my well-being.

Yet I am coming to believe that the most important promise is in understanding the power of motion. It is curious and a mark of our collective narcissism that we humans have forever thought ourselves special only because of the power of our brains. Truly, our brains are special, although in the evolutionary sense it's not clear this is all an upside, all adaptive. The experiment is still in process. I once asked a bird biologist why he thought birds were so interesting, given the fact they are unable to make tools or clothes or houses. His answer was they are so well adapted to their environment, they don't have to do these strange activities. In this sense, our brains are simply compensating for our considerable shortcomings, and a costly work-around at that. Be that as it may, these overactive brains of ours have led us down some dead-end paths like the mind-body separation, but especially in being so engaged with our intelligence, we have underestimated our other attributes, our physical prowess.

Lately, some scientists have worked a whole fertile and corrective field. For instance, neuroscience has begun to appreciate how greatly and effectively our emotional well-being is affected by exercise.

So on New Year's Eve, I am in Bellingham conducting an experiment on my body and my own sense of well-being. As I said, this did not begin today. I have been following the strands of this argument with my own body for well more than a decade, but now, as I follow the science, I begin to see how it all twists together. I have taken this emerging wisdom seriously enough to go the distance.

More to the point, evolutionary biologists and physiologists are examining the simple physical fact of the matter, evidence like our high-arched feet, Achilles tendon, and developed neck muscles that firmly control side-to-side motions of the head while we are running. Their conclusion is this human animal is a running animal, exquisitely built and refined to the conditions of distance running, long distances, perhaps the best distance runner of all mammals. Anthropologists have sought out remaining pockets of hunter-gatherer society and complemented this view. Humans for all of time—all humans, young, old, man, woman—ran, ran something like a marathon every single day.

In the face of such evidence, given such clear and readable direction from the creator, what can I do but run.

ACKNOWLEDGMENTS

In the end, a memoir is a hopelessly circular activity of using one's own brain to examine one's brain, worse, to erect a story on the ricketiest scaffold of the brain, which is memory. Those of us sufficiently self-possessed to become ensnared in this tautology need all the help we can get. Along the way, more people than I can recall (the memory issue again) delivered the support that finally allowed this story of mine to fit between covers. I apologize to those I have forgotten and fail to mention, accept the thanks of those I have deliberately failed to mention, but mostly write here to acknowledge what seems to me a larger debt than a normal book accrues.

The first fact of the matter is, writing this was not even my idea. The genesis occurred maybe a decade ago in a casual conversation with Becky Saletan, my editor then on another project when she was at North Point Press. I was summarizing my weird background, and she responded with the simple imperative: "You have to write it," which seemed an odd idea at the time. I had spent most of my intellectual effort until then trying to distance myself from this story and didn't for a second welcome the idea of wading back into these memories. But as the religious right ascended in our republic, I could see her point. My story seemed less mine alone.

Still, this book suffered a contorted gestation, largely owing to my own inadequacies in figuring out what needed to be done. That problem first surfaced in hammering into a workable and sellable proposal, and that process never would have succeeded without the support of my sage and patient agent, Peter Matson. I'm terribly lucky he was around and on my side.

Likewise, George Witte, my editor, signed on even after what would have appeared to any reasonable observer as a demented meeting in his office. I erupted in full and unchecked babble of hyperarousal for a half hour; he listened, then bought the idea. And then read my draft and delivered the important ideas that made it a book.

My friend, sometimes hunting partner, and dog counselor, Rick Bass, read my draft and generously loaned me some of his supreme command of storytelling. We're all of us grateful Rick is with us, writing and fighting. I more than most.

The work also took a serendipitous turn, and there is nothing unusual in this. Journalism is mostly a matter of hunting and gathering, and discovery is unpredictable. In this case, discovery involved the extraordinary step of my taking an actual paying job, my first in twenty years. For no good reason, I took the suggestion of a friend of mine, Rick van den Pol, that I try my hand at some work at the University of Montana's Institute for Educational Research and Service, which he directs. I had no idea what the work had to do with anything, let alone had to do with my story, but I needed the money, so agreed.

The institute deals with the pernicious effects of child abuse, and working there led me to the massive body of research that is reforming how we understand the forming of the human mind and psyche. Turns out it had everything to do with everything, and my work there allowed a new level of inquiry that greatly influenced this book, particularly in the chapter "Buried in the Family." I am indebted both to Rick and the university for knowingly suffering the presence of (and cutting a paycheck for) a writer working on a full-throated attack on right-wing religious fundamentalism in our country. That's what intellectual freedom is about and what universities ought to be about.

As one might expect, I needed the most help with memory, and got it from a number of sources. I was fortunate enough in this process to reconnect with my old high school friend, David Werth, during a bittersweet trip to northern Michigan in the summer of 2011. His recall always was better than mine. He helped with a lot of details and was kind enough to omit others. Likewise, his sister, my first and favorite colleague in journalism, Betty Werth Westrope, joined in the corrections and read a copy of the manuscript just to be sure. But my debt to both of these remarkable people extends back well beyond this book. I have missed them both in these thirty some years living away from Manning Hill in Montana.

The same trip gave me a wonderful afternoon spent in East Jordan with my father's lone surviving brother, Dale, and his wife, Elaine, their daughter, Diane Boyer, and their extended family, and now I realize, by extension, my family. They continued to offer help through the process.

In the same vein, my sister, Denise, and her husband, Greg Weckesser, took me in and helped with critical details.

Courageously. Denise also was my source for a family history written as a college assignment by my brother Randy. He had interviewed my parents and surviving grandparents, so it turned out to provide a lot of the detail I have used here.

My recollections of my time spent in Idaho were greatly helped by several conversations with Rick Shaughnessy, a competent reporter if ever there was one.

A couple of institutional sources also provided some backup. I was helped out greatly by an afternoon spent with Robert Lyngos at the George N. Fletcher Public Library in Alpena. The extensive historical collection provided abundant detail and documentation. The collection included a Richardson family history prepared by a distant cousin, Clyde Morrison, which provided a wealth of information and detail. Likewise, the Crawford County Historical Museum in Grayling, Michigan, filled in gaps about the town where my maternal grandparents lived.

My research was also greatly aided by the online database Ancestry.com, a source for detail unimaginable or unobtainable only a few years ago. I was able to fill in vast and unexplored facts of my personal genealogy, as advertised, but also to retrieve facsimiles of documents, such as my paternal grandfather's World War I draft card. It is of considerable irony that this all flows from Mormon fascination with genealogy, an example of a quirk of their religion that I have critiqued in this book. Goes to show you.

Along the way in this online research, I encountered a pro in this field, Delynn Flinn, who also has family ties to Alpena County. She provided a number of details and correctives, not the least of which was the newspaper clip of my great-uncle Frank's bizarre suicide.

But as always, my greatest debt is to my wife, Tracy Stone-Manning. As I said, a contorted gestation. She knows this better than anyone and still she believes, a miracle of religious proportions.